I0462934

JC Bruce

THE 'ROGUE' MYTH

Demon Traders or Convenient Scapegoats?

An Alternative Perspective on the 'Rogue Trader'
Phenomenon and
the Underlying Causes of Financial Crises

Copyright © J.C. Bruce

All rights reserved

The moral right of the author has been asserted

ISBN 1449595219

Printed and bound by CreateSpace, USA

Cover design by Nina Faasen

This edition is sold subject to the condition that it shall not, by any way of trade or otherwise, be lent resold, hired out, or otherwise circulated in any form of binding or cover other than that in which it is published and without a similar condition, including this condition, being imposed on the subsequent purchaser.

The scanning, uploading and distribution of this book via the Internet or via any other means without the permission of the publisher or the author is illegal and punishable by law. Please purchase only authorized electronic editions and do not participate in or encourage electronic piracy of copyrighted materials. Your support of the author's rights is appreciated.

Dedicated to my late parents Freddie and Marie Bruce

President Barak Obama commenting on the Wall Street culture, during PBS interview July 2009:

"The problem that I've seen, at least, is you don't get a sense that folks on Wall Street feel any remorse for taking all these risks."

"You don't get a sense that there's been a change of culture and behavior as a consequence of what has happened. And that's why the financial regulatory reform proposals that we put forward are so important." (1)

Arthur Levitt, Chairman United States Securities and Exchange Commission, Chicago Illinois, May 6 1996:

"There will always be incentives to act in ways that are not in investors' interests. If not policed, then over time, people in the industry can come to develop an ethical blind spot, and even form a new 'ethic' that makes it OK to cheat." (2)

"There have been too many instances of so-called 'rogue traders' causing millions, or even billions of dollars in losses – not to mention the demise of some well-known institutions. In my view, there would be no 'rogue traders' if every firm had good internal controls and risk management systems." (3)

Nick Leeson commenting on the morality of, and duplicity in, Financial markets:

"…all of the procedures are wrong, morally and perhaps criminally, some more clearly than others…"

"If the codes of practice were standard, not 'when suits' … perhaps the current ambiguity would be removed." (4)

In a letter to Her Majesty the Queen dated 10 August 2009, 10 eminent economists commented on an explanation by Professors Besley and Hennesey from the British Academy, on why "few economists had foreseen the credit crunch":

"We believe that the narrow training of economists – which concentrates on mathematical techniques and the building of empirically uncontrolled formal models – has been a major reason for this failing in our profession. This defect is enhanced by the pursuit of mathematical technique for its own sake in many leading academic journals and departments of economics." [5]

THE 'ROGUE' MYTH

CONTENTS

PREFACE AND ACKNOWLEDGEMENTS

I have spent nearly twenty years in the financial services industry. Over time I realized that the clients of financial institutions are often mere innocent bystanders blissfully ignorant to the inner workings of an industry that profoundly influences their lives and often the lives of their descendants. Financial collapses today affect the lives of virtually everyone and are often attributed to either 'an act of God' or to the lunacies of some 'rogue' individual or a combination of the two.

From personal experience and research conducted over the last 10 years I came to the realization that neither of these assumptions is accurate and I believe recent events support my view. Although the financial services industries in most countries appear to be heavily regulated it seems to have little effect on either the size and or the frequency of financial catastrophes'. The reason for this I believe is twofold, in the first instance we have little understanding of what we are trying to regulate and secondly our regulatory methodology lacks focus and commitment. There is an old saying "rules are for fools, if there were no fools we would need no rules" or something to the effect. What we are trying to regulate is 'extreme opportunism', the reason why it is so prevalent in the financial services industries is the fact that the short term rewards up for grabs are often obscene in its magnitude, providing extreme incentives for 'success' and very little disincentive or sanction in the event of failure. The old saying; 'a fish rots from the top' alludes to the fact as with most problems, this one also starts at the top and not at the bottom where most attention is often focused. Executive compensation like 'performance' bonuses and share incentive schemes, often has little bearing on the long (or even short) - term profitability and viability of a firm; very large and very real bonuses are often paid based on created 'paper' profits.

*These practices are in many cases dependent on the creative and often negligent utilization of mathematical modeling by financial market practitioners in order to justify greater risk taking in pursuit of larger incentives. This practice is of great concern as the level of apparent risk can easily be manipulated to suit the outcome the modeler desires. These flawed models are then used as justification for engaging in strategies that often end with disastrous consequences for shareholders and investors alike. In an environment where many financial services companies are focused not on making money by providing services **to** their clients; but are focused on making money **from** their clients, these clients often (unknowingly), bear the brunt of such high risk investments.*

As a society we have elevated money to the ultimate symbol of success with little regard for how and at what cost these riches were gained and must therefore bear some of the blame for the culture of greed in financial markets.

The aim of this book is to re-sensitize the public at large as well as regulators, to the simple fact that financial markets are created and maintained by humans and humans are primarily driven by fear and greed. The manifestation of greed is extreme opportunism and this is what we need to control.

I have many people to thank. To Professor Derik Gelderblom, Chair of the Sociology department at UNISA; thank you for your expert guidance and assistance during my years of research and also with the finalization of this manuscript. I would also like to extent my thanks to Professor Erik Lie from the University of Iowa for his permission to reproduce some of his graphs relating to "options backdating".

I would like to express my gratitude to Judy Nokes from The National archives UK for her assistance. Tables 1 and 2 were reproduced under the terms of the Click-Use Licence C2010000330.

As this book is based on a thesis completed for the degree of DPhil in Sociology at UNISA, I want to express my sincere gratitude to the University of South Africa for its permission to publish.

I would like to express my sincere appreciation to Mr. Nick Leeson for assisting me with my initial research. To my friend and colleague Colin Smit; thanks for sharing your wealth of knowledge and experience in the financial markets. To Lizette thank you for all the support over the years. To Beatrix, Jandré and Mark thank you for the proofreading. All the remaining errors and mistakes are mine and for them I apologize. To Riana thank you for the layout and technical editing. To all my friends thank you for your friendship over the years. I would like to extend a special word of thanks to Lee Sanderlin and the staff at BookSurge, without your efforts this book would not have been possible.

Finally to my children Christopher and Nina, my brothers Len and Derick, thank you for your constant motivation love and support. A special word of thanks to my daughter Nina, for the outstanding design of the cover for this book, you are an exceptionally talented artist.

PROLOGUE

The first signs of autumn are starting to show in Somerset West, a picturesque village at the southern tip of Africa. A cold front is moving in from the northwest bringing with it some well deserved rain. I am watching a television program providing a rare insight into the lives of some of the most successful industrialists and financiers in US history. The accounts chronicled the achievements of among other Andrew Carnegie, JP Morgan, and John D. Rockefeller. One thing they all share is the fact that they were all opportunists who often made their money through means that were even then, frowned upon and would today be totally illegal in most jurisdictions. Tales of insider trading, market manipulation and monopolistic practices were part and parcel of the 'competitive' edge of some of these extreme opportunists. Some even described them as 'rogues'. It's around 23-50 CAT and I switched the channel onto CNN to catch a final glimpse of world events. On the other side of the world newly elected US president, Barak Obama expresses outrage at the payment of USD 160 million in bonuses by AIG, with taxpayer money. A few months earlier this behemoth of a company received more than a hundred billion US Dollars, through a hastily constructed bailout package, after it lost more than USD 20 billion due to the "underperformance" of sub-prime related investments. AIG's CEO was forced to resign. (If you feel sorry for him, you shouldn't. According to Reuters his severance package would be between 35 and 68 million USD.)

Similarly Merrill Lynch executives paid themselves bonuses of USD 3.6 billion in 2008 after posting losses of USD 27.6 billion in 2008 and USD 7.8 billion in 2007 [1]. Did anything really change over the last 100 years?

The US government was however quick to respond in a very simple but innovative fashion. In view of the contention by bank and insurance executives that they are legally obliged by employee contracts to pay bonuses, the US Congress, with an overwhelming majority (328-93), voted in favor of legislation (HR1586) that provides for taxing families with an annual income of more than USD 250 000, 90% on certain corporate bonuses. According to the HeraldTribune of 19th March 2009 this tax would apply to bonuses paid by companies that received federal bailout funds as well as Fannie Mae and Freddie Mac. This is an example of innovative and targeted regulation through legislation, specifically aimed at curtailing extreme opportunism. Over the last five years I conducted extensive research into the phenomena of 'rogue trading' as a manifestation of extreme opportunism in financial markets and came to the conclusion that rather than being isolated incidences of human failing we are dealing with a behavior type that is not only widespread, but often promoted, incentivised and applauded. I further concluded that structural factors like regulation, legislation and incentivisation play a crucial role in creating an environment where extreme opportunism is facilitated and promoted and not inhibited. I will in this book endeavor to show that the subprime crises is by and large, nothing more than the consequences resultant from the widespread inclination among financial institution executives to behave in an extreme opportunistic fashion, not dissimilar to the mindset and conduct displayed by those labeled as 'rogue traders'.

For many years the world has been fascinated by 'Rogue Traders'. Individuals whose action we are told crippled some of the most well established financial institutions in the world. The actions of these rogues trigger a wide range of emotional responses, ranging from those that believe 'rogue traders' are some of the vilest criminals that walk the face of the earth and deserve long jail sentences for their heinous deeds, to others that endow them with folk hero status. I analyzed a number of the largest and best publicized events attributed to 'rogue traders' with some very interesting results. I found that sufficient evidence exists to point to a more structural cause for these events and that they are most likely symptoms of a much larger problem. The types of activities engaged in by these so called Rogues, are also not as rare as one might think and the labeling of these individuals as rogues, the criminalization of their actions, as well as the publicity given to these incidences, may also serve very specific purposes.

By attributing these actions to 'rogues' it immediately becomes unforeseeable, unpredictable and virtually unpreventable, thereby exonerating all those that should have created an environment where this type of behavior would by inhibited. Rogues are the perfect scapegoat to shift the blame for incompetence and ineptness on the part of 'very' well remunerated executives and less well remunerated regulators. Executives and regulars alike can wash their hands off these events as it was an unforeseen event, an 'act of God'. It is striking how the executives of Societe Generale vilified Jerome Kiervel for his unauthorized trading loss, while remaining quiet on what punishment they deserve, for even greater sub-prime related losses. Bloomberg reported that Societe Generale suffered subprime related losses in the order of USD 6.8 billion, worldwide banks reportedly lost more than USD 500 billion due to subprime while the IMF puts the figure for all companies at over a USD trillion (2). Against this Kerviel's losses and those of all the other 'rogue traders' in history, seem somewhat insignificant.

In order to hang these different events together in a format that will make it easy to read I will start with an analysis of the most recent 'rogue trader' event, detailing the case of Mr Jerome Kerviel, employed at the time by the French banking giant Societe Generale. In the following six chapters I will discuss some of the most noteworthy 'rogue trader' events spanning a period of more than 20 years. In Chapter 8 I will show that not only 'lowly' traders but also executives of financial and other firms display extreme opportunistic behavior in an environment that is not only conducive to such behavior but actively promotes and rewards such behavior. In the final analysis I will analyze the most recent set of events commonly referred to as the 'subprime' collapse. With the hindsight of the previous chapters these events and the environment in which it occurred should be strangely familiar to the reader as it is in the final analysis the result of widespread extreme opportunism.

Although utmost care was taken to ensure accurate and complete referencing and to prevent any errors or omissions, I apologize for any that slipped through.

THE 'ROGUE' MYTH

INTRODUCTION

Through an analysis of a number of 'rogue trader' events that occured over the last two decades, some light will be shed on the underlying causes of the 'rogue trader' phenomena and the financial market collapses that seem to plague financial systems, with growing regularity and intensity. The perspective I offer will focus on the role of structural factors that facilitated the development of a culture of extreme opportunism present in the environment in which these so called 'rogues' operated. This culture played a motivational and facilitating role for those engaged in the headlong pursuit for profits, through investing in sub-prime based securities and derivatives. Coupled with massive incentives of a monetary and non-monetary nature providing fuel for uninhibited opportunism, a meltdown of global proportions was inevitable. Similarly I will highlight the tell tale absence or ineffectiveness of those factors that could or should have inhibited extreme opportunistic conduct.

Let's initiate on our journey by taking a look at the role of business executives that demand multi million dollar re-muneration packages, for their unique skills and abilities and the possible influence of those remuneration packages that reward uninhibited risk taking. Those that demanded multi million pay packages even after bankrupting the companies they were entrusted to manage, are meeting with growing resistance. For the first time in years their value added are questioned. Nassim Taleb a former derivatives trader and hedge fund manager and author of among other "The Black Swan" made the following observations regarding these matters: "What I saw was that in one of the most prestigious business schools in the world, in the most potent country in the history of the world, the executives of the most powerful corporations were coming to describe what they did for a living, and it was possible that they too did not know what was going on. As a matter of fact, in my mind it was far more than a possibility. I felt in my spine the weight of the epistemic arrogance of the human race." To this he added the following: "I then realized that the great strength of the free-market system is the fact that company executives don't need to know what is going on." [1].

Peter Lynch echoes this sentiment and said "Go for a business that any idiot can run - because sooner or later, any idiot probably is going to run it." [2]. If one merely reflect on the regularity and extent of financial collapses and meltdowns these comments move from mere flippant remarks to a very serious indictment on how executives of large corporations are appointed measured, evaluated, remunerated and controlled. How can an individual earning millions of USD per annum be allowed to claim ignorance and then expect taxpayers and shareholders to bail out his failing firm? An important fact that often escapes our attention is that sub prime investments were made voluntarily. No-one was forced to invest into these assets in exactly the same way as no one was forced to invest into Mr Milken's high yield (junk) bonds in the 1980's or in the dot com shares in the 1990's till 2001. Executives, analysts and traders were rewarded handsomely during the period where these high risk investments showed high paper profits, their bonuses were however paid with real money. I have not seen any of these executives and other beneficiaries offering to pay back their bonuses. If taxpayer's money is to be used to bail out these firms then the executives of these firms should be accountable to taxpayers, until such time as they rehabilitated their companies and maybe themselves. There should be severe penalties in place for executives that repeatedly make themselves guilty of such extreme opportunism.

A chilling reminder of the levels of arrogance that became part of the psyche of executives is the fact that a number of those that nearly bankrupted financial institutions, and had to be saved by taxpayers, had the audacity to apply the assistance money to pay to themselves and other senior staff substantial bonuses. The excuse they offered was that it was essential to retain staff. A case in point was the USD 3.6 billion bonus payment made by Merril Lynch in December 2008. According to a January 13 Bloomberg report, out of Merrill Lynch & Co's 39 000 employees more than 700 received bonuses exceeding USD 1 million with its top four executives sharing USD 121 million. This payment was made not withstanding the fact that a few weeks after paying these bonuses, Merrill Lynch reported a handsome USD 16 billion, quarterly loss. According to The Economic Times of the 4th of March 2009, the firm's top investment banker Andrea Orcel, received a cash and stock remuneration package totaling USD 33.8 million in 2008.

The burning issue is not the fact that the executives and traders at these firms receive substantial bonuses, the problem is the fact that bonuses and other incentives are paid while clients and shareholders are losing money. There appear to be little disincentive for actions that could result in losses, with massive incentives for transactions that may potentially earn profits. The incentive system is highly skewed in favor of extreme opportunism. There appears to exist an unhealthy culture of entitlement that start right at the top of firms. The practice of handing out golden parachutes to incompetent and reckless executives sets a trend of entitlement among other executives and more junior staff. The events of the last two years that are commonly attributed to a collapse in the value of sub prime related assets cannot be analyzed in isolation. An analysis of most of the major 'rogue trader' events over the last decades, contextualized through an analysis of the micro and macro environments in which they operated, will clearly show that a dangerous culture, that condones and even incentivise extreme opportunism, lies at the heart of the factors that caused this financial collapse as well as those that preceded it.

In April 2005, market specialists on the New York Stock Exchange (NYSE) made the news headlines. Individuals from seven specialist firms were systematically and deliberately front running their clients. The disciplinary actions against these firms resulted in penalty and other payments of around USD 247 million (3). How do you get to a situation where specialists from all seven firms are involved in what the NYSE termed "... interpositioning and trading ahead of customer orders..."? Is it possible that this type of behavior became the norm among those insiders/participants and that the new entrants learned this behavior from established players, or was it a deliberate strategy developed and executed by this group of traders to protect their interests, (their virtual monopoly over who may act as intermediaries on the NYSE), that are under severe threat? The answer probably includes influence from both, facilitated by poor oversight and a culture of greed at the top structure of the NYSE. On 17 September 2003, the then chairman of the NYSE had to resign after it became public that he was awarded a USD 187 million remuneration package. This is notwithstanding the fact that complaints were leveled at him for failure to take action after reports of inappropriate "market specialist" behavior were made to him as early as 2002 (4).

Empirical research conducted on the mutual fund (unit trust) industry and the options markets in the United States provides clear evidence that the manipulation of prices of stocks not only exists but is happening on a large scale. Research on the existence of market manipulation in the mutual fund industry published in 1999 showed that "Equity mutual funds earn large positive returns on the last day of the year, and large negative returns on the following day. The same applies on a smaller scale at quarter-ends that aren't month-ends. Empirical evidence from a variety of sources, including portfolio disclosures and intra-day equity transactions, supports the hypothesis proposed by Zweig in 1997, that a subset of fund managers deliberately cause the price shifts with buy orders, intending to move return to the current period from the next." (5). In other words the year end valuations are manipulated to benefit the asset managers. Subsequent research conducted over the behavior of 4 394 optionable stocks (stocks over which options are written) in the United States and 12 001 non-optionable stocks between January 1996 and August 2002 provides clear evidence of price manipulation (6). The researchers calculated that "On expiration date, the returns of optionable stocks are altered by an average of at least 16.5 basis points, which translates into aggregate market capitalization shifts on the order of $9 billion." The researchers attributed this shift to "...hedge rebalancing by option market makers and stock price manipulation by firm proprietary traders..." and show that the firms that hold the larger option positions are the most likely manipulators (7). Both the buyers and sellers of options have an incentive to manipulate the price of the underlying security over which the option is written. The seller of the option would be trying to avert losses when options are exercised against him, while the buyer of the option would try and manipulate the security over which the option is written to make it profitable for him to exercise the options he holds.

This type of conduct was, however, not new. Salomon Brothers, one of the largest Wall Street bond trading firms, admitted in August 1991 that its traders manipulated the bond market over a period of time. The firm paid a $290 million fine and its senior employees also had to pay fines. However, no individual went to jail. What may come as a bit of a shock to readers is the comment of the chairman of the Securities and Exchange Commission (SEC) on the day he announced the fines of those involved in the Salomon incident. The SEC investigation revealed that 98 other banks and investment houses, virtually 100% of the firms active in a particular segment of the bond market, were involved in manipulating the bond market on an organized basis. According to the SEC chairman, the fraudulent activities became "... part of the organizational routine..." (8). In 1993, many Wall Street firms, including Salomon Brothers, began to pay more attention to risk management systems (9).

According to former trader and investment banker Frank Partnoy, today Professor of Law and author of among other F.I.A.S.C.O. and "Infectious Greed", an eighteen-month investigation conducted by a team of more than forty Salomon employees revealed some 'interesting' facts. It emerged that more than USD 250 million worth of hidden losses, built up since 1989, lay undetected in New York and London. The accountants for Salomon, Arthur Anderson, claimed they had no idea of these losses. Lax oversight was, however, to the advantage of John Meriwether's traders at Salomon in two ways. It firstly allowed them to take larger bets more quickly when they spotted an arbitrage opportunity and, secondly, in the absence of strict controls, positions could be left in position longer, allowing for convergence to take place between price discrepancies. This was a major plus, as forced liquidations by nervous managers often resulted in losses from positions that, if left in place, would have been profitable. At the time John Meriwether was head of the Arbitrage Group at Salomon (10) and he later became one of the key figures in the collapse of Long Term Capital Management LTCM, a very large US hedge fund (11). This type of conduct is also not limited to the United States, as clearly demonstrated by the fact that in 1997 Japan's four giant securities firms Nomura, Daiwa, Nikko and Yamaichi all admitted to paying blackmail money to an extortionist to prevent embarrassing information about their firms to be aired at board meetings (12). In 1998, ten of the largest financial institutions in Japan were indicted for bribing officials working for the Japanese financial authorities (13).

In his 2003 account of the corruption of financial markets Frank Partnoy puts a lesser known element of the Enron saga under the spotlight. Although it is a well known fact that Enron's energy trading operation was exceptionally lucrative, the level of profit and loss manipulation by its energy traders has never received the attention it deserved. Not only were profits and or losses manipulated through the use of fictitious accounts and transactions as well as the manipulation of complex computer valuation models, the risk exposure of the firm was also manipulated to misstate the volatility and valuation of Enron's trading positions (14). Behind the façade of high technology, the firm's USD multi billion operations were run on excel spreadsheets. Traders that made substantial profits would hide some of their profits for the next quarter or even the next year to create the illusion of consistency. Similarly traders that were not so successful would hide their losses through the manipulation of portfolio valuation models. On a larger scale the executives of the firm used trading profits to obscure losses made from the firm's core business units. Deceit and manipulation were at the core of Enron and was part and parcel of its culture.

Extreme opportunism is unfortunately not limited to the investment banks of the roaring nineties and their swashbuckling millionaire traders, as some would have us believe. According to Lori Richards from the SEC in the US, they are concerned about the relationships between pension plan consultants and the service providers, such as asset managers they recommend to the pension plans they consult to (15). If an incestuous or generally corrupt relationship exists between an asset manager and the asset consultant who is supposed to oversee transactions, the violation of rules can easily become a widespread and acceptable practice. Therefore, there is sufficient evidence to suggest that factors conducive to extreme opportunism do exist on a substantial scale in the financial services industry and this affects the community at large. In 2006, research conducted by Erik Lie from the University of Iowa into malpractices around the backdating of stock options to executives of around 8 000 US companies (16), revealed that an estimated 30% of firms that granted stock options to their executives between 1996 and 2005 "... manipulated one or more of these grants in some fashion.", in order to boost the remuneration of these executives in an unauthorized manner (17). This research provides very strong support for the argument that opportunistic behavior may indeed be a much wider phenomenon than previously thought.

Professor Mitchel Abolafia an economic sociologist and author of "Making Markets: Opportunism and restraint on Wall Street" (18), asks the question, how is it possible that the violation of rules became so "diffuse" and "routine" in so many firms? He argues that when extreme acts of opportunism exceed the levels of tolerance of powerful stakeholders inside and outside the markets (when someone gets caught), pressures rise to restrain the extremes (the prey were spooked and need to be coaxed back by a false sense of security). This creates the ebb and flow of opportunism and profitability. As restraint increases, opportunism decreases until everyone is relaxed again and the tide of opportunism rises again as restraint and vigilance is relaxed (19). I therefore argue that what we mistakenly refer to as 'rogue incidents' are merely the tip of the proverbial iceberg of extreme opportunistic behavior commonplace in financial markets. The 'rogue' phenomena could probably be attributed to a combination of sensationalism and blame shifting. It was Tartuffe who said "And there is no evil till the act is known / It's scandal, Madam, which makes it an offense / and it is no sin to sin in confidence" (20). In view of this background, I will also argue that the extreme opportunistic behavior so frowned upon and quickly labeled as deviant once these big scandals erupt is in actual fact 'normal' behavior or 'legitimate business strategies' developed to serve the interests of powerful actors and groups of actors in most financial markets and corporations. This behavior is perpetuated as new entrants into the financial markets learn this behavior from the established players around them.

Our first stop on this journey of discovery would be in France where a young man from modest roots found himself working among the best and brightest that France could offer. "Warrior Monks" rather than mere mortals were the magicians that were taking Societe Generale into the world of derivatives and mega profits. A superior mastery of mathematics they believed, gave them ample protection against the risks associated with their profitable strategies. With all their mathematical skill and superior intellect they claimed ignorance at how a young trader managed, without being detected, to first build up substantial profits through unauthorized trading and then generate a massive loss through essentially the same strategies. Their mathematical mastery also offered little protection against multi billion sub prime related losses.

In Chapters 2-6, five similar events will be analyzed. The first will be the activities of two copper traders employed by Sumitomo - at the time the dominant force in the physical copper market. The activities of the two traders spanned a period of more than ten years from 1985 until 1996 and resulted in losses of more than USD 2.5 billion. In Chapter 3, I will look at the activities of a government bonds trader, Toshihide Iguchi, who worked for Daiwa Bank. Mr Iguchi's activities also spanned a ten-year period between 1984 and 1995 and resulted in losses to Daiwa of more than USD 1 billion.

My fourth chapter is dedicated to one of the more bizarre dramas on Wall Street, the events that surrounded the activities of one Joseph Jett, a STRIPS trader for Kidder Peabody. At the time, Kidder Peabody was seen by many as one of the jewels in the crown of General Electric's enigmatic chairman, Mr Jack Welch. Under the veneer of a technological leader, there appears on closer inspection to be little more than headlong pursuit of profit through cost cutting and risk taking. In the fifth chapter, the events surrounding one of the most well known corporate collapses will be analyzed. With the gracious assistance of Mr Nick Leeson, the events that led to the collapse of England's oldest bank will be analyzed. Mr Leeson's activities took place over a three-year period between June 1992 and February 1995 and resulted in an estimated loss of nearly USD 1 billion. In Chapter 6, we shift our attention to the activities of Mr John Rusnak, a trader employed since 1993 by a subsidiary of Allied Irish Banks in the United States, called Allfirst. During 1997 and 2002, Mr Rusnak's activities resulted in losses of nearly USD 700 million to his employer. My research into the activities of Mr Rusnak will be augmented by an analysis of the activities of a former colleague. Mr Victor Gomes, whose activities at Mr Rusnak's former place of employment, Chemical Bank, give us an important perspective on all our case studies. While Mr Rusnak was engaging in his extremely opportunistic activities, a team of Australian currency traders were also testing the boundaries of extreme trading. In Chapter 7, the activities of a four-man team employed by National Australia Bank come under the spotlight. In a period ranging from 2000 to 2004, these traders engaged in activities that resulted in losses amounting to more than USD 277 million. An interesting feature of this case study is the fact that the environment of 'extreme opportunism' in which these traders operated was accepted as a mitigating factor by a court of law during sentencing.

In Chapter 8, the U.S. Savings and Loans crisis, the Enron incident and the Shell 'overstatement of reserves' will be analyzed. The U.S. Savings and Loans collapse will be viewed from two distinct angles. In the first instance, the role of regulators and their political masters will be investigated and, in the second instance, the influence of Mike Milken and his firm Drexel will be analyzed. The moral essence of the actions of Mike Milken will be compared with those of certain Enron and Shell executives in order to determine if there are any similarities. The treatment meted out to these individuals will be compared in a similar fashion to determine the level of consistency in the application of formal and even informal restraints and sanctions in one of the most sophisticated regulatory environments and oldest democracies in the world. In this chapter, research conducted by Erik Lie into manipulation of Executive Stock Options in the United States will also be discussed in order to support my contention that opportunistic behavior is more widespread than generally accepted, even among those who have limited exposure to the financial markets, such as executives from non-financial services companies.

In Chapter 9 the recent financial collapse attributed to sub-prime related instruments will be analyzed against the backdrop of extreme opportunism sketched in the preceding chapters. The readers should not be surprised if they experience a profound sense of 'déjà vu' as the most recent events attributable to extreme opportunism are unpacked. In the final analysis I comment on possible ways of managing this extreme opportunism that so thoroughly clouds our judgement and makes it nigh impossible for us to grasp the reality that neither the future nor human behavior is ours to predict.

CHAPTER 1

JEROME KERVIEL & SOCIETE GENERALE

According to the Telegraph of 25 January 2008 a mystery trader appointed to neutralize the market risk associated with the bank's positions relative to the European indexes, had apparently been taking unauthorized directional bets on market movements, a strategy not dissimilar to those employed by other so called 'rogue traders'. This strategy I will show was neither complex nor unique as similar strategies were also the downfall of other so called 'rogue' traders. At the time of the Societe Generale announcement the estimated loss was put at around 3.6 billion Euros. This figure as we will see rapidly snowballed to a figure of more than 7 billion Euros, making the losses associated with this incident the largest to date. The man blamed for this massive loss is one Jerome Kerviel a 31 years old arbitrageur. In a firm dominated by an exclusive group of intellectuals that viewed themselves as "warrior monks", the son of a hairdresser and a metal-shop teacher seemed a bit out of place. This former 'backroom' boy with an average university education was probably not viewed by the Societe Generale elite as "warrior monk" material but he had something to prove.

Before I start my analysis of what Mr Kerviel did, I believe it is important for us to take a look at the type of environment in which he operated. In an article that appeared in the TIMESONLINE on 16 February 2008 an interesting rendition of the prevailing culture at Societe Generale during the tenure of Mr Kerviel, is presented (1). Think Crusading Knights, "les moines-soldats" or soldier monks on a mission to conquer all opposition, unaffected by human frailties and weaknesses like fear and greed that afflict the masses. To lead this elite fighting force Antoine Paille, the driving force behind Societe Generale's drive to dominate the equity derivatives market, recruited a former paratrooper Jean-Pierre Mustier. Recruited from the best schools these "soldier-monks" armed with their intellect and mathematical models were on a mission to make Societe Generale and themselves a lot of money. By 2007 the income from "market making" and "proprietary trading", generated by the derivatives group formed in the 1980's, rose to 35%. In 2005 income from equity derivatives were estimated to top USD 1.54 billion (2). There were however those that were not so convinced that mathematical modeling can make one as invincible as a medieval suit of armor initially made the knights, or maybe they just remembered a bit of history.

Professor of applied mathematics at Ecole Polytechnique, one of Frances top science training institutions, Nicole El Karoui, expresses concern about the ever growing need for more and more complex products. She is quoted as saying "There's a responsibility to explain that, in fact, the product can be too risky and difficult to analyze." She is however not alone, US regulators expressed similar concerns about a lack of emphasis of the potential losses associated with these complex products (3). Even a fund manager at ABN Amro finds the Societe Generale products too technical and (wisely) refrained from investing in them. Mustier is however not phased and claims that over the past 15 years Societe Generale only lost money on equity derivatives in two months. His superior Paille views options as a product where "math, statistics and computers" are united in unison. The head of structured products trading at Societe Generale, Alexandre Fleury provides us with a priceless summary of the company's attitude towards risk. "...the French have distinguished themselves in equity derivatives because their love of complicated math allows them to take more risks". "We're just trained to do that", he says (4). In response to this article by Simmons published on "NuclearPhynance.com, one of the respondents contributed this little gem of a quote by Ernst Junger, a German writer historian, "...a half-witted mathematician could cause more damage in a second than Frederick the Great in three Silesian campaigns."

Jerome Keviel was not a mathematical genius or a "warrior monk"; he did not graduate from a prestigious school. He obtained a Masters degree in Finance from the Lumiere Lyon University in 2000, after completing his bachelors in Finance from Nantes University. His field of specialization was "organization and control of financial markets" (5). According to Jean-Pierre Mustier he was also not hired directly from university onto the trading floor, in reality he was promoted onto the trading floor as a reward for his outstanding work in the 'backoffice' (6). He did however, (at least for a period), make a lot of money for the warrior monks. Some market commentators dismissed claims by Mr Kerviel of massive profits he generated for Society Generale. Some expressed doubts over whether Mr Kerviel ever made more than 10 million Euros and holding the view that his employer (Societe Generale) would never let him continue with the unauthorized trading. According to Societe Generale's own reports (7) Mr Kerviel did indeed record a profit of EUR 1.5 billion as at 31 December 2007. This leaves us with the questions how did he do it and why was he allowed to?

According to market sources Kerviel took directional bets on the expected movement of a number of indexes. He was apparently holding a EUR 30 billion long position in Dow Jones Eurostox 50, EUR 18 billion 'long position' in the German Dax and a EUR 2 billion long position in the UK FTSE. In other words Mr Kerviel was feeling fairly bullish on these markets. Unfortunately the powers at Societe Generale did not tell Mr Kerviel of their massive sub prime positions that were going South (8). According to Societe Generale Mr Kerviel was supposed to hedge the company's proprietary positions in the market. If Societe Generale for example had certain positions in place Mr Kerviel should have had in place protection to limit potential losses in the event of these positions going the wrong way. In reality Mr Kerviel was however taking very large directional bets on future market movements, by not hedging his positions. It therefore appears that Mr Kerviel was as bullish about the European markets as his bosses were bullish about sub-prime. In order to hide his positions, Societe Generale claims, Mr Kerviel made use of fictitious transactions that he entered into their trading system. This strategy we will see was nothing new, Joseph Jett Nick Leeson, John Rusnack and the NAB four all did it. One would expect that the best and the brightest of the financial world would have learned from history and figured out a way to guard against this type of behavior. The president of the Association of Certified Fraud Examiners in France questions the design and maintenance of internal controls at Societe Generale (9). In the same article the French Finance Minister is quoted as sharing this view regarding the non-functioning of internal controls. An analyst that wanted to remain anonymous claims that the CEO of Societe Generale admitted that their risk control mechanisms were inadequate because of the rapid growth of the firm's derivative business. The analyst however believed that the traders were viewed as "untouchable" as they were making the big money for the firm. Another analyst Pascal Deque points out that the massive sub-prime related loss suffered by Societe Generale, is but a reflection of the fact that Societe Generale was known in the market as a firm willing to take risks. Reports of one of the Societe Generale Directors Robert Day selling shares in the firm days before the firm's sub prime losses were made public does nothing to quell allegations of a culture of opportunism present at Societe Generale. This event was however not entirely isolated.

During August of 2007 unauthorized trading at the New York Branch of another French Bank Credit Agricol's investment arm Calyon, costed the firm USD 347.5 million in fines resulting in a USD 347.5 million decline in third quarter profits (10). The unauthorized trading was executed by traders on the proprietary trading desk, the same area where Mr Kerviel was working. As with Mr Kerviel the trades also exceeded authorized limits and were also bets on the direction of market indexes. The company was severely criticized for the apparent weaknesses in its risk and compliance structures and procedures. Questions were also raised about risk management regimes at investment banks in general. The rating agencies Moody's and Fitch Ratings were sufficiently concerned that they reconsidered the firm's rating. Anyone at Society Generale or the firms that audit them claiming that they were not aware of this incident might find it difficult to find anyone that believe them. Ignorance of this incident is highly unlikely as Calyon and FIMAT merged in January of 2008 and such events had to be covered by the most basic of due diligence exercises. I believe it would not be unfair of anyone to wonder if Societe Generale were aware of this event and did nothing about it.

Another interesting matter that has bearing on Mr Kerviel is the Guillame Pollet lawsuit against Societe Generale. Mr Pollet a former managing director of Society Generale Cowen and Company was charged with insider trading during 2001 by the SEC in the US where the firm was operating (11). After spending 11 months in jail Mr Pollet eventually paid a USD 150 000 fine without admitting to any wrongdoing. The crux of Mr Pollet's lawsuit against Societe Generale is his contention that the present head of Societe Generale corporate and investment bank, Jean-Pierre Mustier and the equities and derivative trading co-heads were not only aware of his actions, but also instructed him to execute some of the illegal transactions (12). One of the former co-heads Luc François were dismissed after Mr Kerviel's actions were uncovered. Mr Kerviel interestingly enough also contends that his immediate superiors Martial Rouyere (head of Delta One) and Eric Cordelle (deputy Head Delta One), were aware of his transactions as far back as April 2007 (13).

Adding to the woes of 2008 Societe Generale was also fined

EUR 300 000 by the French AMF Enforcement Committee following a 2003 case of insider trading at the Societe Generale, Amber Fund (Cayman) Limited (14). This fund was managed by Lyxor Asset Management (a wholly-owned) Societe Generale susiduary. The operational management of the fund was delegated by Lyxor to SG Cowen (sounds familiar?) who acted as trading advisors. SG Cowan a wholly owned subsidiary of Society Generale operated from the Societe Generale offices in New York and reported to the equities and derivatives department (sounds familiar?) of Society Generale. Although Societe Generale was not found guilty on the principal charge of insider trading, the AMF ruled that it "...failed to observe conduct of business rules, particularly the Chinese Wall procedures designed to prevent undue disclosure of confidential information" and issued a fine.

From the abovementioned a number of question marks about the business culture nurtured by the "soldier-monks"can be raised. They may have followed the age old principle of 'All is fair in love and war'. With this bit of Society Generale history under our belts let us now take a closer look at what Mr Kerviel got up to during his tenure at Society Generale.

The primary question on everyone's lips is how on earth no-one detected anything out of the ordinary. According to an explanatory note issued by Societe Generale on 27 January 2008 Mr Kerviel was authorized to conduct arbitrage activities aimed at benefiting from small temporary price fluctuations in instruments listed on European stock markets. The company (Societe Generale) points out that as the price differences are mostly very small very large nominal positions are taken to harvest a worthwhile profit. Market risk is negated by simultaneously taking an offsetting position to hedge the risks inherent in the first position. These second positions appeared to have been fictitious exposing Societe Generale to risks emanating from an unhedged directional position. This explanation seems very plausible and is very similar to other 'rogue trader' strategies. If we however look at the reality of Mr Kerviel's positions his profits and losses appear to swing quite wildly, not the type of pattern one would expect from an arbitrage trader. The very nature of arbitrage suggests that you only take a position if there is a real profit to be harvested. Losses should be non existent or minimal.

Similarly profits would be directly related to the size of positions taken. A EUR 1.5 billion profit would only be achievable from equally very large positions. The swing between profits and losses do not tie up with the signature one expects from arbitrage trading. The argument put forward by Societe Generale is that Mr Kerviel used elaborate measures to obscure his profits from them. According to Mr Kerviel (15) he asked for a EUR 600 000 bonus for 2007. On the basis of what profit did he expect to receive such a bonus if his superiors were not, (at least off the record), aware of his profits? Mr Kerviel's profits and losses however indicate he had good reason to ask for a substantial bonus (16).

In February of 2008 the New York Times ran an article pointing to substantial losses incurred by Mr Kerviel as far back as July of 2007. These losses are significant as futures trading normally require substantial margin to be posted and maintained. Any losses must be settled in cash and as we will show later in the case of Mr Leeson, someone had to authorize the payment of margin that ran into billions. How these cash payments were made without anyone noticing raises a number of serious questions.

In a report by the board of directors to the general shareholders meeting dated 22 May 2008, Societe Generale went to great lengths to explain how Mr Kerviel managed to evade detection of his fraudulent non-existent trades. Although a lot of emphasis is placed on the cunning and deceitfulness of Mr Kerviel, the sheer number of alerts made it very difficult for the executives to avert any blame. Only when we take a closer look at the underlying report the true extent of internal risk management and oversight procedure failure becomes evident.

From the 20 May 2008 "Mission Green" summary report issued by the Societe Generale General Inspection Department (SGGID), a substantial level of insight can be gathered through what was said and perhaps even more from what was not said. In the first instance we need to look at what type of transactions Mr Kerviel was authorized to trade and what was the nature of his unauthorized transactions.

One of the instruments Mr Kerviel was authorized to trade was the warrant or the "turbo" warrant to be specific. Wikipedia explains to us the nature of the animal. The "Turbo **warrant** is a kind of stock option. Specifically, it is a barrier option of the knock-out type. It is similar to a vanilla contract, but with two additional features: It has a low vega, meaning that the option price is much less affected by the implied volatility of the stock market, and it is highly geared due to the possibility of knockout. The term knock-out means that "The strike price (exercise price) of the option is generally the same as the barrier: if the stock hits the barrier, the option expires and becomes worthless. Variations on turbos include: forms where the strike and barrier are not identical; forms where the barrier is only active at, for example, the close of business but the strike is continuously monitored (smart turbos); and forms with no fixed maturity (minis).

For comparison, a regular call option will have a positive value at expiry whenever the spot price settles above the strike price. A turbo will have a positive value at expiry when the spot settle above the strike AND the spot has never fallen below the strike during the life of the option (if it had done so the option would have crossed the barrier (strike) and would have become worthless)." (17).

One of the first questions that have to be answered is how on earth did Societe Generale's internal control system failed to detect any irregularities relating to cash flow. This relevance of this question will grow stronger as we progress to our analysis of the other well publicized "rogue" trader cases. In the majority of these cases poor cash flow oversight was a key weakness. Although one might be forgiven for assuming that financial institutions like Societe Generale would keep very accurate track of any cash in and especially outflows, one would sadly be mistaken. As we will see in the case of Barings and other financial institutions, prudent and proper cash management, appears not to be a prerequisite for running an international bank. According to the internal report generated by the Societe Generale General Inspection department, cash flow related alerts should have came from at least three different sources and if acted upon, could have allowed for the detection of anomalous activities much earlier.

In the first instance Mr Kerviel had to pay an "initial margin", a form of deposit if he wanted to buy a futures contract on the EUREX or any other exchange. Depending on the movement in the price of the futures purchased, a further margin may be required by the relevant clearing house. Mr Kerviel was an active player that took large positions, his deposit requirements was therefore also substantial as was his use of collateral. Since April 2007 Mr Kierviel's trading required 25% of deposit payments by the Global Equity Derivative Section to Societe Generale's Frankfurt clearing house FIMAT. In early November 2007 this percentage ballooned to 60%. These figures were available on the daily intraday margin requirement report received from the clearing house. These figures were however never analyzed by the Securities treasury Middle Office. They also never took the trouble of identifying who was trading on SF 581, the clearing house account exclusively racked up by Mr Kerviel. The Middle Office responsible for securities treasury did not detect any of these anomalies as they contend that it was not part of their explicit brief.

Inititial margin is however only paid in cash if the purchaser of the futures contract is not able to post sufficient bonds as deposit. As the amounts involved could be substantial, bonds are generally used as initial margin while margin calls are mostly done in cash. Traders like Mr Kerviel would have access to a pool of Societe Generale bonds to be used as deposit. This is very similar to collateral posted during securities lending transactions. In practice such a pool of Societe Generale bonds could be borrowed from another party against appropriate collateral. During March of 2007 however, a substantial cash deposit had to be made. On the 13th of that month Societe Generale Futures Back Office made a payment of EUR 699 million to cover Mr Kerviel's trading. One can only assume he depleted the available bond pool. In 2008 during an 18 day span the Societe Generale Futures Back Office made five different cash payment each exceeding EUR 500 million in cash to meet Initial Margin Requirements. One can once again only assume that the available pool of bonds was already depleted. This unusual activity was not detected as "In the absence of any supervision and of any alert threshold for cash amounts paid as deposits in the procedures in place at that time, Back Office failed to detect the substantial increase in cash deposits made under IMR from January 2008 onward." (18).

One must ask the question; didn't anyone keep track of the amount of collateral posted on behalf of individual traders or workstations? The amount of collateral utilized could be detected as such collateral has a cost to Societe Generale and would therefore have to be allocated to an individual trader as this cost would have to be deducted off his profits. The reason offered why this potential alert system malfunctioned was that the report that identified the fact that Mr Kerviel's cost centre GOP 2A was on average responsible for 10% of the financing cost for securities posted as deposit by GEDS to their Frankfurt clearing house from as early as April 2007, was sent to a manager 5 levels above Mr Kerviel and not to his immediate supervisors. This fact is used as justification, for the non detection, of Mr Kerviel's exceptional use of deposts securities. According to the 'Green Report' this was "…a level too high for such data to be analyzed in detail." (19). If this manager was the only one that received this report, how on earth could he be regarded as too "high" to analyze the report he was sent? If he was too important to analyze it himself he could have instructed a junior official to do it for him. Alternatively he should have sat down with Mr Kerviel's Level one and two immediate superiors and discuss the reports with them.

The futures positions taken by Mr Kerviel would also have been subject to daily margin calls if his positions incurred losses. The reason put forward explaining why these margin payment never aroused any suspicion was quite simply that according to Societe Generale, the margin payments made on Mr Kerviel's positions, were paid as part of Sosiete Generale's global payments and was as such hidden from plain sight. The Futures Back Office did not see that Mr Kerviels positions were significant as it was not "…charged with supervising the daily variations in aggregate cash payments, with analyzing the cash payable breakdown per account…". It appears that no one was specifically charged with the monitoring of individual trader's margin payments. If this was indeed true one can only imagine what the impact on the French banking system could have been if there were indeed two 'rogue traders'.

Another element of management information that should have alerted Mr Kerviel's superiors was the relationship between his cash flows and his trading assignments. One has to ask the question; was there any form of oversight in place, to measure the efficiency with which he executed his assignments? According to the "Mission Green report" (20), the cash flow of Mr Kerviel's operational centre GOP 2A had "…no significant impact upon the DELTA ONE balance or upon that of Equity Finance (DELTA ONE's department)." The report further points to the fact that at Mr Kerviel's operational level, red lights should have flashed, due to the fact that "…even if the cash flow level within GOP 2A was in itself not abnormal, it did not correspond to the activity for which JK had authorization." The positive cash flows and the cash flow requirements for GOP 2A seem to range from on average a EUR 400 million negative to a EUR 500 million positive, with cash flow requirements up at EUR 1 billion in early June to late July 2007, while GOP 2A showed an excess of EUR 1.3 billion in the period December 28, 2007 and January 1st, 2008. Was it possible that Mr Kerviel's superiors did not notice these extremes or were they more interested in the potential bonuses that could be derived from a EUR 1.3 billion profit? If Mr Kerviel was only authorized to engage in low risk low return transactions, the amount he had to tie up in the market to achieve such profits had to be very substantial. How did they miss that, taking into account that at least on one account the treasurer of GEDS indeed expressed concerns about two loans of EUR 500 million? At the end of July 2007 the DELTA ONE manager was made aware of these loans and judging from his response to Mr Kerviel was not overly concerned about this fact or even asked him what it was for. His only concern was whether or not Mr Kerviel needed these loans renewed. This behavior seems to tie up with the contention of Mr Kerviel that his superiors were aware of his activities.

During the course of 2007 more than 39 incidences occurred where activities by Mr Kerviel directly related to his "fraud" did in fact elicit formal queries to Mr Kerviel himself. No effort was made by the relevant Middle Office to verify the explanations provided by Mr Kerviel or to alert his immediate superiors. The explanation for this failure was that such actions were "...not explicitly called for by procedures." (21). In other words, nearly forty fictitious transactions designed to hide market risk, failed to elicit any suspicion from the middle office handling Mr Kerviel's trades.

If we move to the alerts identified by the Societe Generale Operations division and the financial and accounting divisions responsible for Mr Kerviels transactions we find a similar picture. In April of 2007 a residual accounting spread of EUR 95 million attracted attention. An alert was indeed issued leading to numerous e-mail communications that among other asked the front office for proof of the authenticity of the transactions. One of the important revelations in the "Mission Green" report is the following comment: "An alert was also issued at the accounts committee meeting on the use of fictitious futures and forwards justified by knocked warrants." (22). There can be no doubt that the accounts department and Mr Kerviel's superiors were aware of the fact that he was using fictitious transactions, the reasons why he did it are irrelevant, the important fact is that proof of the use of fictitious transactions by Mr Kerviel were known to a number of people in a number of departments, as early as April 2007.

These alerts were not isolated and alerts relating to discrepancies were recorded four times during May of 2007 and twice in July 2007. In July of 2007 a transaction with a nominal EUR 7 billion value, is detected that were booked to a "fictitious counterparty (PRE HEDGE) and a EUR 4 billion negative provision flow is identified by OPER." In the same month an earnings discrepancy of EUR 250 million is detected in one of Mr Kerviel's portfolios resulting from a booking entered into the system before the portfolio were recorded, it was then cancelled before the figures were released to the Back Office systems. In August a similar technique was used to record and remove daylight warrants recorded in the ELIOT accounting system before and after the historization of data. This elicited a telephonic enquiry responded to by Mr Kerviel via e-mail. (Historization means ensuring that all relevant changes to master data and transaction data are tracked and recorded and that proper timestamps (depending on availability) are assigned to these changes.) The modification of transactions around historization should have triggered a much more in depth response, as this is a clear indicator of a possible manipulation of oversight systems.

Two other warnings emanating from fictitious transactions were also triggered in May 2007 and January 2008. In the first instance the operations division detected a transaction entered by Mr Kerviel, with a maturity date on a Saturday. In the second instance Mr Kerviel entered two transactions into the accounting system ELIOT that was inconsistent with pre-confirmation information (23). In December of 2007 Mr Kerviel himself queried the high commissions paid on his behalf to the FIMAT settlement house. This was partly as a result of his unauthorized transactions executed during May to October of 2007. The Global Equity and Derivative Solutions Sub Division in charge of financial engineering and aware of the fact that EUR 1.2 million was paid in brokerage on behalf of Mr Kerviel. According to the "Mission Green" report the operations division was "surprised" at this high level of fees but other than verifying that he has indeed traded extensively, did nothing further. If his broking fees were surprisingly high and they verified that it was indeed accurate, it stands to reason that his trading that generated such high brokerage must also have been 'surprisingly' high.

During January to July 2007 the SGIB Finance Division's accounting and Regulatory Reporting sub-division was alerted five times by earnings discrepancies resultant from a number of transactions attributed to the workstation used by Mr Kerviel. The amounts exceeded 2.6 billion Euros in total. In reality this was the result of one of the techniques used by Mr Kerviel to hide his transactions. He entered transactions into the system that appeared to be internal SG transactions. These transactions were from accounting perspective only reconciled monthly allowing Mr Kerviel to cancel such transactions before they were detected (24). The internal entity favoured by Mr Kerviel is referred to as "CLICKOPTIONS" representing a wholly owned SG subsidiary. All these errors were attributed to the use of incorrect counterparties. The operations division was therefore aware of these transactions, together with the exceptional brokerage and all the other alerts brought to their attention. One can only but wonder if nobody really didn't notice anything odd or untoward.

The monitoring of counterparty risk also generated two very noteworthy alerts. Due to fictitious transactions entered by Mr Kerviel the SG Group Risk Management Division was alerted by two breaches of counterparty Value at Risk limits. In July 2007 a transaction entered by Mr Kerviel utilizes USD 760 million of counterparty's allocated USD 1.23 billion limits and in January 2008 a counterparty value at risk of EUR 2.3 billion is detected. The Global Equities and Derivative Solutions sub division in charge of trading sales and financial engineering were duly notified, unfortunately no-one took the time to try and understand the explanation provided by Mr Kerviel. This is strikingly similar to the case of Mr Leeson as pointed out in the chapter dedicated to Mr Leeson by Dr Irene Finel-Honigman from Columbia University, in an article entitled "Societe Generale 2008: Rogues in the trading room, knaves in the boardroom" also highlight the striking similarities between 'rogue trader' events and the lack of proper oversight at the firms that employed them. We also find that the monitoring of market risk by the SG group risk management division yielded 25 alerts between July 2006 and September 2007, most of which were directly related to Mr Kerviel's "unauthorized" transactions. Mr Kerviel and his immediate superiors were advised of these anomalies but the market risk division attributed it to "...recurring problems in recording transactions in computer systems." (25). No-one it seems, took the trouble to find out why these problems occurred so that the 'errors' could be dealt with.

If we disregard alerts that could not be tied directly to Mr Kerviel's 'fraudulent' transactions, we still find that between June of 2006 and January 2008 no less that 63 alerts were indeed triggered by internal Societe Generale systems. From the reasons put forward by all the departments involved, why they did not detect Mr Kerviel's "unauthorized" transactions earlier all boils down to the fact that no-one was specifically tasked with monitoring and analyzing anomalous transactions. One has to ask the question: "How common were these type of alerts, in Societe Generale?" If these alerts were indeed commonplace one can understand why Mr Kerviel's alerts didn't really raise any eyebrows. If the alerts raised by his transactions were isolated incidents one has to question the competence of those that were alerted. If these types of alerts were realy that commonplace, one has to consider the possibility that severe structural shortcomings at Societe Generale, were at the heart of this incident.

The reports generated by the Societe Generale General Inspections department and by the firm's auditors, Price Waterhouse Coopers, both concluded that "... the fraud was facilitated or its detection delayed by weaknesses in the supervision of the trader and in the controls over market activities." The extent of structural weaknesses borders on systemic, including among other the following:

"The trader's hierarchy, constituting the first level of control, proved deficient in the supervision of his activities. The direct supervisor lacked trading experience and was not given a sufficient degree of support in his new role; he demonstrated an inappropriate degree of tolerance in relation to the taking of intraday directional positions and neither he, nor his own supervisor, carried out an adequate review of the trader's activities on the basis of the available figures and reports or reacted to the alerts that would have allowed them to identify the concealed positions."

"The control services (in particular, Back and Middle Offices, the risk control department, the financial and accounts departments, and the compliance department) generally carried out their assignments in accordance with procedures. However, these controls did not allow the fraud to be identified until

January 18, not only because of the efficiency and diversity of the fraudulent concealment techniques used by the trader, but also because of certain weaknesses highlighted in the course of this investigation:

• Difference between the growth in the means (including information systems) available to control and support services and the very strong growth in transaction volumes within the equities division;
• Lack of certain controls liable to identify the fraudulent mechanisms, such as the control of the positions' nominal value or of the transactions used by the perpetrator of the fraud in order to conceal his positions;
• Fragmentation of controls between several units, with an insufficiently precise division of tasks, lack of a systematic centralization of reports and of feedback to the appropriate hierarchical level;
• Priority given to the correct execution of trades, which appears to be the primary concern of Back and Middle Offices, in the absence of an adequate degree of sensitivity to fraud risks;
• Insufficient level of responsiveness for the implementation of the corrective actions identified as necessary by internal audit bodies."

To remedy these shortcomings the following was proposed:

"- The implementation of controls and limits on the nominal value of positions and transactions, and the reintroduction of the review of nominal values into the analysis of daily earnings by the operational hierarchy;
- The reinforcement of processes for the confirmation of transactions with deferred start dates and transactions with internal counterparties;
- The improvement of procedures for controlling the use of counterparties and of technical transactions liable to be used for the concealment of positions, risks or earnings;
- The implementation of controls over cancelled or modified

trades;
- The reinforcement of the monitoring and handling of anomalies and alerts." (26).
All these measures are basic procedures and processes that should have been in place in the first place.

Structural remedies proposed focused on four key areas and are also very basic:

" - The redesigning of the organization of transaction handling, inspired by the principle of the product control model with the aim of reinforcing the integration and cross-departmental cooperation of key procedures relating to the processing and accounting treatment of transactions;

- the creation of an inter-departmental body responsible for trading security whose assignment will consist, notably, of ensuring the quality of all control measures as a whole, both in terms of design and day-to-day functioning. Within this department, one team will be particularly dedicated to the prevention of fraud;

- significant investments in security for information technology, both in terms of securing applications and technical infrastructure and in the management of accounts and authorizations, reinforced authentication systems and detection of anomalies;

- a campaign to raise staff consciousness, focused on a more formal definition of the roles and responsibilities of each person, in addition to training programs on the subject of fraud prevention and rogue trading."

These changes are neither dramatic nor expensive and are indicative of the fact that very little, if any, attention was given to manage any risks other than those their mathematical models exposed. What is of greater concern is that the absence or failure of oversight systems was detectable at virtually all levels. Societe Generale's own internal report acknowledges this fact (27). According to the report Societe Generale operators "...did not have the reflex to inform their hierarchical superiors or Front office supervisors of the appearance of anomalies, even for high amounts, if this was not specifically stated as part of the relevant procedures." Certain basic control measures did not exist. The " Mission Green" report points out that " At no time, controls existed in this area over cancelled or modified trades, over trades with a deferred start date, over trades with technical counterparties, over positions with a high nominal value, over non-trading flows during any given month, all analyses which would probably have allowed identification of the fraud." From this it is quite clear that a risk conscious culture did not exist in Societe Generale.

This problem is further underlined by the fact that the Societe Generale response to external warnings from both EUREX and FIMAT did not get the attention it deserved. EUREX is one of the world's largest derivatives exchanges and as the leading clearing house in Europe were privy to most of Mr Kerviel's transactions. FIMAT on the other hand was part of the Société Générale Group, and at the time of Mr Kerviel, a subsidiary of Société Générale Securities Services. In January 2008 FIMAT entered into a joint venture with Calyon to form what is to day known as "Newedge". In November of 2007 the levels of trading conducted by Mr Kerviel through his FIMAT trading desk resulted in such an increase in banking income for that desk that, FIMAT initiated an internal investigation into the "regulatory conformity" of the transactions entered into by Mr Kerviel. The preliminary investigation highlighted the unusual increase in execution volumes and felt that Societe Generale should be contacted for clarification. Management at FIMAT however delayed until after Mr Kerviel was detected, citing as reason that their internal investigation has not be completed. One will never know if the looming December bonuses may have had anything to do with the delay. In a

Reuters article dated 24 April 2009 Mr Kerviel's lawyer indicated that he requested the judges in the case to question FIMAT's auditors. FIMAT's futures broking arm handled Mr Kerviel's transactions and was therefore fully aware of what he was doing. As FIMAT was at the time a part of Society Generale their contention that, they did not know, appears to be highly questionable.

According to the February 5th 2008 edition of the New York Times EUREX questioned Mr Kerviel's investment strategy behind two substantial transactions involving the selling of DAX futures and the purchase of Eurostox 50 futures. EUREX also questioned the fact that he executed the transactions through FIMAT a Societe Generale subsidiary based in London. As we have seen some at FIMAT were also troubled, (maybe not troubled enough), by Mr Kerviel's trading. The enquiries by EUREX also highlighted these unusual volumes and in one of its communications with Societe Generale refered to among other a purchase trade of 6 000 DAX futures contracts by Mr Kerviel. The trade value was EUR 1.2 billion and was executed in a two hour period. Although the EUREX enquiries contained some inaccuracies Mr Kerviel's superiors should have been alarmed by these volumes, unless of course, they were well aware of his actions (28). The New York Times quotes the compliance officer to whom the EUREX enquiries were addressed; Xavier de la Maisonneuve as claiming that the EUREX enquiries were questioning procedure and strategy and did not raised concerns about the volumes specifically. Although this is technically true it does not absolve him from the responsibility to investigate the issues thoroughly. If he had contacted FIMAT they might have shared the full extent of their concerns regarding Mr Kerviel.

The possible role of the December bonuses may in all probability be central to the inaction of those at FIMAT and at Societe Generale clouding the judgement of those in positions of oversight. As the reader would see throughout this book the 'rogue' traders were all star traders at some point in their careers. Mr Kerviel is no exception. As we have seen his trading created so much income for FIMAT that they investigated it, closer to home it must have been worse. In 2007 his earnings represented 59% of the Delta One desks listed products total. He was furthermore responsible for 22% of Delta One's global proprietary earnings in 2007. On the client trading side Kerviel produced 35% of global earnings in 2006 and 40% of its earnings in 2007 (29). In terms of DELTA ONE Mr Kerviel was a 'rainmaker', a BSD (Big Swinging Dick). It is no wonder that no-one wanted to upset the star trader. With his contributions Mr Kerviel was a significant contributor to the earnings pool that would have determined bonuses of those higher up in the hierarchy than Mr Kerviel.

Lending credence to the abovementioned facts is the increase in profit targets allocated to Mr Kerviel. According to claims made during a televised interview Mr Kerviel claimed that his profit targets and actual profits grew exponentially from 2005 to 2007 (30). Attained profits of one year became minimum profit targets for next year. His profit targets grew from EUR 3 million in 2005 to EUR 55 million for 2008. Although Mr Kerviel outperformed his profit targets significantle between 2005 and 2007 he would only have gained financially from his outperformance from mid 2007 as his position as trader would only become official at that time. This however did not preclude his superiors from receiving performance bonuses based on Mr Kerviel's performance. In the same interview Mr Kerviel also claimed that fictitious trades were standard practice in the Societe Generale environment and he had the tacid approval of the bank for his transactions. He further asserted that his so-called disappearance was in fact on the instructions of Societe Generale.

I do believe that most of you would agree with me that one might be accused of bending the truth if one had to label Societe Generale as an institution with a risk-averse culture.

The type of business they focused on and the way they pursued their chosen niche cannot be consoled with the term risk-averse. The firm pursued a high risk high return strategy on a massive scale. They likened their business approach to warfare and themselves with warrior monks. Casualties would therefore be unavoidable.

Mr Kerviel was however not the only "rogue trader" that came unstuck in 2008. Following the EUR 250 million Credit Agricole loss due to 'unauthorized' trading, in October 2008 a French savings bank, Caisse d'Epargne, announced a EUR 600 million loss due to 'unauthorized derivative trading by a group of six of its proprietary desk's traders [31]. Once again it was the proprietary traders trading with the bank's own assets trying to optimize profits for the banks trough Equity derivative trading. (Sounds familiar?) Once again no proof could be found that the traders were trying to enrich themselves, (other than the obvious bonuses they would have received, if the "hunch" they followed turned out to be correct). One cannot help to wonder if we would ever hear of anyone exposed for profitable 'unauthorized trading'.

As we have seen in the beginning of this chapter the powers at be at Societe Generale were confident that their mathematical prowess would protect them against the dangers of their high risk investment strategies. They were however not the first or the only ones. In a letter to Her Majesty the Queen dated 10 August 2009, a group of 10 eminent economists commented on an explanation by Professors Besley and Hennesey from the British Acadamy, on why "few economists had forseen the credit crunch". "We believe that the narrow training of economists – which concentrates on mathematical techniques and the building of empirically uncontrolled formal models – has been a major reason for this failing in our profession. This defect is enhanced by the pursuit of mathematical technique for its own sake in many leading academic journals and departments of economics." [32]. It appears that an over-reliance on mathematical modeling was a major contributer to the epic scale of the risk management failure experienced by Societe Generale with regard to managing its trading desks and its sub prime exposure. The executives at Societe Generale displayed ignorance, arrogance and incompetence only equaled by their remuneration. They were unfortunately not the first or the only ones.

CHAPTER 2

THE SUMITOMO INCIDENT

On the 28th of March 1998, more than a decade before Mr Kerviel became a household name, a group of traders and executives working for the largest stock broking firm in the world, the London-based Nomura International, tried to drive down the value of a basket of shares listed on the Australian Stock Exchange (ASE) by selling a matching basket of shares totaling USD 600 million a few minutes before the market closed. The USD 600 million represented more than the total trading that normally takes place in one day on the Australian Stock Exchange (ASE) (1). The concept was simple: Nomura amassed a portfolio of USD 600 million in futures contracts that were expiring on the 28th of March 1998. The futures portfolio would increase in value if the All Ordinary Share (All Ord) index of the Australian Stock Exchange (ASE) fell. The USD 600 million in question was apparently the largest futures parcel ever put together on the Australian Futures Exchange. Selling the matching parcel of underlying securities on the Australian Stock Exchange (ASE) would virtually assure a substantial drop in the ordinary share index, increasing the value of the matching USD 600 million futures portfolio. However, as we all know, sometimes the best laid plans don't work out. Due to a combination of factors, Nomura were only able to dump +/- USD 450 million worth of shares, and the index only fell 26 points or around one percent in the last 30 minutes of trading on the 28th of March 1996. Although the profits for Nomura were less than expected, it must still have been substantial as the key players, Channon, Moss and Mapstone, reportedly received several million dollars in bonuses. The Australian authorities reacted strongly against

Nomura and on the 11th of December 1998 the Sydney Morning Herold reported that in the Federal Court, Justice Ronald Sackville found that Nomura (International) Plc, the oldest and largest financial conglomerate in the world, was "not simply using accepted or standard market techniques to achieve legitimate commercial objectives" and that "Nomura engaged in deliberately misleading conduct designed to achieve illegitimate ends" (2).

Nomura was, however, no stranger to controversy. In July of 1997 the company agreed to pay USD 84 million to Orange County, California. Orange County suffered a USD 1,6 billion loss in December of 1994 resulting from speculation in high risk securities (3). In June of 1997 Nomura was also making news headlines for all the wrong reasons. In Tokyo charges were filed against two former senior officials of the bank for apparently paying a racketeer to prevent a shareholder meeting from being disrupted, presumably by unhappy shareholders. Its trading privileges on the Tokyo Stock Exchange (TSE) were also curtailed, resultant from payments made to a gangster. The individual in question was apparently compensated for trading losses (4). I believe it is safe to say that a culture of extreme opportunism did indeed exist at Nomura – could it also be found in other international firms? The answer is yes.

On the 26th of March 1998, two years and two months after the massive Nomura positions matured Yasuo "The Hammer" Hamanaka (also known as Mr 5%) was sentenced in a Tokyo District Court to an eight-year prison term (5). From around 1984 until his discovery in 1996, Mr Hamanaka engaged in a range of activities that culminated in a loss of more than USD two and a half billion to Sumitomo Corporation (6). Sumitomo, at the time, was the world's largest trading firm in physical copper (7). In the London Metal Exchange forward market for copper, participating firms would normally have a three-month exposure through the buying or selling of an options contract. These positions could, however, be rolled over, whereby losses or profits could be deferred through deferring the settlement date. The trading team, of which Mr Hamanaka later became the head, traded around 500 000 metric tons of copper per year, a figure that represented approximately 5% of the total annual global demand for copper. The firm of Sumitomo was very proud of their position as the dominant player in the copper market and attributed their dominance to their "...expertise in risk management". In this case study we will analyze the events that culminated in the eventual loss. By analyzing the evidence led and outcomes of court cases and disciplinary action by regulatory authorities in Japan, the United States and the United Kingdom, as well as relevant newspaper and academic articles, we will construct a model of events that will assist us in determining if this loss could be attributed to the actions of a 'rogue trader' at work or to the culmination of other factors and the actions or inactions of other role players involved.

Yasuo Hamanaka pleaded guilty to charges of forgery and fraud and, in March of 1998, he was sentenced to 8 years' imprisonment with hard labor less the 400 days he had already served at the date of sentencing (8). During his trail, however, it emerged from evidence given by Mr Hamanaka that during 1985 the head of Sumitomo's copper dealing team at the time, Mr Steve Shimizu, was the one who proposed speculative trading to Mr Hamanaka as a way to recoup pre-existing losses resultant from physical trading activities (9). Mr Hamanaka testified that Mr Shimizu said that "unauthorized futures trading" was the only possible way to recoup the copper team's existing losses. Mr Hamanaka also testified that, at that time, he suspected that his superior, Mr Shimizu, was already conducting speculative transactions to recoup losses, as his volumes of trading were "more than normal". By March 1986 the losses of the Sumitomo copper trading team rose to around USD 50 million. At that time the decision was made by Mr Shimizu and Mr Hamanaka not to reveal the losses to their superiors, as they were "too great". At that time fate dealt Mr Hamanaka a cruel blow. Mr Shimizu was to be reassigned to Manila by Sumitomo and he decided to resign, leaving Mr Hamanaka to handle the losses. Mr Hamanaka further testified that, although the task was initially daunting, he was convinced that over time he could make back the losses through careful and cautious futures trading. Mr Shimizu testified that he was well aware of the fact that Mr Hamanaka would be left to shoulder the responsibility for the USD 50 million in accumulated losses. He also suggested a hypothetical limit that would have triggered disclosure to his superiors, by saying that it would probably be around USD 100 million (10). Another interesting point that emerged from the testimony of Mr Shimizu was his contention that "all data concerning transactions and contracts were entered into Sumitomo's computer system" (11), alluding to the fact that with proper oversight and risk management these transactions should have been detected. During the trial it also emerged that Mr Shimizu set up his own firm, Scat Ltd, which conducted business with Sumitomo. As a result of such transactions, Mr Hamanaka was paid a portion of the profits made by Scat. It appears that the court viewed the acceptance of money without company approval as an indicator of the way Mr Hamanaka conducted his affairs.

According to the 1997 testimony of Yoshio Takeuchi, the then assistant general manager nonferrous metal, chemicals and petroleum group of Sumitomo, there were newspaper articles in the British press that claimed that Sumitomo were acquiring massive positions in copper warrants on the London Metal Exchange (LME) (12). This, according to Mr Takeuchi's testimony, sparked an internal investigation by Sumitomo. The internal investigation, aimed at determining if Sumitomo were manipulating the copper market, found that those allegations of market manipulation were unfounded and untrue. A few weeks later, Mr Takeuchi was on the stand again (13). This time he testified to the fact that Sumitomo Head Office in Japan had an agreement with its subsidiaries, like Hong Kong, where contracts that exceeded credit lines could only be approved after a process of mutual consultation. This limit was, in the 1980s, set at USD 1 million for the Hong Kong subsidiary but was, however, changed in 1994 after Mr Hamanaka regularly exceeded his limits, in one instance by USD 100 million in a transaction with Credit Lyonnais Rouse (CLR). Mr Takeuchi testified that the General Manager of credit and controlling was alerted to this transaction, but took no real action other than rapping Mr Hamanaka over the knuckles. Mr Hamanaka's defense proved that all the Hong Kong subsidiaries' transactions were conducted under instructions and with the funding of Tokyo. When confronted with Sumitomo records of numerous transactions conducted by Mr Hamanaka that exceeded his trading limits, Mr Takeuchi responded by saying he could not remember, did not know or that he "…was not in a position to be able to know". These bouts of amnesia also affected other Sumitomo executives.

During the trial, the former credit manager for Sumitomo Corporation, Mr Hiroshi Nishino, was questioned by Mr Hamanaka's defense team on how it was possible that all these massive positions remained hidden from himself and senior management at Sumitomo (14). During questioning that lasted nearly two hours, Mr Nishino's standard responses to virtually all the questions that were put to him was either "I don't remember", "I have no memory of it" or "I have no recollection of it" and, when he was shown incriminating documents, he responded with "I have never seen it". Some of the documents related to the huge copper transactions that were shown to Mr Nishino included correspondence between the president of Sumitomo and the president of its Hong Kong subsidiary, clearly indicating their knowledge of at least some of these very large transactions. Similarly, when asked how he as head of credit missed the transactions between Credit Lyonnais Rouse and Morgan Guaranty Trust & Co, in a regime where all transactions by any subsidiary over USD 20 million needed approval from Tokyo, Mr Nishino's memory failed him. Similarly, Mr Hamanaka's defense also proved that senior management was at least aware of one suspicious transaction of USD 320 million that was detected as an unpaid account during September of 1993. At roughly the same time, credit lines were set for all dealers and brokers with whom Sumitomo was dealing. When questioned on this, Mr Nishino's response was one of denying that such a document was ever sent by his staff to Tokyo on his orders. In 1994 numerous efforts to obtain letters of approval from Tokyo for extraordinary transactions (one can assume executed by Mr Hamanaka) were fruitless. It is clear from the evidence presented by Mr Hamanaka's defense that there were numerous occasions when his transactions could have been detected over an extended period of time. It is, therefore, not surprising that in May of 1998 the United States Commodity Futures Trading Commission (CFTC) took action against Sumitomo Corporation for manipulating the copper market. Sumitomo eventually had to pay the FSA GBP 5 million to cover its time and effort and had to pay the CFTC USD 125 million (15); a mere slap on the wrist for the multi-billion dollar multi-national.

During 1995 both the US Commodities Futures Trading Commission (CFTC) and the Securities Investment Board (SIB) in the UK initiated investigations into the behavior of the international copper price (6). These investigations eventually led to action taken against firms in both the UK and USA. The SIB was later known as the Securities and Finance Authority Limited (SFA). On the 30th of June 1999 the CFTC announced that an administrative enforcement action had been settled with the two Merrill Lynch companies. Without admitting or denying the allegations, the two companies agreed to the order being entered into the CFTC records (16). The order found that, at minimum, these two firms assisted Sumitomo Corporation and other firms in the following respects: "by providing more than one half billion dollars of credit and finance to the manipulators, which the manipulators used to purchase and hold a dominant position in futures contracts and London Metal Exchange warehouse stocks of copper; by providing trading facilities, accounts and trading capacity through which the manipulators acquired their dominant position in a combination of futures contracts and warehouse stocks, and through which the manipulators sold or lent a small portion of their holdings at artificially high absolute prices and artificially high backward dated spread price differentials; and by providing trading advice which the manipulators used in the execution of their strategy of withholding their copper from the market."

The CFTC findings also make it clear that "…Merrill (B&D) and Merrill International possessed the requisite knowledge and intent to find that they aided and abetted the manipulators' violations. In addition, the Order finds that Merrill (B&D) benefited from the manipulation by providing financing, trading facilities and credit to the manipulators, and by earning profits through its proprietary trading" (17). It is very clear from the wording used by the CFTC that they do not view these actions as a "rogue" event. This was a very clear strategy that was well planned, extensively funded and meticulously executed over an extended period of time. Merril Lynch agreed to pay a USD 15 million penalty to CFTC and a further USD 10 million to the London Metal Exchange (LME). CNN Money (18) reported that Merrill Lynch claimed they entered into the settlement as it was to avoid the "expense" and "distraction" that a drawn-out court case could entail, after initially dismissing CFTC allegations as groundless.

On the first of March 2000 the Securities and Futures Authority in the United Kingdom announced penalties imposed on a number of firms and individuals (19). These penalties resulted from proceedings instituted during November of 1997, following an investigation into the dealings of these firms with Sumitomo Corporation and Mr Hamanaka, the general manager at the time of the non-ferrous metals department, in particular. Mr Harker and Mr Wolff were both reprimanded and fined GBP 30 000 and GBP 15 000 respectively and had to make contributions of GBP 15 000 and GBP 6 000 to the SFA's costs.

Mr Tazaki lost his SFA registration for a period of seven years, during which he also could not register with the SFA in any other capacity. He was also fined GBP 45 000 and had to contribute GBP 5 000 to SFA costs. Similarly, the firm of Rudolf Wolff & Co. Limited was reprimanded and fined GBP 375 000 over and above a contribution of GBP 125 000 that they had to make towards the expenses incurred by the SFA. In essence, the abovementioned individuals and firms that were penalized admitted to breaching a number of SFA principles. This included failing to "act with due skill, care and diligence" to "observe high standards of market conduct" and to "organize their affairs in a responsible manner" [20].

During the SFA investigation it became clear that the relationship between Rudolf Wolff & Company, as a firm, and some of its staff with Sumitomo was essentially corrupt in nature. A large portion of its business consisted of fictitious "cross trades", which were essentially accounting entries that created a false perception of turnover. It was furthermore found that SCAT, the company owned by Mr Shimizu, was appointed as a consultant to Rudolf Wolff & Company and, on at least one occasion, money from a Sumitomo account managed by Rudolf Wolff & Company was paid to SCAT under instructions from Mr Hamanaka. No-one ever confirmed that these instructions were authorized. Rudolf Wolff & Company also provided Sumitomo with false trading volume confirmations over a 5-year period between April of 1991 and April of 1996. The information used in the confirmations was information supplied by Mr Hamanaka and was never checked. Similarly, Rudolf Wolff & Company staff provided Sumitomo with month-end confirmations of its copper trading activities without actually confirming that the confirmations sought by Sumitomo tied up with actual transactions that were executed. In essence, Rudolf Wolff & Company provided third party confirmation to Mr Hamanaka of transactions that never took place. Similarly, Rudolf Wolff KK, the Japanese subsidiary of Rudolf Wolff & Company, admitted to providing Sumitomo (usually on the request of Mr Hamanaka) with numerous false documents over the 5-year period from 1991 to 1996. These false documents included confirmations of the existence of fictitious copper warrants, confirmations of fictitious transactions, as well as false or incorrect invoices and "difference" accounts (21). An internal memo from Mr Tsukuda, a director for Rudolf Wolff KK, to Mr Tazaki, the managing director, clearly indicated that confirmations of Sumitomo positions were signed without the supporting documentation attached and that both Rudolf Wolff KK and Mr Hamanaka were aware that the warrant holdings that were confirmed referred to non-existent positions. It also made it clear that Mr Hamanaka's requests for the altering of trade dates and confirmations for non-existent transfers were done without the knowledge of Sumitomo. One possible explanation for the reasons behind the assistance provided to Mr Hamanaka might be found in his authorization of the use of USD 500 000 of Sumitomo's funds to invest in TAO, a "fund management vehicle", established by Rudolf Wolff & Company.

In April of 2002, without admitting liability, JP Morgan agreed to pay more than USD 120 million to Sumitomo Corporation. This payment resulted from claims by Sumitomo Corporation that JP Morgan assisted Hamanaka in his activities by providing him with a "loan" of more than USD 150 million during 1994 (22). Sumitomo argued that the "loan" was disguised as a "series of copper transactions" that had an initial premium (the loan) of USD 154 million payable to Sumitomo attached to it. By structuring it in such a way, Sumitomo argued that it was virtually impossible for their auditors to detect the loan. The effective interest rate charged by JP Morgan was also "hundreds of basis points" more than what Sumitomo would normally pay in the markets for such loans. This led Sumitomo to suspect that those at JP Morgan involved in the transactions had to have guessed that Mr Hamanaka was desperate and acting without authorization. One of the JP Morgan bankers, Ms Kieran Sykes, had done business with Mr Hamanaka at her previous firm,

ING. During 1993 she assisted Mr Hamanaka to secure a USD 100 million line of credit from ING. There were, however, one or two oddities around this loan. In the first instance, the banking fees of USD 750 000 for the Sumitomo loan were paid by a UK firm called Winchester Commodities and, secondly, there was no second signature on the Sumitomo request for the loan. When the loan came up for renewal, a senior official from ING was dispatched to Tokyo to secure a signature from a Sumitomo main board director before ING would be prepared to renew the facility. Mr Hamanaka's response was odd, to say the least, and the official was not allowed access into the Sumitomo building by Mr Hamanaka. In response, ING cancelled the loan, but took no steps to advise Sumitomo of the treatment their banker received. Another interesting twist in this event is the fact that, on the day that the JP Morgan facility was approved, Winchester Commodities made a payment of USD 100 000 to a firm registered in the British Virgin Isles belonging to Ms Sykes. Ms Sykes denied that the two events were tied to one another in any way, thereby denying that she was paid a fee or a bribe.

The initial losses incurred by Sumitomo's copper division resulted from the trading of physical copper in the Philippines (23). In order to recoup these losses, Mr Shimizu began speculating on derivatives through the LME. The losses of the copper section had, however, risen in 1987 to USD 58 million and we know that Mr Shimizu had by then resigned.

During 1993 Mr Hamanaka engaged in the unauthorized sale of deep in the money put options, to Morgan Guaranty Trust and lost USD 393 million on the transaction. This method of funding was also used by others, including Mr Leeson and Mr Rusnak, and will be discussed in detail later ino this book. During 1994 Mr Hamanaka ran out of funds again and this time he started selling a combination of puts and calls in order to raise USD 150 million. Mr Nick Leeson also sold a combination of puts and calls called a straddle. In my interview with him, he confirmed to me that he chose this instrument because of the high premium he could generate out of it. One can only assume that Mr Hamanaka used this combination of instruments for the same reason. In the case of Mr Leeson, his losses resultant from using these instruments greatly contributed to the demise of Barings Bank in 1995. In the case of Mr Hamanaka, the losses that resulted from the sale of these puts and calls amounted to USD 253 million.

In August of 1998 Sumitomo agreed to pay USD 99 million following legal action taken against it in a New York court and followed it up with a payment of USD 42.5 million after similar action in a Californian court. The applicants in these actions alleged that Sumitomo Corporation, with the assistance of a firm called Global Minerals, manipulated the copper market between 1994 and 1996 (24). In essence, an artificial copper shortage was created through the purchasing of physical copper, by taking delivery of option and future contracts and storing the copper in LME warehouses. Mr Hamanaka resisted speculators like George Soros, who were trying to short the market by selling copper that they didn't have at lower than market prices, with the hope that they could buy the copper at the time of delivery at even lower prices. Mr Hamanaka, however, used the extensive resources and, more importantly perhaps, credit-worthiness of Sumitomo to buy the other side of these options sold by the speculators, thereby neutralizing the downward pressure created by these sales. When Mr Hamanaka was removed from his position in May of 1995, no-one was countering the short selling and the copper price collapsed. This collapse caused copper prices to drop sharply, causing massive losses resulting from Mr Hamanaka's positions that were dependent on high copper prices. Total losses to Sumitomo eventually rose to the unprecedented amount of more than USD 2.5 billion.

One of the first indications that something was amiss came in 1991, when David Threlkeld, a metal broker trading on the

LME, reported a request by Mr Hamanaka for an invoice for non-existent trades (25). As we know from the trial, Sumitomo was advised but did nothing about it. This was, however, not all. In 1994 the SFA investigated the trading activities of Winchester Commodities and a Chilean trader acting for a firm called Codelco. During this investigation they uncovered the fact that Winchester made virtually all their profits from their broking activities for Sumitomo. This information was purportedly shared with Sumitomo but elicited no apparent response. The third warning was probably the most compelling. By early 1996 both the UK and USA regulators expressed concerns about the behavior of the copper price. As mentioned earlier, production was outstripping demand by a substantial margin and the price of copper kept on rising. It is difficult to believe that, as the largest player in the copper market globally, the executives of the firm that would have had access to most research on the behavior of the copper price did not seriously question this anomaly, unless they were aware of or at least suspected the reason for it.

How is it possible for the executives of a firm that prides it self on being the largest and most dominant player in a particular industry not to know how they attained and maintained their position? Why, even when made aware of very large and repeated transgressions of trading limits, was nothing done? In this chapter, we have seen that Mr Hamanaka was not the initiator of the events that led to one of the largest losses in corporate history. The initial losses were created not by him self, nor did he invent the "solution" to the dilemma his superior created. He learned from his superior how to behave, who in all probability learned from someone else that hiding your losses is an acceptable practice. We also find that, according to the CFTC, some of the largest financial institutions in the world, Merril Lynch and JP Morgan, were actively involved in assisting Mr Hamanaka in his efforts to manipulate the copper market, an exercise he believed would give him the competitive edge that would allow him to make back the massive losses he was sitting on. It is also an enigma how Mr Hamanaka's superiors and the board of directors can plead ignorance to how their firm managed a stranglehold on the world's copper market over many years. There is evidence to support the view that Sumitomo was, in all probability, aware of the fact that Mr Hamanaka was trying to manipulate the copper market and also allowed him to operate outside the internal rules and limits with impunity. In what became something of a trademark for many of the events we will analyze in later chapters, we find that Mr Hamanaka incurred very large losses resultant from the sale of deep in the money options. He sold deep in the money options to generate financing for the positions he was holding or wanted to take.

Market manipulation appears to be part and parcel of the strategies employed by financial market operators, in their pursuit of personal wealth and corporate profits. We have seen here a number of different companies, all very successful and "respectable", which operate on a multinational and global level over a range of jurisdictions. The markets are largely impersonal and it is very difficult to identify 'victims' of these opportunistic behaviors. It is very difficult to portray Sumitomo or Nomura as typical victims, as they appear to be active participants rather than hapless victims, and are at least as liable as the so-called rogues. Rewards are substantial for those who succeed, while informal and even formal restraints are weak and ineffective. There is a definite imbalance between the facilitator side and the inhibitor side in an environment of very strong motivators like preserving face, especially in the Japanese culture.

CHAPTER 3

TOSHIHIDE IGUCHI & DAIWA BANK

On the 13th of July 1995, a mere three months after the arrest in Germany of Nick Leeson, Barings Bank's "star" trader, the executive vice president of Daiwa Bank's New York branch, confessed in a letter to the president of his bank the fact that he had, over an 11-year period, lost the bank an estimated USD 1.1 billion. In this chapter we will analyze the events that led up to and followed Mr Igichi's confession, with special attention to the corporate environment in which he had to operate. Newspaper and other articles, magazine interviews, court records and Mr Iguchi's own account of the events at Daiwa Bank will be used to determine the corporate culture at Daiwa Bank at the time of Mr Iguchi's tenure at the bank.

Toshihide Iguchi was born in Kobe in Japan (coincidentally, the city that was hit by an earthquake during 1995). He became a US citizen and majored in psychology at Southwest Missouri State University in Springfield USA [1]. In 1974 he joined the New York branch of Daiwa and in 1977 he was put in charge of the custody department [2]. In 1980 he was placed in charge of securities trading and in 1984 was promoted to the position of trader and he started trading in US Government bonds. He however retained his back office duties and went on to supervise the New York back office up until 1995. In this period of controlling both front and back offices Mr Iguchi, according to his own confession, conducted more than 30 000 unauthorized transactions [3]. The original loss was incurred in 1984 and amounted to USD 200 000 at the time. However, as Mr Iguchi tried to trade himself out of this loss, it grew to over USD 1 billion in the eleven-year period [4].

Mr Iguchi was described as a workaholic and, although he was divorced, he was granted custody of his two sons (5) and stayed in a USD 300 000 house in Kinnelon, New Jersey. The New York office that opened in 1950 initially only dealt in US treasury securities as a service to their pension fund clients. During the 1980s, however, Daiwa became a major player in the US government debt market and the firm was designated as a primary dealer in 1986. A Primary dealer is "a designation given by the Federal Reserve System to commercial banks or broker/dealers who meet specific criteria, including capital requirements and participation in Treasury auctions" (6).

Mr Iguchi placed a large portion of the blame on the ineptness of the formal regulators, both in Japan and in the USA. He used specific examples to illustrate this. In one case during 1992, an inspection by US Federal Reserve Bank regulators that was supposed to last two days only lasted 15 minutes. Mr Iguchi also claimed that one of the Federal officials smelled strongly of alcohol (7). Mr Iguchi also accounts that he believed that the US Federal authorities suspected Daiwa of improper conduct as far back as 1993 and that Daiwa also made concerted efforts, such as filling his trading room with cardboard boxes, to conceal the existence of his trading room in New York. The failure of the formal regulators was not, however, limited to the US. During 1994 an inspection to the New York offices of Daiwa, conducted by inspectors from the Japanese Ministry of Finance and which was supposed to last a week, was wrapped up in a day, apparently to allow time for the inspectors to fit in a visit to Las Vegas. (Maybe they wanted to see some real gamblers in action.)

During an interview with TIME Magazine Mr Iguchi accounts that, before 1992, there were about six or seven cases of unauthorized trading at Daiwa Bank that led to losses of between USD 100 million and 300 million each. In not one of these cases were those responsible either charged or arrested (8).

Another interesting characteristic of the Iguchi affair was the fact that the transactions executed by Mr Iguchi were not intricate derivative transactions. Mr Iguchi was selling and buying the same vanilla type bonds for a period of twelve years and he believed that there were a number of his superiors who had the ability to completely understand exactly what he was doing. The problem in the case of Daiwa, Mr Iguchi pointed out in his interview with TIME magazine (9), was not a lack or inability to understand, but rather an unwillingness to see. This induced blindness he attributes to the fact that his department accounted for more than 50% of the profits generated by the New York branch of Daiwa and that this dependence on his profits is at the root of the problem.

However, this all changed in 1995 when Mr Iguchi advised the President of Daiwa, Mr Akiri Fujita, of his activities (10). In a letter in Japanese addressed to the President of Daiwa, Mr Iguchi (in his own words) made an "honest confession" of his activities. This letter, commonly referred to as "the confession letter", was incidentally sent only a few months after the collapse in February of 1995 and the subsequent arrest of Mr Nick Leeson, the General Manager of Barings Securities Singapore. During the proceedings of a Federal Grand Jury and subsequent court procedures, a tale unfolded itself reminiscent of those we normally find in spy novels (11).

In evidence led before US courts it was revealed that, over a period of nearly two months, no less than five letters were drafted by Mr Iguchi. The first letter, drafted before July 21, 1995, was the initial "confession letter" that started the whole process and was written of Mr Iguchi's own accord. The fifth and last "revised confession letter" was written on instruction from Mr Iguchi's General Manager, Mr Masahiro Tsuda. According to evidence led, the first "confession letter" stated that Mr Iguchi, as an employee of the New York Branch of Daiwa Bank, caused losses of just over USD 1 billion from the trading in United States Treasury bonds. Mr Iguchi stated further that he concealed his losses by selling treasury bonds that the bank was holding on behalf of its clients. As the custodian bank for clients, the bank was tasked with the duty of the safekeeping of securities belonging to its clients. In his "confession letter" Mr Iguchi identified the United States Treasury Obligations that he sold from a Bankers Trust account, together with the ultimate owners of the sold securities. Mr Iguchi revealed that, without authorization, he sold USD 377 million worth of United States Treasury Obligations (12).

The owners of the US treasury obligations were entitled to routine coupon payments on their bonds from the Federal Treasury and also the market value of the securities in the event that they sold the US Treasury Obligations they owned or thought they owned. In order to fund the Daiwa customers in the event of a sale or a coupon payment, Mr Iguchi sold the US Treasury Obligations of other clients in order to raise the required amount of cash that he needed. In his "confession letter" Mr Iguchi not only spelled out the losses he incurred, he also warned his superiors against the possibility of detection by the US authorities and states that, without him being present and able to handle the situation, an investigation would be a certainty. This would be triggered by any sale of securities no longer there or a coupon payment due to clients whose bonds he sold to finance an earlier transaction. He went further and warned of dire consequences for the bank if the matter was handled outside the realm of Daiwa and the Japanese authorities, as a result of the "current relationship" between the US and Japan, which we can only assume was not warm. Mr Iguchi did, however, provide a solution to this problem. In the first instance, he made it clear that he needed to be there as the architect of the problem to ensure the unauthorized trades remained undetected over the short term and he also proposed a permanent remedy for the dilemma. He suggested to the powers that be at Daiwa to replace the securities that he sold without authorization to ensure that the loss would not appear on the books of Daiwa's New York branch and could, therefore, not be detected by the US authorities. In his "confession letter" Mr Iguchi also played his trump card by refreshing the Daiwa President's memory of similar events of unlawful conduct at Daiwa including, as he phrased it, a "big accident" that was concealed in the past. This obviously substantial trading loss was concealed through the filing of, among other things, "false documents to US Federal Reserve" and other acts necessary to deceive the US authorities (13). Mr Iguchi followed this "confession letter" up with a second letter in which he assured the President of Daiwa that, based on his experience, there was no possibility of detection by the US authorities if Daiwa bought back the missing securities.

With this as a backdrop it is, therefore, not surprising that on the 24th of July 1995 Mr Iguchi was contacted by a trio of Daiwa officials via telephone to discuss the two letters that he sent to the President of Daiwa. The trio included no less than the Deputy President of Daiwa, one of the Managing Directors of Daiwa and the General Manager of the International Treasury Division. During this conversation, the state alleged it was made clear to Mr Iguchi that the New York Branch of Daiwa had to be removed from the equation and Mr Iguchi was asked for his assistance and some suggestions on how best to accomplish this and to keep on concealing the loss from detection by the US authorities. This elicited a third letter from Mr Iguchi, dated 25th of July 1995, which was now addressed to the Deputy President of Daiwa, who it appears had taken charge of this matter. In his letter, Mr Iguchi warned against fiddling the books of Daiwa New York, as this would be committing an offense clearly falling under the jurisdiction of the US authorities. It is clear from this warning that Mr Iguchi felt that the only way of mending the situation was to replace the missing securities. In response, the Managing Director involved contacted Mr Iguchi by telephone and arranged for a meeting in New York. This meeting took place around the 28th of July 1995 at the Park Lane Hotel in New York. Present were the Managing Director involved, the President of the Daiwa Trust, the General Manager of the New York Branch of Daiwa and, obviously, Mr Iguchi. During the meeting, the State alleged that the Managing Director involved disclosed that Daiwa intended to announce the loss in late November, after the announcement of the Daiwa half-yearly results scheduled for 30th September 1995. He assured those present that no-one would be prejudiced and he also enquired from Mr Iguchi if he would be willing to accept a transfer to an affiliate of Daiwa in Japan. Mr Iguchi pointed out to those present the interest-bearing nature of the missing US Treasury Obligations, which entitles the rightful owners of these securities to predetermined periodic interest payments. If the missing securities remained secret, it would necessitate the selling of more securities to generate the funds required. The Managing Director involved gave Mr Iguchi the go-ahead to continue selling the necessary securities to ensure that payments could be made to clients, as and when was necessary. He also went further and instructed Mr Iguchi to do whatever necessary to conceal the USD 1.1 billion loss and asked him to also prepare a detailed letter containing the events that surrounded the loss (14).

This meeting was followed by the meeting that took place at the Park Lane hotel in New York around the 29th of July 1995. As instructed, Mr Iguchi had produced a detailed account (the "Fourth Iguchi Letter"), of how he incurred the initial losses and how he covered them up though the unauthorized sale of securities belonging to clients, as well as Daiwa's proprietary stock and through entering false information into the books of Daiwa New York.

One of the crucial means of deception described in the "Fourth Iguchi Letter" was falsifying the Bankers Trust accounts that reflected the actual holdings of United States Treasury Obligations held on behalf of Daiwa and its clients. Because of the time it took to falsify these Bankers Trust reports by hand (obviously using a typewriter), Mr Iguchi turned to technology and used a word processor, which allowed him to only change the necessary areas once he had the original loaded. Mr Iguchi provided the original Bankers Trust statements to his superiors at the meeting. Through these, they could verify that the extent of the "missing" securities was nearly USD 600 million in short-term United States Treasury Obligations. Of this amount, +/- USD 377 million belonged to Daiwa clients and +/- USD 134 million was the property of Daiwa itself. After satisfying themselves as to the exact extent of the missing obligations, Mr Iguchi was instructed by the General Manager involved to destroy the computer disk on which he prepared his confession letter (one can only assume he referred to all four letters). A few days later, purportedly around the fourth of August 1995, Mr Iguchi once again received instructions from Mr Tsuda. He was, firstly, instructed to draft an undated confession letter in which he only discusses his own fraud, losses and unauthorized activities, and he was also instructed not to discuss any of the omitted issues with anybody. The amended letter (the Fifth Iguchi Letter) was subsequently drafted by Mr Iguchi.

Once in possession of the sanitized letter, the executives of the bank decided it was time to reveal their "problem" to the authorities. On the 8th of August 1995 the President of Daiwa informed the Banking Bureau Chief of the Japanese Ministry of Finance, Mr Yoshimasa Nishimura and, on the 18th of September, the matter was reported to the Federal Reserve Bank of New York by Daiwa and the Japanese regulators (15). Mr Iguchi was (according to him), not informed of this decision (16) and to his surprise he was arrested by the US authorities on the 23rd of September 1995.

A collection of US authorities, including the New York State Banking Department, the Federal Reserve Bank of New York, the Board of Governors and the Federal Default Insurance Fund, also jointly issued "cease and desist" orders against Daiwa Bank and the Daiwa Trust Company. These orders not only curtailed the activities of these two entities in the US, but also called for an independent forensic investigation to be conducted by an independent firm. As part of their brief, they had to make a thorough assessment of, among other things, the internal controls and risk management procedures. As it turned out, there was more to the Daiwa incident than Toshihide Iguchi.

On the 2nd of November 1995, the US authorities terminated Daiwa's operations in the US by instructing the company to wind up its operations by February of the next year (17). Daiwa was also indicted on 24 charges that included "conspiracy, mail and wire fraud, obstructing the examination of a financial institution, falsification of bank records, failure to report felonies, and the affirmative concealment of felonies". Daiwa pleaded guilty to these charges on 28th February 1996 and was sentenced to a fine of USD 340 million. Krane & DeTrask (18) quotes from the sentencing of Daiwa by Judge Kaplan: "Daiwa has manifested extraordinary culpability both with respect to [Iguchi's] scheme ... and otherwise ... Daiwa bank has acted with exceptional contempt of US law and US regulatory authority. It has refused to cooperate with US authorities to this date. It has little claim on the sympathies of an American court" (19).

The General Manager who attended the meetings in the hotel rooms with Mr Tsuda was also indicted, arrested and charged with "conspiracy to deceive the Federal Reserve by concealing the bank's $1.1 billion trading loss, making false statements to the Federal Reserve, making false entries in the books and records of Daiwa, and the misprision of a felony". Mr Tsuda pleaded guilty to one count of conspiracy on the 4th of April 1996, for which he was sentenced during October of that year to a fine of USD 100 000 and two months in prison (20).

In a November 30 report prepared for the US Congress it is claimed that, as far back as 1989, Daiwa officials, including Mr Iguchi, were engaged in actions to mislead officers of the New York Banking Department who were conducting an inspection. Their actions included the relocation of traders and back office staff (21). These actions were also employed to deceive auditors conducting a 1992 inspection by the Federal Reserve Bank of New York. When examiners from the New York Federal Reserve Bank became aware of the fact that Mr Iguchi was in fact running the securities trading and custody services, the matter was taken up with Daiwa management. In response, the Daiwa management provided Federal officers with written confirmation that the custodial and trading oversight functions had indeed been split. By November of the next year, Daiwa was once again cautioned by the New York Federal Reserve and the State Banking Department concerning, among other things, the relocation of traders and audit deficiencies in the accounting function at Daiwa New York. During a joint examination, inspectors from the two regulatory bodies were once again assured that Mr Iguchi was only responsible for custody services, while the trading function resorted under another senior Daiwa official.

After Mr Iguchi's July 17 confession to the Chairman of Daiwa, a number of transactions were executed with the approval of senior Daiwa officials. To prevent detection of Mr Iguchi's indiscretions, this included the filing of a false report to the Federal Reserve. By August the 8th of 1995, the Japanese Ministry of Finance was advised, but did not advise their US counterparts until Daiwa advised the New York Federal Reserve Bank on the 18th of September 1995 (22). It is important to note that, at the time, the Japanese banking crisis was in full swing and an estimated USD 400 billion of non-performing loans were strangling the Japanese banking industry (23). One of the inherent causes of this massive accumulation of bad debts was the accounting practices of Japanese banks.

Japanese banks never adjusted the market value of property held as security downwards, even after such property became virtually worthless. After Mr Iguchi's arrest on September 24th US officials were also alerted to the losses of nearly

USD 100 million between 1984 and 1987 that were concealed by Daiwa through using a Cayman Island subsidiary. Some of these losses were the result of unauthorized trading by Daiwa staff. One wonders if Mr Iguchi would have volunteered this information had he been timeously advised by his superiors of their intention to inform the US authorities of his actions.

During his interview with Time Magazine (24) Mr Iguchi provides us with important insights into the 'motives' for his actions. Initially he tried to recover a loss he made, through a legitimate and authorized transaction. In his mind admitting to the loss would have caused him to "lose face" and possibly his job. The alternative was to keep the loss a secret for a period of time, trade out of the loss, and all would be well. Mr Iguchi also made reference to an obvious, but often discarded, piece of evidence, "No-one ever goes into the market thinking he is going to lose money". This often overlooked fact is crucial, as it identifies the fundamental driver to Mr Iguchi. His status, self-worth and security depended on his ability to make money, and lots of it. In fact, Mr Iguchi also felt responsible for the status, self-worth and security of a number of people in his firm. According to him, he was responsible for more than half the profits of the New York office and this dependence, in turn, acted as a blindfold to those who should have supervised him. This is evidence of the role of structural deficiencies inherent in the Bank. These facts should also be seen against the backdrop of the fact that Mr Iguchi believed that, by hiding his loss and trading out of it, he was at the worst in violation of a couple of internal rules. He was further strengthened in this belief by his knowledge of at least half a dozen cases of unauthorized trading in his firm, involving amounts of between USD 100 million and USD 300 million. In not one of these cases was anyone arrested or even charged with a crime. According to Mr Iguchi, he only realized as late as 1993 that making a false statement to a Federal examiner was a crime. It is noteworthy that he still appears not to view his unauthorized activities as criminal.

There is a school of thought that associates financial collapses with the use of exotic financial instruments. In the case of Mr Iguchi, this appears not to be the case. Mr Iguchi traded US Government Bonds, also known as Treasury Obligations, for twelve years. According to him, there were a number of managers above him who were capable of understanding what he was doing (25). There was, however, one report (26) claiming that Daiwa management admitted to the fact that Mr Iguchi was dealing in derivatives.

Mr Iguchi primarily traded in US Government Bonds. There is an inverse relationship between the price of a government's bonds and the rate at which that same government is prepared to lend money to its banks through the central bank. This borrowing is referred to as the 'discount window' or 'repo' rate. In *Figure 1* we have a graphic representation of the repo rates of the New York Federal Reserve Bank from the time Mr Iguchi started working for Daiwa until his confession in 1995. As we know, Mr Iguchi started working for Daiwa in 1974 and became head of securities trading in 1977. He started trading in 1984 and by 1989 he had built up a loss of nearly USD 600 million.

Mr Iguchi experienced a movement in US interest rates from 7.5% in January 1974 to 5.25% in January 1977, when he became head of securities trading. Thereafter, rates rose to 14% in 1981 before moving to 8.4% in 1984, when he began trading US Government Bonds. From this time onwards, interest rates in the US steadily declined to as low as 3% in 1993/94. If you held the view (we assume Mr Iguchi held) that interest rates will bounce back, you would have lost a bundle over this period.

If we analyze the Daiwa event, or should we call it events, it is clear that there was indeed a culture of deceit present in the company. The young Mr Iguchi who started working for Daiwa

FIG 1

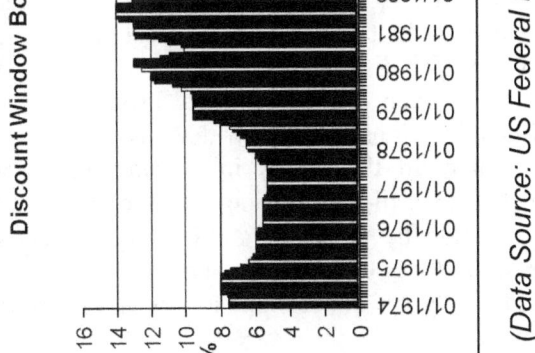

Discount Window Borrowing Federal Reserve Bank of NY

(Data Source: US Federal Reserve)

was learning his trade from those who created that culture and he also learned how to operate in it. Mr Iguchi experienced events where other traders who engaged in unauthorized trading were actively assisted by Daiwa executives in covering up these indiscretions. Coupled with the advantage he had of being in charge of both the front and back office, as well as his very good understanding of how the company's systems worked, this created an environment conducive to Mr Iguchi conducting his activities undetected for a very long time. It is quite clear that formal US regulations were often circumvented by Daiwa staff. It is also abundantly clear that the accepted procedure of dealing with an irregularity was to hide it, even if it meant going to great lengths to achieve this. There can be little argument that all layers of the firm, up to the Board, not only approved some of these actions but also actively participated in them. There is also evidence to suggest that the Japanese Regulator, the Ministry of Finance, actively assisted Daiwa in keeping their transgressions secret. It is, therefore, no surprise that Mr Iguchi kept his mistakes secret for a very long time, as the fear of losing face and possibly his job was a very strong motivator. I do believe that, at least in part, of Mr Iguchi's motivation for disclosing his deeds to the chairman of Daiwa may have been the arrest and prosecution of Mr Leeson. Mr Iguchi obviously believed that his transgressions would be treated like all the others in Daiwa and he was absolutely correct. Daiwa did act in line with the culture of the company and so did the Ministry of Finance in Japan. It is very interesting that, even while serving his sentence, Mr Iguchi defended Daiwa's decision to try and resolve the matter internally.

During his February 10 interview with Time Magazine he also defended their decision not to report the matter to the US authorities, citing the fact that they had to completely understand the nature of the problem and its "...implications to the bank later on" (27). Mr Iguchi's biggest gripe with Daiwa was the fact that they didn't warn him of their intention to eventually disclose the matter to the US authorities, putting him in a disadvantageous position with regard to retaining a lawyer and constructing an appropriate defense.

Mr Iguchi's motivation was a combination of trying to protect his position in Daiwa and his own prestige. This in itself was not an extreme motivation, as he was not earning millions per annum. The Daiwa problem was the strength of facilitating factors like a lack of efficient risk management regimes, such as splitting the control of front and back offices and enforcing adherence to internal and external regulations. On the contrary, management on the highest levels assisted staff in evading regulations (on a number of occasions), rather than insuring strict adherence. As an inhibiting factor, formal regulatory efficiency on both the Japanese and US sides was questionable at best. From Mr Iguchi's perspective there was, therefore, precious little to inhibit extreme opportunism. Even without extreme salary incentives and highly geared exotic derivatives, Mr Iguchi's opportunism was extreme. The billion dollar losses through around 30 000 unauthorized transactions over a more than ten-year period was largely made possible by an overwhelming body of facilitating factors.

In March 1999 Mr Iguchi was released from the federal correctional institute at Allanwood (28).

CHAPTER 4

JOSEPH JETT & KIDDER PEABODY

During the week of April 11 1994 Michael A. Carpenter, the CEO of Kidder Peabody, a highly rated US investment bank, had the unenviable task (1) of telling the Chairman of his parent company and longstanding friend that his firm experienced an "accounting glitch", a euphemistic way of saying 'we lost a substantial amount of money'. The parent company was General Electric and its chairman was none other than John F. Welch Jr., better known to most people as "Jack". The amount of money involved was around USD 300 million in false profits and USD 85 million in hidden losses, according to reports; Mr Welch lost his lunch on hearing the news (2). The losses resulted from a massive overstatement of profits resulting from the manipulation of Kidder's accounting system by their 'star' trader, Joseph Jett.

In order to grasp the culture at Kidder, it is important to understand the business philosophy of the General Electric chairman. Any business owned by General Electric had to be a sector leader – if not, it had to be "fixed, closed or sold" (3). After eliminating numerous layers of management at General Electric, a flat structure was implemented. This gave executives of companies in the General Electric stable a lot of autonomy. Jack Welch was interested in results, and results meant profits. In order to achieve this goal, he gave his executives a lot of freedom and the potential of making large amounts of money for themselves. One observer was quoted by Partnoy as saying the "GE's culture is results oriented, that's the reason they do well and also break rules. It's the opposite side of the same coin" (4). After its purchase of Kidder, General Electric pumped around USD 500 million into Kidder and, after the trouble in the fixed income market, another USD 200 million was required in 1994 (5). Nineteen ninety-four was not a particularly good year for Jack Welch (6). During January of that year, Kidder's derivatives vice president Clifford Kaplan was sacked after it was discovered that he was simultaneously employed by Kidder and the US section of a Parisian Bank. The individual in question was also involved in selling an Italian derivative transaction without the required license and, in the process, caused cost overruns in excess of USD 2 million. During the first quarter of that same year another trader had managed to hide losses amounting to USD 11 million after a less than successful bond derivative transaction with NationsBank. This was, however, not all; adding insult to injury, it also became known that yet another Kidder options trader was also less than forthcoming about the fact that he had lost USD 6 million on trading options on French and Spanish government bonds. In April 1994 Neil Margolin was fired for hiding his USD 11 million in losses and, in June of 1994, Peter Bryant was fired for hiding his USD 6 million in losses (7). These losses, in themselves, are not alarming. Losses are, after all, part and parcel of investment banking. What should have raised the alarm bells was the fact that no-one detected these losses. This clearly indicates inadequate oversight on a wide front, not only limited to Mr Jett.

Part of the problem had been attributed to the hands-off approach followed by the man who built the derivatives business at Kidder. With a Ph.D. in mathematics, Melvin Mullin managed his area in Kidder as Jack Welch managed Kidder: hands-off, with profit as the be all and end all (8). He was, however, credited as the one responsible for allowing Kaplan to practice unlicensed and for ignoring cautions regarding a transaction that contravened Japanese banking regulations. His wife also worked for Kidder and managed to cost the firm USD 2 million when she, by accident, double-hedged her own portfolio. This in itself is once again not such a big issue, mistakes do happen. The problem was that Mullin appointed and supervised his wife and found it justifiable to approve a USD 900 000 bonus for her efforts. Mullen was, however, transferred to another position in Kidder during February of 1993 and was replaced by none other than Mr Jett as the new Managing Director of the government desk (9). Mr Jett now reported directly to Edward Curello, who was overall in charge of the fixed income division.

However, there were other problems right from the day that General Electric bought Kidder (10). One of Kidders traders was found guilty of insider trading, raising questions about management at Kidder. In response to this and other problems Jack Welch appointed a close personal friend, Michael A. Carpenter, as CEO of Kidder. He had no experience in running a broking firm and was not licensed by the SEC to run a broking firm up until 1993. Under his leadership, Kidder embarked on a massive expansion of its Mortgage Backed Securities (MBS) book through the use of extensive leverage. The firm was so highly geared that outsiders calculated that a 3.2% drop in the value of Kidders assets would have wiped the firm out. By September 1994 Kidder was the number one underwriter of MBS debt in the US. However, this expansion went hand-in-hand with cost control, which meant that systems and controls were viewed as overheads. This led to inferior systems and the use of inexperienced traders in favor of more experienced staff that usually cost more money. Reporting to Michael Carpenter was Edward Curello who, by all accounts, was a very trusting but capable manager who was largely given carte blanche to run the fixed income division of Kidder. This entailed managing a staff of 750 people who generated USD 1 billion of earnings per annum through executing USD 20 billion worth of transactions per day. To assist him in this process, he employed a dedicated risk and compliance manager, David Bernstein. Although highly respected, he had a policy of getting rid of those who didn't produce, and traders were often underreporting profits in good months to have a reserve in lean months. This saved them from having to tell Curello when they made losses. Curello would apparently go to great lengths not to report losses (11). During the investigation of Walter Mahailovich, a trader accused by Curello of false bookkeeping, former traders reported that Curello would allow traders to 'massage' their books by assisting the back office in valuing their positions. There was a definite culture of hiding losses and profits from Curello. If one takes into consideration that Kidder was scrutinized by General Electric's auditors every 18 months, a question has to be raised about the quality of these audits. In the report produced by Gary Lynch, inexperience on the part of auditors was quoted as a contributing factor to the causes of the non-identification of Mr Jett's activities. Another trademark of Kidder's trading strategy was the dominance of proprietary trading executed by their traders relative to trading on behalf of outside clients (12). An explanation for this is that proprietary trading is potentially much more lucrative than agency trading. The Chief Financial Officer of Kidder, Richard O'Donnel, was tasked with the responsibility to oversee compliance with internal and external control measures and regulation. In April of 1994 he still believed that the controls at Kidder were better than any of their competitors. On the 22nd of that month another trader who reported to Cerrulo, one Neil Margolin, was also dismissed for hiding losses through improperly valuing his positions. He was also conducting proprietary trading for Kidder and the amount reported to be involved was only around USD 10 million (13). These failures in oversight at Kidder were not isolated or new to the company. As far back as 1985, Kidder was involved in a transaction in which Curello participated, when regulatory provisions were breached and a client was severely overcharged. In a transaction with a Texas thrift bank (a bank whose main purpose is to take deposits from consumers and make home mortgages) (14), Kidder exceeded the permissible 5% profit margin by 480% and charged the client 29%. The case was only settled in 1990 through Kidder agreeing to pay USD 3.7 million in order to prevent the case from going to arbitration. During 1988 (15) both Kidder and

Curello were fined by the National Association of Securities Dealers (NASD) for failing to reverse a transaction through which a trader working for Curello, one Ira Saferstein, exploited a pricing error by CS First Boston. Even after the NASD ruled that the profit had to be repaid, Kidder objected strongly. Although Mr Curello was strong on profits, he was apparently not so strong on being on top of how these profits were generated. Comments by outside managers alluded to the fact that those at the top of Kidder did not fully understand the source of their profits (16). This problem was not unique to Kidder, as illustrated by the fact that it was recently highlighted as one of the most important risks facing companies today. The 2003 report of the Centre for the Study of Financial Innovation (CSFI) on the risks that face banks posted as their largest threat a lack of thorough understanding of "complex financial instruments" (17). The combination of high levels of use and low levels of understanding, in their view, was a lethal cocktail.

Mr Jett used STRIPS or the forward reconstitution of STRIPS to create unprecedented "profits" for Kidder. These instruments were largely unregulated at the time, and were viewed as a type of over-the-counter (OTC) derivative that companies need not disclose (18). Bonds are normally made up of two components: an interest portion that pays an interest payment or coupon at regular intervals, and a principle capital amount payable at the end of the term of the bond. Investopedia describes STRIPS as "An acronym for 'separate trading of registered interest and principal securities'. Treasury STRIPS are fixed-income securities sold at a significant discount to face value and offer no interest payments because they mature at par". In essence, the non-interest portion of a bond and the coupon payments are all treated as capital only payments at future dates. While interest payments are often heavily taxed, in many tax regimes capital gains is often tax free or taxed at a lower rate, and because of this a lucrative market for created STRIPS developed. Once stripped, the individual capital only future payments trade at a discount to face value due to the time you

have to wait before you receive your payment. This period
could be six months or even up to thirty years. If you could buy
a STRIP that matures tomorrow and entitles you to receive
USD 1 000, you would probably be prepared to pay USD 999
for it. However, if you have to wait six months for your
payment, USD 800 might be more palatable. The most
important determinants of the price would be the time left till
maturity, the ruling interest rates and the risk associated with
the issuer of the instrument. However, the pieces of what used
to be a Treasury bond, for example, can be reunited and this is
referred to as reconstitution. If you have all the necessary
pieces, you can go to the Federal Reserve and they will give
you a complete Treasury bond. As these pieces all trade at a
discount, there is an inherent potential for profit as there may be
slight variations in what people would be prepared to pay for
the right to receive a capital amount on a future date. An
arbitrage opportunity therefore exists, as there can be a price
difference between the price of a complete bond and its parts
priced individually. These trades are easy and cheap to execute,
but margins are always very thin (19).

The little bit of 'genius' was realizing that the computer system
used by Kidder took into consideration the increase in value of
a STRIP as it neared maturity when the transaction was entered
into the system. The future value was, however, inadvertently
interpreted by the system as a current profit. It was, therefore,
possible for Mr Jett to record a profit every time he bought a
STRIP and entered the transaction for reconstitution at a future
date into Kidder's system. Another problem is the possibility
that you might incur a loss on that future date. Such a loss could
materialize if there was a sudden change in interest rates; for
example, if interest rates rose sharply, the value of your
STRIPS and the reconstituted Treasury bond would drop,
leaving you with a loss. The beauty of the scheme, and the part
that allowed Mr Jett to evade a lengthy jail sentence, was the
fact that all Mr Jett had to do was enter the transaction into the
Kidder accounting system and, 'voilá', there was a profit. There

was no need to actually conduct a transaction – it could all be fake. The bulk of his transactions were in reality fake, explaining why it was possible for him to have more holdings in a particular government security than was available in circulation. All Mr Jett had to do to keep his scheme alive was to increase the size of fake transactions into the system in order to generate more fake profits than the fake losses generated by the Kidder accounting system and the actual losses he generated from actual trading. As the fake transactions approached maturity, the price of the STRIP converged with the face value of the instrument, wiping out Mr Jett's illusionary profits. This is clearly demonstrated in tables released by the SEC in 1998 [20].

The pyramid scheme nature of what Mr Jett was doing is clearly visible, as the losses would realize the moment Mr Jett stopped entering new transactions. It is also noteworthy that, although there was a perception on Wall Street that the Kidder accounting system was very advanced, it was in actual fact running on software that was written before 1969 [21].

In the first instance, Mr Jett had a less than illustrious career up until 1991. He was less than successful during his short spell at Morgan Stanley and was subsequently fired by First Boston, which was his second place of employment [22]. Similarly, in his first few months of employment at Kidder, Mr Jett was less than spectacular and, at the end of 1991, his performance rating only justified a USD 5 000 bonus. His turnaround was, however, dramatic – a 'profit' of USD 32 million earned him a bonus of USD 2.1 million at the end of 1992 and a USD 151 million trading profit at the end of 1993. His performance bonus was a spectacular USD 9.3 million and he was Kidder's 'man of the year'. No-one took the trouble to determine exactly how this miracle was achieved.

One of his co-workers was, however, not dazzled by Mr Jett during the early stages of his career [23]. During 1992 Hugh

Bush, a trader who worked closely with Mr Jett, complained to superiors about the way in which Mr Jett was valuing his positions. This complaint was ignored by Dr Mullen and Mr Jett ensured that there would be no further complaints by providing Dr Mullen with recorded evidence that the complainant was engaging other banks in search of alternative employment. The complainant's 'reward' for this dastardly deed was summary dismissal [24]. Cullen refuted the claims that Bush made allegations against Mr Jett. In the same year Scott Newquist, a senior executive and member of the inventory committee at Kidder, also claimed to have raised concerns with Carpenter regarding the positions held by Mr Jett. He complained about the fact that the "inventory committee", which had to keep track of what the company owns, were finding it difficult to get clear answers on what positions Mr Jett held [25]. Newquist also claimed that Mr Carpenter took no action because, in his view, Mr Carpenter was focused only on profit and nothing else; Mr Carpenter denied these claims. A former Kidder trader, Robert Dickey, also claimed that Mr Jett's predecessors knew about the defect in the system [26], which raises the possibility that someone in Kidder might have told Mr Jett about it. During May of 1993 an accountant at Kidder, Charles Fiumefreddo, realized that there was an error in the computer system and recommended that it be corrected [27]. However, Mr Jett objected very strongly and nothing was done. According to Fiumefreddo, the suggested change would have exposed Mr Jett's scam. In the spring of that same year Jim Rizzi, who worked on the repurchase desk at Kidder, noticed something odd [28]. As the repurchase desk was responsible for borrowing securities if there was a shortfall or converting bonds into cash through the repurchase mechanism in the market when cash was needed, they had a unique view of Mr Jett's trading activity. Rizzi noticed that Mr Jett was managing unusually large volumes of transactions and his forward settlements would often not settle, even though the necessary STRIPS was acquired by Rizzi to reconstitute a complete bond. He also noticed that STRIPS that were reconstituted were promptly stripped again after a few days. Rizzi started to have doubts about whether or not Mr Jett's transactions were actual transactions or mere paper entries. He shared his concerns with his boss, Brain Finkelstein. Finkelstein already had serious doubts about Jett's meteoric rise and frequently questioned the unusual profitability he achieved. He again raised the matter with Bernstein who, at the time, was Currello's confidant. Bernstein apparently responded by confirming that Curello was aware of Mr Jett's trading strategy.

In the early months of 1994, a number of high profile collapses of fund managers dominated news headlines. Early in 1994 Askin Capital wiped out USD 600 million and in April Robert Citron bankrupted Orange County (29). Kidder Peabody just happened to be the largest investor in Askin Capital Management (30). At Kidder Peabody, however, Mr Joseph Jett was swinging for the fence and recorded a record USD 66 million in 'profits'. During the same time, the computer system at Kidder started to buckle under the massive volumes of trades (31) and computer specialists were called in to remedy the situation. What they found was astounding. Mr Jett had, in the period he worked at Kidder, entered USD 1.7 trillion in trades into the computer system. Of these transactions, none were ever consummated, allowing for profits to be recorded without any securities actually changing hands. They advised senior executives, including Edward Currello. When he looked closely at Mr Jett's positions, he realized that he was holding an estimated USD 40 billion in forward reconstitutions. At the time it appears that Mr Currello did not fully appreciate the fact that the profits declared by Mr Jett were false, and all he initially tried to do was to prevent these massive transactions from appearing on the balance sheet of General Electric (32). It was only when he asked Mr Jett to explain his trading strategy in writing that the realization struck home that Mr Jett's trading "strategy" was a farce and that losses could be substantial. An in-depth audit by David Bernstein (33), which was responsible for risk management, revealed a USD 300 million anomaly in Mr Jett's trading book. Further investigation revealed that Mr Jett hid nearly USD 85 million in losses and reported around USD 350 million in false profits.

Jack Welch immediately contracted Gary Lynch, a former SEC chairman, to investigate the Jett incident (34). In August of 1994 the damning report was released and its findings are of great relevance for this book. The conclusion of the Lynch Report was summarized as follows "The report concluded that the ultimate problem was the emphasis throughout Kidder on profits and greed." Although "Jett was provided the opportunity to generate false profits by trading and accounting systems," it was his supervisors who allowed Jett to use that opportunity for over two years because they never understood what Jett was doing in his day-to-day trading activity, or the reason for his apparent profitability. "The door to Jett's abuses was opened as much by human failings as by inadequate formal systems," It also said of Mr Jett's supervisors that "Their focus was on profit and loss, and risk-management data provided no insight into the mechanics of Jett's trading."

Subsequent to the Report, Orlando Joseph Jett was charged with fraud amounting to nearly USD 83 million but subsequently, in 1996, he was found not guilty of fraud. A securities arbitration panel also found that Kidder could not prove that Mr Jett engaged in "fraud, breach of duty and unjust enrichment" and ordered the release of a portion of his assets frozen in Kidder accounts. This was, however, not the end and "civil administration" charges were brought against Mr Jett. In July 1998 an administrative law Judge, Carol Fox Foelak, found after two years of deliberation that Mr Jett was technically not guilty of committing fraud, as his actions could not be tied to the physical purchase or sale of securities. However, the Judge found that "...Jett, with intent to defraud, booked hundreds of millions of dollars in illusionary profits through an anomaly in Kidders trading and accounting systems, thereby deceiving the firm about his trading performance and obtaining large bonuses and other benefits" (35). He was ordered to pay a civil penalty of USD 200 000 and was "barred from association with a broker or dealer". He also had to give up USD 8.21 million in money he received through his illegal activities. The judgment was appealed by the Division of Enforcement and Mr Jett. Mr Jett appealed his conviction on "recordkeeping violations" and the finding that he "engaged in a scheme to defraud". The Division appealed the finding by the judge that, technically, Mr Jett did not contravene a number of antifraud provisions, as his activities could not be tied to the actual purchase or sale of securities. On March 5 2004 the Commission hearing the appeal found that Mr Jett did indeed violate antifraud provisions (36).

Mr Jett was by no means the only one who suffered sanction. On June 22 1994, Michael Carpenter had to resign from his position at Kidder (37). One month later, he was joined by Edward Curello, whose supervision was questioned by the Lynch Report. He was subsequently charged by the SEC for failure to supervise and had to pay a USD 50 000 penalty to settle the SEC charges. On top of the fine, he was suspended from operating in the securities industry for a year. However, these blows were softened by a USD 9 million settlement that he received from Kidder. A similar fate also awaited Melvin Mullen, who also had to resign on the 3rd of August 1994 after he managed to settle civil sanctions. He paid a fine of USD 25 000 and could not work in the industry for a period of three months. David Bernstein, the man credited by some for exposing Mr Jett (38) was demoted but never charged for any wrongdoing.

Although there is evidence to suggest that a culture of opportunism existed at Kidder before it was taken over by General Electric, there can be little doubt that the management style imposed by General Electric was a contributing factor that exacerbated the problem. The headlong pursuit of profit had two important elements – cost cutting and high incentives – with little restraint or interference for those making money.

The effect was antiquated systems and incentives to take risk in order to get to the profit levels that would generate bonuses. The hands-off management style towards successful traders has the potential of becoming one of the golden threads running through this book and, although it might work in other industries (like making light bulbs), it is quite clearly a dangerous way of managing an investment bank. It was also clear that the senior executives at Kidder, especially those appointed by General Electric, had very little knowledge of the practical workings of an investment bank, especially on operational level. Another important contributor was the misplaced faith that the Chief Financial Officer had in the abilities of the auditors of the parent company and, quite possibly, in his own internal and external audits. The fact that the Lynch Report cited inexperience of the auditors as an excuse for them not detecting Mr Jett's activities cast a grave shadow over the hazard created by executives that rely heavily on audits to identify irregularities. The regulators, in the case of Kidder Peabody, are also not without blame. The massive positions that Mr Jett was building up were reported and should have alerted the regulators.

Although many would like us to think that the eventual demise and sale of Kidder Peabody could be attributed to Mr Jett, in reality the owners, General Electric and its management, were the only ones to blame for its inability to prevail. The losses at Kidder continued through 1994 (39) and at the end of that year total net losses were approximated at nearly USD 1 billion, the worst in Kidder's 129-year history. At that time, General Electric decided to sell the firm to Paine Webber, putting more than 2 200 Kidder employees out of work, but making it possible for General Electric to once again declare record profits for the year. Through this sale, or as some called it a merger, Paine Webber Inc took over a number of business units. In return they received 25% shareholding in Paine Webber, totaling USD 670 million, and a seat on the board of General Electric while General Electric absorbed the ailing Mortgaged

Backed Securities (MBS) book (40). Expert opinion expressed by Professor Roy C. Smith from the Salomon centre at NYU and a follow-up article published in the Wall Street Journal both identified the strain exerted by the massive USD 12 billon MBS book suffering under interest rate hikes in 1994, as the real culprit that paralyzed Kidder Peabody. The strategy to grow its exposure in MBS was conceived and implemented under the leadership of Carpenter and Cerullo (41). As Kidder financed most of its MBS expansion through debt, it had to be with the consent and approval of General Electric. In fact, Kidder was so highly leveraged that every USD 93 of assets they financed with borrowed money was only supported by USD 1 worth of equity. One implication of this ratio was the fact that the net assets of Kidder could be wiped out by a mere 3.2% reduction in the value of its assets. This aggressive policy propelled Kidder from the number 10 spot in the MBS market in 1990 to the first spot in 1994 when it was the largest MBS underwriter in the US, controlling 25% of the market. This "achievement" meant that they met the criterion laid down by Mr Welch to be either first or second in their sector. This strategy did, however, expose Kidder to some serious risk. As the underwriter of an issued security, Kidder buys the entire issue of such security with the intention of on-selling it to the public. Any reduction in the value of such an inventory of securities will be for the account of Kidder; this is especially relevant in the interest rate sensitive MBS market.

There can be little doubt that a number of structural factors were key to the actions of Joseph Jett and the eventual demise of Kidder Peabody. Formal and informal regulatory procedures were either not in place and/or failed dismally, Joseph Jett had a competitive advantage as he managed to detect and exploit a severe weakness in the Kidder accounting system and the potential for spectacular short-term gain was on everyone's mind in Kidder and its parent company, General Electric. There is clear evidence presented in this case study indicating that the type of behavior manifested by Mr Jett was no anomaly at

Kidder. The question then is why were all these structural and other factors present? The answer is fairly straightforward – the Kidder and General Electric culture was one that encouraged profits at all cost and to minimize expenses, even at the expense of proper oversight. If Joseph Jett did not learn this very quickly at Kidder he had to be very stupid, something he undoubtedly wasn't. If your traders and those responsible for managing them know that profit is the sole and only yardstick for success, they will use whatever means necessary to achieve it. If everyone, including managers, is hiding losses and parking profits because they know that showing a loss could cost them their jobs, what prevents them from taking advantage of incompetent and inexperienced managers and antiquated accounting systems? We know that there were others before Mr Jett who was hiding losses without being detected and that even the computer error that allowed Mr Jett to book his phantom profits was also known to people at Kidder before Mr Jett started abusing it. Kidder and General Electric were also known for having scant regard for regulations, why should their staff have a different philosophy?

The environment at Kidder was a very good example of a total lack of balance between factors that facilitate extreme opportunism and those that could inhibit it, in an environment of very strong monetary and status motivators. General Electric under Jack Welch did not display a balanced approach when it came to making money. Every effort was made to facilitate this goal; if you failed you were severely sanctioned. There is very little if any evidence that any inhibitors like advanced internal audit systems or hands on operations management procedures were implemented to ensure effective oversight of Kidder. In the presence of such a glaring imbalance, the probability for extreme opportunism is very high.

CHAPTER 5

NICK LEESON & BARINGS BANK

On the 25th of February 1967, a son was born to a plasterer and a nurse in the King Street Maternity Hospital in Watford, on the outskirts of London (1). The boy was the first of four children born to Harry Leeson, a hardworking self-employed man, and his wife Anne, who by all accounts was a loving mother. The name of this boy is Nicholas William Leeson. As a man, he would first become known in his own firm as a "Turbo Arbitrageur" and a mere two years later he would become internationally known as the man who destroyed one of the oldest banks in the world. The bank was Barings Bank, which could even count HRH Elizabeth Mountbatten-Windsor as one of its clients.

In this chapter we will investigate the events that led up to the collapse of Barings Bank and the eventual arrest of Mr Leeson. The culture and environments in which Mr Leeson learned his skills and operated will be thoroughly analyzed. The sources that were consulted are newspaper and other articles, his authorized biography, as well as unauthorized works regarding the Barings collapse, formal investigations by the Bank of England and the Singapore authorities, as well as court records. These will all be put into perspective by comments from Mr Leeson himself. The activities of Mr Leeson can be divided into a number of categories. We will firstly look at an analysis of his trading strategy and how his losses were incurred and, secondly, at how he managed to hide these losses. Attention will also be paid to how he funded his activities and what role the corporate culture and organizational structure at Barings played in creating an environment conducive to the events that led up to the collapse of Barings Bank.

The office politics in Barings were described as "savage" and Andrew Tuckey, the Chairman of Barings Brothers & Co. and Barings Securities, was quoted as describing the investment banking and securities-broking as "…'tension businesses' run by people who were moving and jockeying, and who were judged by their profits. That is the nature of the investment business…" (2). What this extract tells us is that personal position and advancement appeared to be the number one priority at Barings, consuming a lot of time that could have been spent on managing the firm.

Mr Leeson was posted to Barings Futures Singapore only in April 1992, to establish the settlements operations for Barings Futures Singapore. This posting came after Mr Leeson managed to clear up a GBP 100 million settlements mess in the Jakarta office. Senior management at Barings was made aware of these problems in the settlement areas of Barings' Far East offices. The Following extract from a letter to Ian Martin (the then Finance Director of Barings Securities Limited) from Mr Tim Easun a member of Business Development Group of Barings shows that, in September of 1991, at least one senior manager was warned (3).

"The non-segregated client account has been continually overdrawn over the last few months. Futures and Options cash accounts should never be overdrawn. This factor highlights a fundamental problem. Either margin calls have not been made or collateral balances are not being utilized correctly. Situations which should not occur in an efficiently run operation."

In another memorandum dated 26 December 1991, we find the cause of this situation and much more. Mr Bruce Benson, Manager of the Agency Sales Team (Japan), sent a memorandum to Mr Andrew Bayliss, (at the time the Deputy Chairman of Barings Securities Ltd) which, according to the

Singapore report (4), reported the following:

"I realize Carl and Lynn have been working very hard, and I greatly appreciate Nick Leeson's help (even though he has been dying to get out of that area for two years). Nevertheless, I must tell you, that the settlements area is struggling to stay above water. We will lose clients, we will waste more interest income, and we will inevitably incur large trading errors if we do not make this area a top priority (even **more than we are doing now)** …". He went further and wrote "…I have found out that …(2) we never properly collected hundreds of millions of Yen in margin money to begin with (more interest income out the window) (3), there are many other "bigger" "potentially HUGE" problems to be sorted…". To this he also added, "… Andrew, you know how much money we lost in interest income last year. Huge money. Millions of pounds. Do you know that we have a temp handling all our margin money? Do you know that the margin money regularly represents multiples of the net worth of the entire company?" In what can only be described as prophetic words, he concluded with a stern warning, "…If the back office causes us to lose money and clients from this point forward, it is not their fault, it is our fault for not recognizing how urgently they need help."

What is clear from these communications is that, at the end of 1991, both the Finance Director of Barings Securities Ltd and his Deputy were made acutely aware of the fact that there were serious deficiencies in the back office capacity of Barings that were already costing the bank millions of pounds every year and had the potential to cost much more. These deficiencies were nothing new to Barings. Stephan Fay (5) quotes John Guy, the individual who managed settlements at Barings up until the early 1990s, as confirming that settlements were not viewed as a priority by Barings management. No efforts were made to develop computer systems that would allow management to be on top of all their worldwide positions or even to help them manage their risk. "It was all done on the back of an envelope" is how Mr Guy apparently described the Barings back office. The reason why the back office was deprived of well trained and qualified staff is attributed to the focus of Barings management on maximizing bonuses and minimizing overheads. Back office was regarded as an overhead in a culture where "...money became the main, perhaps the sole, standard of judgment of a person's value...". In my interview with Mr Leeson he confirmed to me that he was acutely aware of these deficiencies. (He made it very clear to me, in response to two different questions, that he did not set out intentionally or unintentionally to exploit these weaknesses.) According to him, the culture of Barings was to try and be the first to exploit new markets and to do things first. However, Barings concentrated on their research and execution ability, and the administration and settlements areas had to look after themselves. To underline this, he recounted two incidents that reflected this bias. When the stock market in Jakarta was opening up, Barings apparently decided to open an "office" in Jakarta first; William Daniels was sent to operate from a hotel room with a telex. There he would start in the mornings, getting a telex with 150 trades on it. Six months later, when Mr Leeson was sent to Indonesia to sort out a GBP 100 million in share certificates that couldn't be delivered to clients Barings transacted with, he was still operating from a hotel room with no effective infrastructure to support him. Mr Leeson also recounted to me that, when he arrived in Singapore, he wanted to recruit someone who was working for Chase Manhattan Bank and with whom he had previously worked at Morgan Stanley. This person, called Stella, was in his view extremely efficient and experienced. However, due to the fact that the salary he wanted to pay this woman was twice the salary those in the equity settlement area were getting, the decision was made by Simon Jones not to employ her. Mr Jones then hired someone fresh out of the National University of Singapore, with no experience, at the lower salary. Mr Leeson did note to me that the decision may have been, in part, Mr Jones flexing his muscles to show him who was boss. Mr Leeson believes that his inexperienced staff, with no template to measure his actions against, was to a large extent moulded by him and would, therefore, not question any of the instructions that he gave them. Mr Leeson identified this lack of having experienced staff in the key settlement areas as a very early cause of the breakdown of control. Without quality staff in the right positions, the right questions were never asked. When those questions were eventually asked in February 1995, he knew his days were numbered. According to him, the means to detect what he was doing was very simple. "There were only two trading accounts, a London and a Tokyo account. You pull up the report from SIMEX, you compare these two versus the SIMEX report and there is a massive difference." Mr Leeson ascribes even the most recent 'rogue trader' events as a systems and oversight failure due to a lack of quality people in key positions. Even though the advances in systems can reduce some of the risk, quality people, in Mr Leeson's view, still remain the key.

One of the most important, and often overlooked, factors is the role of learned behavior. We know that traders, like most young employees in the financial markets, do not walk into their new positions with a fully developed set of skills. They learn how to handle situations and what behavior is deemed appropriate and what is deemed inappropriate from the people they work with and work for. Mr Leeson was taught how to handle mistakes. By his own account, the use of fictitious transactions to rectify errors was a widespread practice (6). It is also of vital importance to stress the fact that Mr Leeson did not invent the 88888 account. When he started trading in Singapore, an error account No. 99905 already existed. Trading errors were booked into this account and were then reported to London, where the losses resultant from such errors, were eventually written off against Barings' profits. The head of derivatives settlements in London, Gordon Bowser, who was responsible for all derivatives settlements for Barings, requested Mr Leeson to create an alternative error account and asked him to "keep them all in Singapore" (7), as the errors may draw the attention of the auditors. Mr Leeson was provided with the tool to hide errors and was instructed on how to use it.

In 2001, Stephen J. Brown and Onno W. Steenbeek produced an analysis of Mr Leeson's trading activities. These can roughly be divided into the categories of authorized and unauthorized.

The now infamous 88888 account was opened on the 3rd of July 1992; a mere two days after Barings became a member of SIMEX. This account was opened on instructions from Gordon Bowser in London, who was responsible for Barings' derivative settlements (8). The first transaction purportedly booked into the 88888 account was an error by one of his staff. An inexperienced trader apparently inadvertently sold twenty lots of Nikkei 225 futures instead of buying twenty lots of Nikkei 225 futures. The effect of this error was +/- GBP 20 000. According to Mr Leeson, he felt sorry for the girl and booked the error into 88888 (9). The Report of the Singapore inspectors indicated that, on the contrary, Mr Leeson started using the account the same day he opened it. According to the Report, Mr Leeson lost GBP 20 000 when he bought and sold 2 051 Nikkei futures. This loss was the first entry into the 88888 account. The Report also points out that Mr Leeson apparently gave specific instructions on the 8th of July 1992 that the software of the computer system they used should be changed to ensure that the 88888 account would not be reflected in any market activity reports and would be used solely by them internally to estimate SIMEX margins (10). Towards the end of August, Mr Leeson bought 189 long Nikkei futures without the appropriate hedge, indicating that he was following a very bold strategy of taking 'naked' or unhedged positions or bets on the direction and the way in which the market will move (11). On the 26th of August, a form BC4 was faxed to SIMEX by Mr Leeson to identify the owner of account 88888 as "Barings Securities London – Error Account". This was necessary because SIMEX required that all accounts for which more than a hundred contracts were traded be identified.

However, this form was "corrected" later in the day with an identical form differing only in the fact that the words "Error Account" were omitted. Fay speculates that this was probably done because Mr Leeson realized that the volume of activity in the account may not tie up with the volumes expected from an error account. Mr Leeson also convinced Mr Gordon Bowser, the Risk Manager at Barings Securities Limited, to provide him with funding for the margin calls of clients that he traded for on SIMEX even before SIMEX had asked for the margins. The reason he gave was that it was difficult to borrow from Japanese Banks when clients needed cash in a hurry to meet margin calls. This practice, although technically illegal, was obviously allowed so as not to inconvenience clients of Barings. By the end of August the losses in the account had risen to GBP 320 000.

During September Mr Leeson's losses from his futures positions were rising from GBP 300 000 to more than GBP 3 million. In the next month, this figure ballooned to GBP 4.5 million. During October Mr Leeson started selling un-hedged options on the Nikkei 225 and quickly ran up a loss of GBP 70 000. This loss was, however, offset by a profit of GBP 75 000 during the month of November. In this month his cumulative losses fell to around GBP 2 million. Mr Leeson apportioned most of the blame on the inability of the SIMEX system to reconcile all transactions. According to him, system errors often left him with naked positions due to unreconciled transactions from a previous day's trading. It was these errors that initially ended up in the 88888 account, he claimed (12). By the end of September, Mr Leeson instructed his staff to credit his 88888 account with an amount of GBP 4 million while debiting a Barings account at Citibank with a similar amount. This transaction was reversed when the next month began, to bring the positions back to where they were. This was done to hide the deficit from the eyes of the Deloitte Touche auditors, who would start with their work after the September 30 year end of Barings. Shortly hereafter, the auditors received a fax purportedly from Gordon Bowser, the Risk Manager at Barings Securities Limited, advising them that account **88888** did not have to be reconciled, as it was an error account with an insignificant balance. Although Mr Bowser could not definitely remember if he, in actual fact, wrote the fax in question, there is evidence to suggest that this fax was indeed Mr Leeson's first forgery. The possibility exists that Mr Leeson took another fax, sent on the 2nd of October by Mr Bowser and referring to account 99002, and altered it to reflect the date as the 7th of October 1992 and changed the account number to **88888** (13). It is important to remember that the use of fictitious transactions to "balance" the books was a common technique employed at Barings and not something invented by Mr Leeson (14).

During the best part of 1993 the **88888** account was seldom used by Mr Leeson and, as a result of a strong market, he managed to wipe out the accumulated losses in the **88888** account (15). Unfortunately, Mr Leeson reverted back to using the **88888** account the very next Monday and he acknowledged the fact that, by that time, he was addicted to using the **88888** account to hide his losses (16).

By October of that year he was also promoted to General Manager and Assistant Director. Mr Leeson was now officially in charge of trading and settlements. It must be noted that, to outsiders, it appeared as if Mr Leeson did a very good job of executing trades for the proprietary traders in Tokyo (17). There was, however, a dark side to his 'ability' as a trader. He used the **88888** account to absorb smaller losses he incurred by providing false execution prices to the traders in Tokyo. For example, he would sell at USD 100 but would indicate to those he executed for that he sold at USD 101. This bolstered his reputation as a trader. The main purpose of the **88888** account was, therefore, to generate fictitious profits for Barings Securities Limited and Barings Securities Japan. Although a strong market helped Mr Leeson to clear his losses, it didn't take long before Mr Leeson was back in trouble again. By the end of 1993 the losses in account **88888** once again grew to USD 35.8 million (18).

The main problem facing Mr Leeson was the margin calls he had to pay on his futures positions on SIMEX. This problem was overcome by a combination of strategies. In the first instance, unhedged transactions for account **88888** were first booked into accounts of Barings Securities Japan and Barings Securities Limited. However, these transactions were offset with similar and opposite transactions seconds before the close of market. These offsetting transactions were booked to **88888** and gave the appearance of a hedge. The prices of these transactions were once again manipulated to favor Barings Securities Japan and Barings Securities Limited and the corresponding losses were absorbed into the **88888** account. The second technique used by Mr Leeson was to transfer unhedged positions in the accounts of Barings Securities Japan and Barings Securities Limited to the **88888** account through the entry of fictitious trades. This gave the illusion that no unhedged positions in the accounts of Barings Securities Japan and Barings Securities Limited existed. The third manipulation used by Mr Leeson had the effect of actually fooling the SIMEX margin call system. By instructing his settlement staff to execute fictitious trades in the accounting system just before market closure, and then reversing those same trades the next morning, Mr Leeson was able to reduce the margin payments required by SIMEX.

Not even these elaborate efforts could negate the need for margin payments on Mr Leeson's growing futures positions. Once again a set of 'solutions' was used to tackle the problem (19). Mr Leeson convinced London that he was involved in low margin arbitrage, which means that volumes must be high to make the level of profit generated worth their while. As the transactions were essentially 'riskless', which it can be if done properly, the amounts involved should not be of concern to Barings. He also explained that, as he was arbitraging across two exchanges, each exchange would require its own margin payments and netting could not be used between the exchanges. He convinced Barings London that, due to market volatility, SIMEX was demanding intra-day margin calls and, as it was difficult for him to get the money from his clients as a result of time zone differences, Barings Securities Limited should finance these on behalf of its clients. Although such funding is technically illegal, the rest of Mr Leeson's stories sound plausible as they all have an element of truth in them. Someone without any reason to doubt him would probably accept the story at face value.

From October 1992 Mr Leeson was selling options on the Nikkei index. This he managed to do quite profitably using his 88888 account and, at some stages, such as by the end of December 1994, the value of these options totaled USD 178 million. As his futures positions grew, he had to sell more and more options to fund his SIMEX margin calls. The premium he received from selling "in the money options" went directly to fund his margins. By his own account [20], he could not sell options during October of 2004 and resorted to a fraudulent journal entry on the Citibank account to create the perception of a zero balance in the 88888 account. In November he had to attend a "strategy" meeting in Tokyo and didn't have time to sell options to cover his margin calls and had to, once again, resort to a fraudulent entry in the Citibank account totaling GBP 65 million [21]. The option-selling exercise also exacerbated the doubling strategy followed by Mr Leeson when, after the Kobe earthquake, the USD 178 million profit was converted into a USD 108 million loss by the end of February 1995.

To put this into perspective, it must be understood that the amount of options sold by Mr Leeson had the effect of reducing the volatility in the underlying market of, for example, the Nikkei 225 futures contract over which he was writing options. Fay [22] quotes Mr Leeson from an interview with David Frost, during which Mr Leeson explained the influence of his options trading on his activities. In essence, the price of an option is largely dependent on the volatility of the market in the instrument over which the option is written. The higher the volatility, the higher the option premium, which the writer can demand. According to Mr Leeson, in 1992 when he started writing options, the price he could demand due to volatility was 40% to 45% of the price of the underlying security, for example the Nikkei 225 futures contract. As he was selling options every month to offset his losses, over time he was flooding the market, which reduced the volatility by the end of 1994 to 10 %. The effect was that, to achieve the same income, he had to sell very large amounts "thousands" of options. Mr Leeson confirmed to me that he primarily started selling the more dangerous straddles in order to gain the higher premium attached to them, in order to counteract the effect of the lower volatility in the market on his income from selling vanilla options. As early as 1993 Mr Leeson was "...attracted to the large premiums from straddles..." notwithstanding the fact that he realized that his losses could be unlimited if the market moved against his view (23). He also admitted that he didn't hedge his positions, as he needed his entire premium to cover his existing losses. In the next chapter we will see that Mr John Rusnak was in the exact same position, with very much the same end result.

As we by now know, the net effect of Mr Leeson's activities was the collapse of Barings Bank. Although this statement is a fact, it doesn't tell us the whole story. In *Figure 2* I have used information published in the Singapore Report (24) to graphically demonstrate the cumulative losses on account 88888.

Excluded from this graph is the eventual tally for the losses as reflected in February of 1995. At the end of this month, the losses rose from the 590.3 million Singapore Dollars to a staggering 2.210 billion Singapore Dollars, which is equal to nearly USD 1 billion.

FIG 2

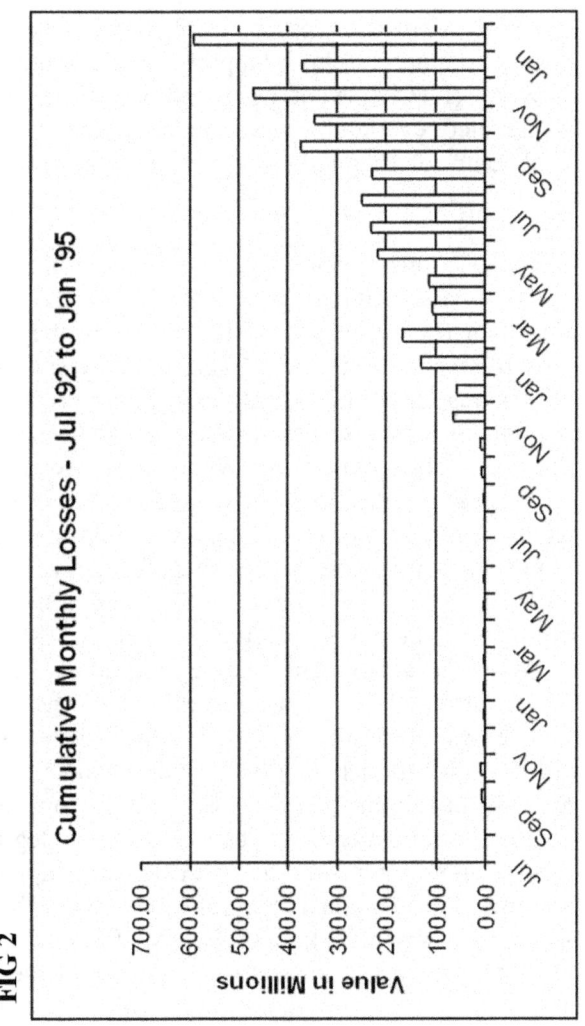

(Values in Singapore Dollars)

The main reasons for this dramatic escalation were the 1 000 point drop in the Nikkei 225 on 23 January 1995 after the Kobe earthquake (25) and Mr Leeson's increase in his exposure in the belief that the market would rebound. According to the Singapore Report (26), the collapse of Barings could have been averted as late as January 1995. I support this view and, if one looks at how the LTCM event described in "When Genius Failed" was handled, eventual losses may have been drastically reduced if the Bank of England had taken the appropriate and decisive action.

One of the accusations leveled against Mr Leeson was the suspicion that he was generating real profits for Barings by front-running their (his) clients. Ron Baker, Head of Financial Products Group Barings Investment Bank, strongly supported a GBP 130 000 bonus for Mr Leeson at the beginning of 1994 (27). Baker was impressed by the way Mr Leeson, as he termed it, "worked the information curve" (28). When he received a large purchase order that needed to be executed on SIMEX for a client from the Barings Tokyo office, he would purchase a similar amount of contracts on the Osaka exchange. If the price rose, he would sell the client his own Osaka holding at the higher price; if it fell, he would execute the deal on SIMEX and cancel his Osaka transaction. This strategy would also work in the event of a large sale. At least James Baker, the internal auditor of Barings Securities Limited, was aware of this activity. In his audit report he condoned this conduct as legal, because the "front-running" order was placed on another exchange and should, therefore, be viewed as legitimate arbitrage and not front-running. Although apparently insignificant, this is once again a clear reflection of the 'blurred-lines environment' in which traders like Mr Leeson operate. The Report by the Singapore inspectors (29) questions the whole matter of the so-called "information curve", which undoubtedly includes the fact that traders who handle both agency and proprietary business would be in an unfair "advantageous" position due to their insider knowledge of the positions that clients intend to take. The report highlights the fact that senior Barings management was aware of this fact and had no ethical difficulties with it. The Head of Barings Group Compliance at the time of the collapse, Ms Val Thomas, is quoted by the Singapore Report as saying that she was never aware of this "use" of client trading information and comments that it should have raised ethical difficulties inside Barings because it borders on front-running. In his book "Rogue Trader" Mr Leeson, however, denies that Barings were involved in front-running their clients (30). In my interview with Mr Leeson he said to me that, although Barings as an organization was always trying to bend the rules as far as possible, he could not confirm any instances of front-running other than his own. He did, however, confirm that the Singapore office would often receive orders from clients across the world. The clients would be operating in different currencies, and using the exchange rate most advantageous to Barings over the day to settle the executed trade would generate profits for Barings. The client would get a very good execution price, but incur slightly less than the optimum exchange rate for settlement purposes. This activity made the Singapore office GBP 2 million per year. However, Mr Leeson sees this type of conduct as normal for financial organizations similar to Barings. The use of questionable conduct to enhance profits was undoubtedly a skill Mr Leeson learned at his places of employment, rather than something he brought to them.

When we look at figures reflected in the Board of Banking Supervision Report (**Table 1**), it appears that Mr Leeson overall never made a profit for Barings Bank, even though he was regarded as a "turbo arbitrageur". Although these figures may be technically correct, they are disputed by Mr Leeson.

According to Mr Leeson, the report only looked at the losses he made in the 88888 account without taking into consideration his profitable transactions (32). During our interview, he also pointed out that the mistakes of all the other traders working for him in

Singapore all found their way into the 88888 account. It is also important to take note of the fact that, during July 1993, the 88888 account was down to virtually zero (33).

TABLE 1

Facts versus Fantasy: Profitability of Mr. Leeson's Trading Activities.			
Period	Reported (million)	Actual (million)	Cumulative actual[1] (million)
1 Jan 1993 to 31 Dec 1993	+GBP 8.83	-GBP 21	-GBP 23
1 Jan 1994 to 31 Dec 1994	+GBP 28.529	-GBP 185	-GBP 208
1 Jan 1995 to 31 Dec 1995	+GBP 18.567	-GBP 619	-GBP 827

1. The cumulative actual represents Mr. Leeson's cumulative losses carried forward.
Source: Report of the Board of Banking Supervision Inquiry into the Circumstances of the Collapse of Barings, Ordered by the House of Commons, Her Majesty's Stationery Office, 1995.

(31)   Reproduced under the terms of the Click-Use Licence.

If Mr Leeson never made profits, this would obviously have been impossible. This is one of the important differences between Mr Leeson and Mr Jett. Mr Leeson managed to generate actual profits from executing actual transactions, albeit very risky transactions and, if not for the Kobe disaster, may have made a very large real profit for his company. Mr Jett's 'profitable' transactions, albeit very risky transactions and, if not for the Kobe disaster, may have made a very large real profit for his company. Mr Jett's 'profitable' transactions, on the other hand, were little more than a pyramid scheme based on fictitious entries into an antiquated accounting system. However, Mr Jett used fictitious trades to enhance his income.

Why he wasn't convicted of more serious offences is open for debate.

An analysis of the crimes that Mr Leeson committed has two sides to it. In the first instance, we have the charges brought against him by the Singapore authorities and, secondly, we have a set of 'crimes' that he himself confessed to and compiled in his efforts to get extradited to the UK for trial. The list of crimes he confessed to in a document provided to the Serious Fraud Office (SFO) can be divided into seven sets of actions (34).

- "The communication of false information by Mr Leeson to the auditors of BFS in relation to the sum of 7.7 billion yen... This false information was accepted by the auditors and resulted in incorrect financial information being forwarded by them to Barings in London."

- "The exclusion by Mr Leeson of Account Number 88888 from the consolidated record of accounts sent daily to London. In this way the month-end balances could be manipulated by Mr Leeson to hide the losses appearing in that account and thereby give the false impression of profitability to Barings in London."

- "The repeated requests by Mr Leeson to Barings London for further sums to be paid to SIMEX by way of margin. These false requests resulted in sums being provided by Barings in London for one purpose (the payment of margin on authorized trades), that money actually being used in addition for another purpose (the payment of margin on unauthorized trades in the 88888 account)."

- "The false indication by Mr Leeson to his superiors in London that he was trading in conformity with the restriction that he maintain no overnight positions."

- "The false indication by Mr Leeson to his superiors in London that his trading was no more than arbitraging through a balanced book between Singapore and Osaka. Barings in London repeatedly and regularly received reports indicating that Mr Leeson's overall trading was profitable, whilst in reality it was making losses."

- "The entering by Mr Leeson or on his behalf of false prices in relation to account number 92000."

- "The false manipulation by Mr Leeson of the month-end equity balances on 88888 account as communicated to London."

According to Mr Leeson's own estimates, the list of charges brought against him by the Singapore authorities were far less complete than the list he provided to the Serious Fraud Office (SFO) and it was clear that the authorities in the UK were not keen to have him stand trial in England. When asked about possible reasons for this inaction, Mr Leeson said to me that the powers that be were probably concerned that a jury could have found it difficult to convict him, as happened in the Maxwell case when one of the jurors indicated that he didn't understand the case. He also pointed out to me that the Singapore authorities could have drawn up a much more extensive charge sheet if they wanted to cite each and every transgression. The charges that he pleaded guilty to were, in essence, the result of a plea bargain exercise between him and the Singapore authorities. It was only after this arrangement that he agreed to fly to Singapore for trial, where he then pleaded guilty and was sentenced to the agreed-to jail term. The essence of Mr. Leeson's crimes was the fact that he lied about the profitability of his transactions and that he entered into unauthorized transactions on behalf of Barings in order to recoup his hidden losses.

One of the favorite transactions used by Mr Leeson was the

"short straddle". This transaction is "an options strategy carried out by holding a short position in both a call and a put that have the same strike price and expiration date. The maximum profit is the amount of premium collected by writing the options" (35). As mentioned previously, Mr Leeson was writing these options in order to generate money to pay his margin calls from SIMEX (36) as early as 1993. Mr Leeson confirmed that he chose the straddle ultimately because of the high premiums he could gain from selling them. He needed the premiums to meet the margin calls on his other positions (37).

In practice, the effect of holding these positions can be demonstrated as follows: "If a trader writes a straddle with a strike price of $25 and the price of the stock jumps up to $50, the trader would be obligated to sell the stock for $25. If the investor did not hold the underlying stock, he or she would be forced to buy it on the market for $50 and sell it for $25." In reality, Mr Leeson sold more than 370 000 straddles over a period of just over a year (38),(39). If we analyze the anatomy of a straddle it clearly emphasizes the fact that the gain to the writer of the puts and calls can be no more than the premium he received when he entered into the sale transactions. If the market kept within a predetermined band he would gain the premium amount, as the two options would expire worthless, because the price of the underlying security did not breach the upper or lower threshold. However, if the market moved vigorously up or down, the problems would start. This is exactly what happened after the Kobe earthquake, and Mr Leeson's option positions were showing a loss of around USD 178 million by the end of February 1995 (40).

If short straddles were medicine, the leaflet that accompanied them would most probably include a word of caution to those about to use them. The Investopedia Dictionary gives us an idea of what these warnings, in all likelihood, would have looked like. It firstly cautions the reader about the fact that "the short straddle is a very risky strategy an investor uses when he or she believes that a stock's price will not move up or down significantly" and, in the second instance, it warns that "because of its riskiness, the short straddle should be employed only by advanced traders due to the unlimited amount of risk associated with a very large move up or down" (41). Mr Leeson should have been acutely aware of this fact. Whether or not he had another choice, other than to face the music, is another matter.

The second, and most devastating instrument used by Mr Leeson, was his naked long positions in Nikkei futures and his naked short futures position in Japanese Government Bonds. It must be remembered that the buyer of a futures contract is under legal obligation to either exercise or close out his position by buying an equal but opposite position. The seller of an option or future is equally under obligation to perform if the options or futures that he sold are exercised. A naked position is "a securities position that is not hedged from market risk. Both the potential gain and the potential risk are greater when a position is naked instead of covered (a covered position is hedged from market risk)" (42). Once again, a basic source like Investopedia cautions that "whether to have a naked position is rarely a concern for most small investors, but it is a concern for large investment holders and institutions". The reason is obvious: large unhedged positions in highly leveraged instruments like futures contracts can produce devastating losses.

In Mr Leeson's case, his positions could only have been described as staggering. The volume traded through the 88888 account grew from a mere 2 051 contracts for July 1992 to 96 121 in September 1994. Mr Leeson held 49% of the March 1995 contract and 24% of the June 1995 contract (43). Mr Leeson also had substantial positions in futures on Japanese Government Bonds. By November 1994 trading trough his 88888 account accounted for 24% of the SIMEX volume for Japanese Government Bond futures. At the time of the collapse, Mr Leeson held an unhedged short position of more than 28 000 contracts (44). In **Table 2** we see a summary of Mr Leeson's positions shortly before the collapse of Barings Bank. It was clear that Mr Leeson held 85% of the Japanese Government Bonds (JGB) March 1995 contracts and 88% of the June 1995 contracts (45). These positions became known in the market and made Mr Leeson extremely vulnerable. It must always be remembered that, for one party to make money, another party must lose the equivalent amount of money. Due to the sheer size of his positions, the counterparties must have included some of the largest investment banks in the world.

The extent of his positions was such that Swiss Bank apparently produced a paper at the end of 1994 in which no less than five potential explanations were put forward as reasons or motivations for Barings' positions in the market. Indicative of the size of these positions was the fact that one explanation that was put forward cited potential cooperation with a Government to support the market (46). During January of 1995, numerous individuals at Barings were questioned regarding the size of the Barings positions (47). It would be wrong merely to assume that these were calls made from individuals with the best interests of Barings at heart. In the cutthroat world of derivatives trading, information is worth gold and anyone working for a firm that was on the other side of Mr Leeson's positions would have been useful to try and find out what they could about the Barings strategy and/or who they (Barings) were trading for. As the Salomon strategy showed us (48), having deep pockets is often more important than a brilliant strategy. It is, therefore, quite conceivable that these rumors were viewed by Barings management as panic from worried counterparties about to lose a lot of money. The other comforting factor to those attending a Barings Asset and Liability Committee (ALCO) meeting at the time, was the fact that although large, these positions were supposedly hedged, making them essentially benign. The alarming part of the gossip was the call from the former Barings employee working for the Bank for International Settlements (BIS) in Basle regarding a rumor that Barings missed a margin call in Asia. This type of gossip in a market, whether true or not, could destroy a bank, as public perception dictates the standing of a bank much more than actual capitalization. As the news reached Peter Norris, Mary Walz contacted the Barings traders in Asia, including Mr Leeson, who advised her that she and her team should talk to the press. In hindsight, this instruction may seem odd. In reality, misinformation is a valuable and powerful tool for those operating in financial markets. It is quite possible that the wrong comment made in innocence about, for example, the actual positions of Barings could undo the well-laid plans their star trader, Mr Leeson, put in place to outwit the competition and earn them all spectacular bonuses. At the Barings executive committee meeting EXCO, Peter Norris explained that he instructed the Tokyo positions to be reduced purely for PR reasons and not because he saw any threat in the size of the positions (49). The problem was that no-one took the trouble of verifying the facts. **Table 2** clearly reflects a summary of the staggering extent of the positions held by Mr Leeson.

TABLE 2

Fantasy versus Fact: Mr. Leeson's positions as at end February 1995.		
Number of contracts nominal value in US$ amounts		Actual position in terms of open interest of relevant contract[2]
Reported[3]	Actual[4]	
Futures		
Nikkei 225	30112 $2809 million	long 61039 $7000 million	49% of March 1995 contract and 24% of June 1995 contract.
JGB	15940 $8980 million	short 28034 $19650 million	85% of March 1995 contract and 88% of June 1995 contract.

Euro yen	601 $26.5 million	short 6845 $350 million	5% of June 1995 contract, 1% of September 1995 contract and 1% of December 1995 contract.

Options

Nikkei 225	Nil	37925 calls $3580 million 32967 puts $3100 million	

1. Expressed in terms of SIMEX contract sizes which are half the size of those of the OSE and the TSE. For Euro yen, SIMEX and TIFFE contracts are of similar size.
2. Open interest figures for each contract month of each listed contract. For the Nikkei 225, JGB and Euro yen contracts, the contract months are March, June, September and December.

3. Mr. Leeson's reported futures positions were supposedly matched because they were part of Barings' switching activity, i.e. the number of contracts on either the Osaka Stock Exchange, the Singapore International Monetary Exchange or the Tokyo Stock Exchange.
4. The actual positions refer to those unauthorized trades held in error account **88888**.

Source: The Report of the Board of Banking Supervision Inquiry into the Circumstances of the Collapse of Barings, Ordered by the House of Commons, Her Majesty's Stationery Office, 1995

(50)   Reproduced under the terms of the Click-Use Licence.

These positions were, however, built up in a relatively short space of time. After the Kobe earthquake, Mr Leeson embarked on a very substantial strategy to increase his net long futures positions on the SIMEX and Osaka exchanges. As the Nikkei average was falling, the straddles sold by Mr Leeson began showing their true colours (51). The put options that Mr Leeson sold obliged him to buy the Nikkei 225 average based contracts at a fixed price, even though the underlying value may have decreased substantially on the expiry date. If the market kept on falling, his losses would mount continuously until the expiry date of the contracts. Mr Leeson also had the problem of a substantial rise in the market. As we showed, the call options that he sold as part of his straddles would also become valuable to their holders if the average of the Nikkei 225 showed a substantial rise, breaking out of the 19 000 - 20 000 range Mr Leeson was hoping for. This is clearly demonstrated by information released by DataStream and the Osaka Securities Exchanges illustrating Baring's Long Positions against the Nikkei 225 Average (52).

The key to Mr Leeson's ability to create false profits and hide his actual positions could be attributed to a well-used trading transaction called a cross-trade. In order to increase efficiency, a Member of an Exchange that represents both a buyer and a seller from two different accounts, and who have a matching interest (the buy order matches the sell order in price) in the same security, is allowed to execute the transaction on the floor of the Exchange. According to SIMEX rules, he is allowed to cross or execute the transaction after he declares the bid (buy) and offer (sell) prices three times in the trading pit. If no other member wants to take up the transaction, he can execute the transaction at the ruling market price (53). Mr. Leeson executed a substantial number of transactions between the Barings London-Euro yen Arbitrage account number 98008, the Barings – London JGB Arbitrage account number 98007, the Barings Securities Japan-Nikkei and JGB Arbitrage account number 92000 and his own 88888 account. In order to create the fictitious profits, the entries into the CONTAC system used by Barings and a number of other SIMEX members, were manipulated. Each cross-trade executed on the trading floor was then broken up into a number of smaller trades. The prices of these smaller trades were then changed to create a fictitious profit in one account and the corresponding losses were booked to the 88888 account.

In other instances, he executed smaller switches, in which case he merely changed the prices at which the trades were executed on the floor to create a fictitious profit. It appears that the subdivision of trades was designed to lead Barings Securities Japan into believing that the transactions (and profits) were real. One can only assume the undivided trades were for accounts that were both under his control. A substantial number of transactions were also entered into the CONTAC system, although they were never crossed on the SIMEX floor. These off-market transactions, although legal and perfectly acceptable on many international exchanges, were not permitted by SIMEX. The effect of these actions was twofold: in the first instance, it created false profits while hiding the losses, and the second and ultimately more important implication was the fact that no-one could detect the very large unhedged positions that Mr Leeson entered into on behalf of the bank. This latter implication is clearly reflected by the Nikkei Position of Account '92000' contained in the "Report of the Board of Banking Supervision Inquiry into the Circumstances of the Collapse of Barings" (54). The "Report" shows that it appears as if there is a substantial decline in the positions of Barings, which is in line with the instruction from the ALCO meetings held in February 1995 (55); in reality, however, there was a substantial increase in the positions that Barings were holding.

As we have seen in the previous chapter, one of the most blatant warnings that should have alerted the management of Barings was the exposure in April of 1994 of a Wall Street trader called Joseph Jett. Mr Jett fabricated a USD 350 million profit through manipulation of his firm's (Kidder Peabody) accounting system (56). The Joseph Jett incident did spark an internal review of risk procedures, which identified the fact that the existing procedures were not up to standard. The Board of Barings was apparently informed that a system was under development to allow Barings in London to monitor their overseas activities. The Director Settlements of Barings Investment Bank at this time was aware of the potential hazards associated with the fact that his department was dependent on the relevant traders supplying figures regarding trade prices, as well as volume traded (57). Risk controllers were, interestingly enough, appointed in London, Tokyo and Hong Kong, but not in Singapore, as Simon Jones viewed it as not necessary (58).

During January of 1995 the external auditors of BFS, Coopers & Lybrand, noted a substantial discrepancy between the BFS general ledger and the SIMEX yen settlement variation account. When Mr. Leeson was approached for an explanation, he blamed a computer error for the discrepancy (59). He later changed his explanation. As early as January 30, 1995 this USD 86 million receivable from a New York trading firm called Spear Leeds & Kellog, or SLK, was questioned by the external auditors of Barings Futures Singapore (60). The external auditors conveyed their concerns to the Group Finance Director of Barings Investment Bank, Geoffrey Broadhurst, who in turn claimed that he informed Peter Norris, the CEO of Barings Securities Limited. The head of Barings' Futures and Options Settlements office in London claimed that she offered to Broadhurst that she would call SLK on the day of the 30th of January when they first became aware of the USD 86 million receivable; however, he told her not to do it. According to Broadhurst, he was told by Norris not to do anything until it was confirmed that a real problem existed and was further instructed by Mr Norris to advise Coopers and Lybrand that they would prefer to investigate the matter internally. Spear, Leeds & Kellogg from New York was not unfamiliar to Barings, as their SIMEX trades were cleared through the Barings office in Singapore (61). Broadhurst himself was, however, not familiar with SLK and he was, on enquiry, advised by the Barings credit department in London that the credit limit of the firm with Barings was only USD 5 million, a lot less than the USD 86 million involved in this transaction (62).

The matter was apparently never fully investigated and apparently, on the 8th of February 1995, Mr Norris referred to the matter as an "operational error" during a meeting of the Asset and Liability Committee (63). This was not out of the ordinary as, on the 2nd of February 1995, Mr Leeson provided the Coopers and Lybrand auditors with a forged letter purportedly signed by the managing director of SLK, Mr Richard Hogan (64). The letter acknowledged the existence of the receivable in question. However, this did not totally satisfy Coopers and Lybrand. They also needed confirmation that the trade was authorized by Barings in London and confirmation by SLK that the USD 86 million would be paid to Barings. To achieve that, Mr Leeson went further and forged a fax from Ronald Baker, head of the Financial Products Group at Barings Investment Bank, acknowledging and authorizing the transaction, as well as another fax from Richard Hogan confirming that the premium would be paid. Mr Leeson also provided the auditors with forged documentation "confirming" that the money in question was indeed received by Barings. This satisfied the auditors. It is possible that Coopers and Lybrand conveyed their satisfaction to Mr Norris who, in turn, accepted the view of the auditors and conveyed such at the (ALCO) meeting of the 8th of February 1995.

The forgeries were fairly clumsy and the second fax that supposedly came from Hogan clearly showed that the header on the New York fax was from "Nick and Lisa". This per se can be explained by the fact that, due to time differences, Mr Leeson could have asked Mr Hogan to send the fax to his home rather than to the office. He may have claimed that he left the fax at home and asked his wife to fax it to him at the office. What is of greater importance is the fact that, in a handwritten memo to Simon Jones, Director Barings Futures Singapore and Finance Director Barings Securities Singapore, dated 1 February 1995,

Mr Leeson admitted that he was involved in an unauthorized trade (65).

The Report by the Singapore Inspectors (66) raised a number of questions regarding the handling of the SLK receivable. In the first instance, no less than seven different explanations were provided for the discrepancy.

-   When first questioned by the C&L auditors about the discrepancy between the two accounts, Mr Leeson blamed it on a computer error.

-   The second explanation he offered was that the shortfall was due to an outstanding refund of a margin deposited with SLK for an OTC Nikkei option that expired on the 30th December 1994.

-   At the request of SLK and BNP, an option trade between the two parties had been recorded in the BFS accounting records. BNP sold an option maturing on 30 December 1994 to SLK. Due to a BFS booking error, the BNP leg of the transaction was incorrectly marked for maturity on the 3rd of December 1994. On the third BFS paid the option premium to BNP, causing the shortfall as the payment of the option premium by SLK was only due on the 30th of December. This SLK payment was, however, outstanding and overdue. Mr Leeson admitted in writing that the transaction was unauthorized.

-   The fourth version put forward in a letter from Coopers & Lybrand stated that a Barings client, SLK, purchased Nikkei options from BSL and didn't exercise the options or pay over the option premium due to BSL. The outstanding option premium was paid over to BSL on 31 December 1994.

- According to Ms Waltz, she was told by Mr Broad-hurst that a booking error of a transaction between SLK and BNP gave rise to the SLK receivable.

- The sixth version of the problem put forward by Mr Broadhurst to C&L in London in February 1995, was that the problem arose because SLK traders wore BFS jackets when they traded on SIMEX. The front and back office function in Singapore has been split and extra staff had been employed to cope with the increase in trades. Mr Leeson's role, and the fact that he admitted to an unauthorized trade, was omitted. The auditors were also asked to omit the incident from the audit management letter, as it could cause problems for Barings at SIMEX. Everything in this account is false.

- On the 9th of February 1995, Mr Leeson told Mr. Hawes during a meeting that SLK sold an option to BNP and, on maturity of the option, the amount of 7.778 billion yen in question was payable by SLK to BNP.

The obvious question is why no-one noticed the conflicting stories, why no action was taken against Mr Leeson and why the auditors were misled. There can be very little doubt that this matter was covered up, clearly implicating at least some of the Barings management. Ironically enough, in the three weeks up until the 24th of February 1995, nearly a billion USD was sent to BFS by other Barings entities. It is, therefore, quite conceivable that the collapse of Barings could have been averted if proper care and diligence was exercised by management when they became aware of the shortfall.

On 11 January 1995 Soo Yu Chuan, the Senior Vice President Audit and Compliance SIMEX, in a letter to Simon Dominic Jones, Director Barings Futures Singapore and Finance Director Barings Securities Singapore, questioned an apparent shortfall in margin requirements for account 88888 (67). He also questioned the ultimate identity of the owner of this account. It appears he was led to believe that account 88888 was a non-proprietary account and, therefore, pointed out that the fact that Barings were funding the margins in this account would be in contravention of SIMEX rule 822 prohibiting SIMEX member firms from financing the margin calls of their clients.

SIMEX officials started to watch Barings traders very closely in the beginning of 1995. It is noteworthy that Tony Hawes had to assure SIMEX officials during a meeting on 8th February 1995 that "...the entire assets of the Barings Group were available to ensure that Barings Futures in Singapore could meet its liabilities to the exchange" (68). During this meeting Mr Hawes was corrected by a SIMEX official when he said that Barings was short in Singapore. Mr Leeson was long in Osaka. The implication of this was an unhedged position, which carries great inherent risk. To his credit, Mr Hawes raised the matter with Mr Leeson, but was told that the Simex official was in error and that the said official conveyed this to him (Mr Leeson) in a telephone conversation (69).

On 16 February 1995 the company secretary of Barings Bank was telephoned by a senior director from another merchant bank in London called Schroders (70). Apparently, a rumor was doing the rounds that a counterparty of Barings was about to default on a large position (20 000 contracts) on the Osaka Exchange. The call and the rumor were discussed by the Barings ALCO and dismissed. As they did three weeks earlier, they once again decided that the Singapore positions should be reduced. Once again, no concrete measures were put in place to monitor whether or not these decisions were in fact implemented. Once again, as with the SLK receivable, any thorough analysis would have exposed Mr Leeson's activities and, even at this very late stage, might have averted the collapse of Barings.

I asked Mr Leeson for his comments regarding the inaction of management and their apparent efforts to conceal the SLK issue. He attributes it to the fact that the event occurred shortly before bonus allocations took place. He credits the possibility that anything untoward may jeopardize the bonuses of management as their motivation to smooth over things.

In September of 1993 the head of settlements raised some concerns regarding the controls in Mr Leeson's area, but was apparently rebuffed (71). Similarly, the concerns about data integrity raised by Tony Gamby after the investigation following the Joseph Jett exposure didn't lead to any serious risk control measures (72). One of the individuals at Barings who expressed his concerns about Mr Leeson was the Group Treasurer of Barings Investment Bank (BIB), Tony Hawes. He briefed James Baker, who was tasked to carry out the audit of Barings Singapore during the spring 1994 (73) about the necessity for Mr Leeson's control of both the front and back offices to be investigated due to the potential for abuse. He further expressed concerns about the amount of margin payments made by Barings Securities Limited London without a clear understanding of why and on whose behalf these payments were being made. As we mentioned before, Mr Leeson claimed these were margin payments made on behalf of his clients. Another voice of concern came from an assistant to Peter Norris, Sajeed Sacranie, who questioned whether or not SIMEX rules allowed the mixing of agency and proprietary trading, as done by Mr Leeson. The motivation for SIMEX to disallow such activity would probably be the potential for front-running of client orders.

During the autumn of 1994 a Tokyo trader working for Barings reported an odd experience he had with Mr Leeson to Mary Walz (Global Head of Equity Financial Products Barings Investment Bank), one of the managers Mr Leeson reported to (74). According to the Tokyo trader, he detected a discrepancy between what he was led to believe regarding Mr Leeson's trading activity in Japanese Government Bonds on the SIMEX

market and what he could see on his own screen. On drawing
Mr Leeson's attention to this anomaly, he was advised by
Mr Leeson that this was the effect of cross-trading that hadn't
been reflected by SIMEX. A short while later, the Tokyo
trader's screen reflected trades more in line with what he
thought Mr Leeson executed. They both assumed that the
SIMEX officials turned a blind eye to his after-hours trading
because of the amount of business he conducted. A few months
later, in July 1994, Fernando Geuler (Head of Proprietary
Equity Derivatives Trading Barings Securities Japan)
complained to Mary Walz about a lack of sufficient information
to monitor Mr Leeson's positions (75). The solution was to give
Mr Leeson his own trading book for Nikkei arbitrage. In
October the exceptional profits generated by Mr Leeson once
again fueled Geuler's suspicions (76). There was a lack of
activity in the Nikkei 225 index that normally manifests in low
volatility, which should translate into fewer money-making
opportunities, which is reflected in lower profits. Mr Leeson,
however, was making even more profit. The only explanation
he [Geuler] could find was that Mr Leeson was, as a matter of
course, front-running orders to allow such profits. Geuler once
again shared his concerns with Mary Walz and warned of the
consequences to Barings. Walz took the issue up with Ron
Baker, Head of Financial Products Group Barings Investment
Bank who, according to Geuler, contacted him to assure him
that the audit conducted by James Baker cleared Leeson. Ron
Baker later denied that either Walz or Geuler ever expressed
concerns about the way in which Mr. Leeson was generating his
profits. Fernando Geuler also made Mary Walz aware of an
incident during January of 1995 when Mr Leeson, apparently
without provocation, started to shout abuse at him in the course
of a routine conversation (77). It is quite clear that Mr Leeson
was under tremendous strain at this point in time.

In an article in the Wall Street Journal, Sydney Finkelstein
reported (78) that he was told by clerks at the Singapore Barings
office that Mr Leeson's activities were an "open secret". This is

confirmed by the fact that he enlisted their assistance in hiding his activities on a regular and consistent basis. During a visit in October 1994, Tony Hawes met one of the back office staff, called Linda, and was shocked by her lack of understanding of futures and options (79). Mr Leeson also used his floor traders to execute large orders 30 seconds before the end of daily sessions. Mr Leeson confirmed to me that his settlement staff were very inexperienced and were very loyal to him. Their lack of experience giving them a point of reference from which to judge his actions, and the relationship he built up by protecting them when they made mistakes, would explain their loyalty. The question that deserves to be asked is why Mr Hawes did not act when he realized that Norhaslinda Haji Hassan (Linda), the settlements officer for Barings Futures Singapore, had a very limited knowledge of futures and options.

The Report to the Board of Banking Supervision Inquiry into the collapse of Barings also identified a number of "indicators" that should have alerted the Barings management (80). Some of those highlighted were:

- The identification of the lack of separation of duties between the front and back offices reported in the internal audit report following the July and August 1994 review of the activities of Barings Futures Singapore (BFS).

- The high levels of funding required by Barings Futures Singapore, as well as the fact that no reconciliation took place of funds transferred from Barings in London to Barings Futures Singapore.

- Another red light would have been the extraordinary profits generated by Barings Futures Singapore through a perceived low-risk activity such as arbitrage (low risk, low return and vice versa).

The report pointed out the following other factors that, if viewed collectively, should have raised the alarm: the SLK receivable and the two SIMEX letters, reporting very large Barings positions; market rumors in the beginning of 1995, as discussed previously; and the high levels of inter-exchange arbitrage allowed without the application of gross trading limits.

If any of these warnings were treated with the attention it deserved, a catastrophe could in all probability have been averted. On Thursday the 23rd of February 1995 however, one day before Mr Leeson was to receive his bonus and two days before his 28th birthday, everything became too much. Mr Leeson left his trading desk and with his wife he made his way to Borneo. On Monday morning the 27 February 1995 a newspaper headline confirmed his worst fears, "BRITISH MERCHANT BANK COLLAPSE" (81). The massive positions showed in **Table 2** were too much for even Barings to bear. Within a few days Mr Leeson was arrested on his arrival at Frankfurt, on his way back to England. From there he was extradited to Singapore, where he was tried and sentenced to six and a half years in prison (82). Barings were taken over by the Dutch firm ING for a token 1 GBP (83). If any of you experience a sense of 'dejavue' you are not mistaken. The similarities between Mr Leeson and Mr Kerviel's cases are striking.

Lynn T. Drennan points out the fact that the huge media interests that accompany events like the Barings collapse and the types of events similar to it are at least in part fueled by a desire to blame either an individual or a group of individuals for what happened (84). Drennan continues and highlights the apparent obsession with the media to portray individuals as "demons" or "rogues". This irrational feeding frenzy often helps to obscure the fact that the circumstances in which the abuse took place are usually created by a whole series of failures that can be attributed to, among other things, management and system inefficiencies. This fact underlines the "culpability" of an organization as a whole. It is, however, very difficult to crucify an entity if the crowds are baying for blood. It is unfortunate for the likes of Rusnak, Iguchi, Leeson and Kerviel that the culpability of these collectives is often only exposed after the media frenzy is over. In the case of Mr Leeson, the Report of the Singapore inspectors highlighted their conviction that Mr Leeson was not solely responsible. Mr Leeson partly contributes the apparent unwillingness of the UK authorities to have him tried in the UK to the possibility that blame would also be apportioned to the powers that be at Barings (85).

Drennan summarizes her analysis of the events that led to the collapse of Barings Bank and the Mirror Group of companies of which Robert Maxwell was the CEO, by arguing that to attribute the collapse of these two companies purely to two individuals acting unethically and socially irresponsibly would be a gross oversimplification of the true facts. We should investigate the very important, although very often obscured, role of "...a failure in the corporate culture and management systems of the organization that allowed, if not encouraged, such behaviour" (86),(87). Mr Leeson himself had the following to say when he reflected on what he did: "I tried to remember the pressure I'd been under to perform and produce profits, but then I realized that this was just looking for excuses. These were my crimes, and I had to acknowledge them, plead guilty to them, and then put them behind me and get on with my life" (88). However, he went further and said: "...I did know that I could never even have begun these crimes in any other bank". This, as we have seen in this book, unfortunately turned out not to be true.

During my interviews with Mr Leeson he made it quite clear that he accepts responsibility for his actions. His motivation was twofold: a combination of his need to be successful in order to gain the respect and admiration of his family, his wife, superiors, co-workers and friends. He cites his inability to accept the fact that he was failing as one of the major reasons for trying to trade out of his positions while hiding his losses. This, as we have shown and will further show, was not unique to Mr Leeson. The potential loss of status, standing, respect and maybe your work seems to be a very strong motivator to hide and trade out of your losses rather than admitting to them. Mr Leeson also recounted to me an incident in December of 1994 in which a debt trader in London traded in something he shouldn't have and lost nearly USD 10 million. This loss was covered up by the institution that he worked for. This course of action, Mr Leeson believes, was and still is standard practice in the industry. Mr Leeson is adamant in his conviction that, if he was aware of a 'rogue trader' incident that ended like his did, he would not even have considered going down the road he traveled. He does, however, lay some blame at the doors of his superiors at Barings for creating an environment in which his activities could remain undetected for so long.

This question is essentially made up of two components; in the first instance, one needs to determine if Mr Leeson's activities were as a whole or in part motivated by his remuneration package. Secondly and potentially more importantly, was the inability of the management at Barings to detect Mr Leeson's activities resultant from their own need to have the company generate profits in order for them to get their very substantial remuneration packages? We will show that the answer to this question, analyzed from both perspectives, undoubtedly has to be yes.

During his holiday in the UK at the end of 1994, Mr Leeson recounts that he told his wife that he wanted to resign his position at Barings. Her response was that he must first go back and collect his bonus which, according to her "will set us up for life!" (89). One of the most astounding facts about this incident was that, according to his own account (90), Mr Leeson was trying to hang on only until he had received his bonus (91). He had two options; he could leave or try and trade out of his losses. As he could not leave, his only remaining option was to start doubling up in order to make inroads into his GBP 200 million losses. He would have received his bonus on the 24th of February, the day before his birthday on the 25th of February. According to the Bank of England report, his superiors considered paying him a bonus of more than GBP 700 000. This figure is about double the amount that Mr Leeson recalls was offered to him in November 1994 by Ron Baker, the Head of Barings Financial Products Group (92). By his own account, the bonus Mr. Leeson was expecting would have been around GBP 400 000. There is also more than sufficient evidence to suggest that senior executives at the bank may have been more concerned with their bonuses than the long-term interests of the shareholders of the company. This would provide us with some explanation for the seeming inability to question any of Mr Leeson's activities. A clear example was the audit conducted by James Baker. As we have seen previously, Mr Baker was armed with all the right questions. The failure of his audit to expose Mr Leeson appears to be directly linked to his focus (93). Mr Baker was apparently ultimately concerned with threats to the flow of profits to Barings. One of these threats he identified as a drop-off in volatility of the markets and the overall volumes of business available in the market. The second threat he identified was the potential loss of Mr Leeson. It is clear that Mr James Baker appreciated and confirmed the perception in Barings of the direct correlation between the presence of Mr Leeson and the present and future profitability of Barings.

During my interview with Mr Leeson, he confirmed that money undoubtedly played a role as a motivator for, among other things, his actions and the action or inaction of those in Barings who benefited from the "profits" he was generating through the Barings bonus structure (94). He said that the prestige and the status that went along with being a highly successful trader was probably the principle motivator. He wanted desperately to be the successful trader, son, friend and husband. When I asked him why he started using the 88888 account again after he cleared it in 1994, he said it was the fear of failing that made him use the 88888 account. Mr Leeson was, in other words, dependent on the 88888 account to maintain his status. He could not admit to himself that he was not the superstar trader that he so desperately wanted to be. Mr Leeson also recognizes the fact that he was, by that time, addicted to his 88888 account. The ease with which he could manipulate the books, resultant from being in charge of both the front and back office functions, coupled with the absence of any real oversight by Barings internal risk management systems, allowed him, as he described it, to be "probably the only person in the world to be able to operate on both sides of the balance sheet" (95). As we have shown and will further show, Mr Leeson was unfortunately not in a unique position and nor was he the only one who showed signs of addictive behavior.

Like Societe Generale Barings employed a very fragmented reporting system, which resulted in a situation in which Mr Leeson was reporting to product managers in London who were responsible for the profitability of his transactions. The product manager for proprietary trading was different from the product manager for agency trading. From 1 January 1994 Mr Leeson reported to Mr. Ron Baker, director of Barings Bank & Company (BB&CO)/Head of Financial Products Group (FPG) of Barings Investment Bank through Mary Walz, also a Director of Barings Bank & Company (BB&CO)/Global Head of Equity Financial Products, Barings Investment Bank (BIB). He also reported to a local manager at Barings Securities Singapore, who was responsible for operational and administrative matters. He had a further reporting line to the regional operations manager for Southeast Asia. In practice, Mr Leeson reported to both Mr James Bax, Regional Manager South Asia/Director Barings Futures Singapore (BFS) and Mr Simon Jones, Regional Operations Manager South Asia/Director Barings Futures Singapore (BFS)/Chief Operating Officer Barings Securities Singapore (BSS) (96)

The argument being made is that it is not uncommon for this so-called matrix system to be employed in financial businesses with global operations. In the case of Barings, the shortcomings of the system were brutally exposed. In practice, an overseas manager would have local reporting lines of an administrative nature, together with a product or operational manager at a regional or head office. In Mr Leeson's case, it appears that everyone wanted him to report to them as he was reporting large profits, while no-one took the time to determine exactly how he was achieving his profits. This view was confirmed by Mr Leeson (97). Mr Leeson made it clear to me that the reporting structure at Barings was far from ideal. This was further complicated by the fact that the "profit" and loss accounts reflecting the "profits" he was generating most probably served as an incentive to individuals to create the impression that they in some way contributed to this profit and/or were entitled to share in the glory, as he was in one way or another reporting to them. This, together with the constant turf battles in the organization, created the environment in which questions about his profitability were viewed by his immediate superiors as an attack on their turf rather than a genuine effort by someone to solve some of the questions that were raised from time to time. Mr Leeson described his reporting lines as "…hazy and inbred as the Barings family tree itself" (98). The already unwieldy structure before 1993 became even more complicated after the 1993 merger (99). It was at this time that the "matrix" system of reporting was introduced. Mr Leeson pointed out to me that, although the group of people who had the responsibility to oversee his actions all had experience in a range of different areas of the financial markets and trading in them, no-one had experience of the whole process from trading through to settlement and reporting. It was this lack of a thorough understanding of the total process, coupled with an already fragmented reporting structure, which became a major contributor to the environment that allowed him to trade unauthorized, hide his losses, inflate his profits and fraudulently receive funding to sustain his activities.

Mr Leeson also emphasized the unwillingness of his superiors to ask questions if they didn't understand something as a key element of failure in the overall oversight structure. Although he holds the view that it is possibly only human nature for people not to ask questions out of fear of looking stupid, it nevertheless allowed him to talk himself out of many tight spots. This phenomenon is unfortunately not restricted to Barings, and played a role in a number of these failures. A striking example of this type of behavior was the claim by Joseph Jett's manager that he didn't understand what Jett was doing, when asked why he didn't detect Jett's activities (100). Coming from a man with a PhD in mathematics, how was that possible? Was that precisely the problem; was he afraid of asking because he was afraid of looking stupid?

The question of regulatory failure, in the case of Barings, has two elements to it. In the first instance, the role of British regulator, the Bank of England, needs to be investigated and, secondly, the role of the Singaporean regulator deserves our attention.

There is sufficient evidence to suggest that the Bank of England and the SFA had grave concerns about Barings as far back as the early 1990s. The Bank of England was apparently informed by the banking side of Barings, Barings Brothers that a distinct possibility existed for the closure of Barings Securities if the losses in this area persisted and grew (101). In reality, the operating loss for the preceding 12 months up until 30 September at Barings Securities was nearly GBP 40 million, which translated into an after-tax loss on ordinary activities of nearly GBP 12 million. During its June 1992 inspection of Barings, the Securities and Futures Authority (SFA) detected a number of breaches of its rules by Barings. By early 1993 the Bank of England was still very concerned by the state of Barings. During a meeting between a Barings delegation and Christopher Thompson, the Bank of England supervisor responsible for Barings, Mr Thompson apparently advised the Barings delegation that there was a real fear that the earnings collapse at Barings Securities was threatening the very existence of Barings Brothers & Co. and that this may result in the collapse of the merchant bank that has been around for more than 230 years (102).

Mr Leeson himself viewed the role of the officials at SIMEX as a very important contributing factor to the environment in which he was able to conduct his activities and was allowed to build up his massive positions. A SIMEX official apparently asked him to increase his positions only weeks before the collapse of Barings. This is a very critical issue, as SIMEX was the one organization that knew exactly what his positions were (103). SIMEX not only knew what positions he was holding, they also knew the ultimate ownership of the 88888 account, as they requested Mr Leeson to identify the owner of the account. As the Barings positions on the Osaka and Tokyo exchanges were reflected on Bloomberg on a daily basis, SIMEX was the only role player other than himself that knew exactly what the overall Barings positions were. According to Mr Leeson, a senior SIMEX official asked him to put more business through SIMEX only a few weeks before the collapse of the Bank. Mr Leeson holds the view that SIMEX did not have the expertise to conduct the levels of business they were conducting at the time. He noted to me that the most experienced and best staff was poached by the major banks, leaving SIMEX at a disadvantage. This phenomenon, according to Mr Leeson, is not only confined to SIMEX. In his view, the best people are usually working for the banks, trying to break the rules, and not for the regulatory bodies trying to enforce the rules. Even in the case of Barings, Mr Leeson feels strongly that there was a lack of emphasis on the importance of proper administrative systems, and experienced staff. A reflection of this is the fact that he was not allowed to pay for experienced back-office staff, a fact that contributed to the eventual collapse of the bank. Because of Barings trying to save costs in all non-profit-generating areas, he was only able to appoint inexperienced staff. This not only led to a lot of mistakes, it also allowed him to conduct his activities without fear that his staff would understand exactly what he was doing.

The Daily Telegraph, in reporting on the Bank of England report, expressed astonishment at how Mr Leeson's activities remained undetected for so long. The following line from their report may be truer than we think: "Mr Leeson is neither a victim nor a hero, merely the latest in a long history of young men entrusted with responsibilities for which they proved unfit" (104). The report purportedly continued to question the portrayal of senior Barings management as "sublime incompetents" and the possibility that Mr Leeson would be the only one to be punished with a jail sentence while the board of Barings would come off scot-free.

I asked Mr Leeson to comment on how often traders try to trade themselves out of losses and/or unauthorized positions. He commented that he believed it was human nature to try and trade out of a difficult position rather than just accept it, but added that, although he didn't believe it was rife, it happened more frequently than the financial institutions would like to admit. In his time at Barings he could recall about six or seven occasions when someone in the debt products department, other than himself, overtraded. When asked how the profitability of a trader affects the diligence of management with respect to enforcing rules, he recalled that during his time at Morgan Stanley there was a successful trader who was sitting in an armchair rather than the normal traders' chairs and was allowed to smoke big fat cigars while everyone else had to smoke outside. He also noted that individuals like that, with bigger-than-life personas, could be very intimidating to junior and/or inexperienced staff and that it would be quite possible for such an individual to dominate such inexperienced staff. It was, therefore, quite obvious that the rules didn't apply equally to everybody in these trading operations. I believe it is very easy for inexperienced staff to not only be dominated, but also to be so impressed with the 'status' of such a star trader, that they would find it difficult to question transactions and/or actions of such a revered trader.

Mr Leeson commented that it would be very difficult to remove money as an incentive for extreme opportunism, due to the competitiveness of the industry, unless it was done on an industry-wide basis. If you don't pay the player what he can get elsewhere, he will just move. He noted to me that Deutsche Bank had recently restructured their remunerating structure, a decision he believed would place them at a disadvantage in retaining their best traders and attracting new ones. With regard to the influence of bonuses on the actions of management at Barings, Mr Leeson said that when the auditors (I assume the internal auditors) were conducting their audits of his trading activities, it was quite possible that they didn't scratch as hard as they could have because they were afraid of jeopardizing their bonuses. He did, however, add that he had no hard evidence to support this view, as only those actually involved would know the true motivation for their actions or inactions. Mr Leeson was asked if it was possible, that the decision by senior management of Barings to spend money on administration and systems could have been clouded by the fact that the Barings bonus system made it a choice between an improved IT and administration capability and higher bonuses for themselves. Mr Leeson responded that this was possible, as Morgan Stanley had an IT department of around 200 people while Barings had one person when he started there. However, he said this situation did improve during his time at Barings.

I also asked Mr Leeson if he believed that more regulation would prevent unauthorized activities within trading firms. He held the view that more regulation would do very little to prevent such occurrences. Mr Leeson also pointed out to me, in response to another question, that whereas one used to find (in the time that he worked at Morgan Stanley) very large IT departments because of their focus on service and settlements, the emphasis had somewhat shifted, and today one would find very large legal departments, which are needed to bend the regulations. This, he believes, will always be the case and regulators will always be playing catch-up. He believes that the prevention should take place through internal controls within trading firms. He believes measures to prevent these activities need not be complicated or expensive. He also believes complacency plays an important role; as people do the same checks over and over, they tend to lose their vigilance. On the matter of the reliance by firms on the work done by outside audit firms, Mr Leeson pointed out that in the few weeks that even a major audit entails, only a snapshot of the company is taken, at a time when everybody is expecting a snapshot. If you send people without the proper experience, they have no chance to understand or appreciate the impact some of the complex products could have on a company's balance sheet. To solve this problem, audits should be a continuous process conducted by experienced and seasoned individuals with a thorough understanding of the business they have to audit. Advanced automated audit systems tailor-made to audit investment transactions would also be invaluable to less experienced auditors. The "ELECTRONIC TRUSTEE" [105] system is an example of such a system capable of conducting continuous automated audits of investment transactions. By combining technology with common sense oversight practices, unauthorized transactions or other anomalies could be detected within hours instead of months or years after the event.

In this chapter we clearly demonstrated that a combination of factors played a role in creating this tragic event. The role of learned behavior cannot be overemphasized; one of the most crucial insights into the soul of Barings was provided to me in an e-mail from Mr Leeson responding to questions I put to him regarding the NAB event in Australia. Mr Leeson acknowledges the fact that most companies engage in questionable market practices and traders may find it difficult to differentiate between what is acceptable and what not. He also commented that "...all of the procedures are wrong, morally and perhaps criminally, some more clearly than others..." and that "if the codes of practice were standard, not 'when suits' as above, perhaps the current ambiguity would be removed" (106). The balance between factors facilitating or inhibiting extreme opportunism was non-existent, to put it mildly. Even the most basic systems and staff needed to ensure back office efficiency were too expensive for the Barings management. Auditors were inexperienced and inefficient and were useless as an inhibitor for opportunism of extreme proportions. The personal interests of senior management outweighed the interests of clients and bond holders of Barings. Money and status were strong motivators in an environment of limited oversight and control.

CHAPTER 6

JOHN RUSNAK & ALLIED IRISH BANK

On the 7th of February 2002 the BBC reported that Allied Irish Bank discovered a shortfall of USD 750 million in the accounts of its US subsidiary [1]. Reports indicated that evidence pointed to Mr John M. Rusnak as the culprit. Two days later, on the 9th of February 2002, PRAVDA also covered the story and asked a few interesting questions. The article questions the haste with which John Rusnak was declared a swindler by the management of Allied Irish Banks. He has been described as "…a 'family man' with two children and a Labrador called Barney…" [2]. Investigators described him as "unusually clever and devious" [3]. With the benefit of hindsight, maybe he was just a good student.

According to his court records, he never "stole" money in the conventional sense of the word [4]. His activities did, however, help him to earn bonuses based on fictitious profits, totaling USD 850 000 between 1997 and 2001 [5]. Other than the bonuses of +/- USD 170 000 per year, there is no evidence that he otherwise enriched himself through committing a fraud totaling nearly USD 700 million. For every USD 1 000 he lost, he earned a one-dollar bonus, a very puzzling 'crime' indeed.

In analyzing this event, official and unofficial reports will be used to reconstruct the activities of John Rusnak and the environment in which it took place. Among other things, we will look at the report by Promontory Financial Group LLC and the Wachtell, Lipton, Rosen & Katz legal firm to the AIB and Allfirst Boards of Directors; court records of UNITED STATES OF AMERICA v. JOHN M. RUSNAK IN THE

UNITED STATES DISTRICT COURT FOR THE DISTRICT OF MARYLAND; and commentary by Sharon Burke from the Department of Mathematical Sciences at Villanova University, together with work by Colm Kearney, Professor of International Business at Trinity College in Dublin and a Dublin Finance Specialist, Dr Elaine Hutson. This information will be augmented by numerous newspaper reports and records of a debate in the Irish Parliament regarding Allied Irish Banks (AIB). Attention will also be given to an investigation into allegations that senior officials of Allied Irish bank were also involved in irregularities relating to, among other things, "inappropriate dealing transactions" and tax evasion as early as pre-1996 (6). Court records detailing the events in 1994 at Chemical Bank will also be used to provide an interesting perspective on the activities of Mr Rusnak.

In 1999 an investigation initiated by the Irish parliament identified Allied Irish Banks (AIB) as being a substantial player in a tax avoidance scheme (7). The bank later paid a total of USD 140 million in penalties and unpaid taxes.

Two years after John Rusnak was sentenced to jail for seven and a half years, Allied Irish Bank was in the news once again for all the wrong reasons. May of 2004 was an interesting month for Allied Irish Bank. Early that month the bank admitted that it "...had overcharged many of its foreign-exchange customers since the mid-1990s..." (8). Later that year, after initially refusing to testify in public to the Irish parliament's Finance and Public Services Committee, the Chief Executive and the Chairman of Allied Irish Bank admitted that bank investigators identified more than one million instances of charging "illegal amounts" to 173 000 customers between 1996 and 2004 (9). Later, in May, the bank also admitted that it "... had overcharged customers who had invested in trust funds established before 1971" (10). Senior officials at the bank reportedly established offshore accounts for managing clients' money in a way that was disadvantageous to their clients. We assume the bank was the advantaged party. The extent to which the bank has benefited is not clear; they were, however, ordered by the government-controlled Central Bank to deposit EUR 25 million with it, to cover potential claims against Allied Irish Bank (11).

This was, however, not the end of it. The bank, reportedly "under pressure from external auditors" (12) admitted that ten of its current and former directors who invested in some of the bank's tax-evading offshore accounts "...may have received unfair investment advantages versus other bank investors". According to a report published in the Washington Times, the group included three current executives and seven former executives. The Washington Times, quoting the Irish Times, reported that the group included "...Gerry Scanlan, chief executive from 1985 to 1994; Roy Douglas, a former head of AIB's British division who currently is chairman of another Irish heavyweight, Irish Life & Permanent; David Cronin, former treasurer at AIB's one-time US subsidiary, Allfirst Inc.; Darmuid Moore, AIB's former director of corporate strategy, who retired in 1993; and former deputy chief executive, Paddy Dowling, who is deceased" (13). These revelations led to the resignation of Tom Mulcahy as chairman of Aer Lingus, the state-owned Irish Airline. Mr. Mulcahy was the chief executive of Allied Irish Bank between 1994 and 2001 and was identified as a participant in the scheme. The Irish Deputy Prime Minister reportedly used the words "deeply shocking" in reaction to the actions of the executives and added that "...the Irish public was getting 'fed up' with sloppiness and unethical behavior exposed at the bank" (14).

What is interesting is the level of people involved in the scam, in that they included only the very top echelon at the bank. Mr David Cronin was, therefore, part of the inner circle of executives of the bank and, as a participant, obviously privy to the fact that they were engaging in illegal and immoral activities. The relevance and importance of this fact will become clear as we analyze the report following the investigation by Eugene Ludwig of Promontory Financial Group LLC of Washington DC.

As a currency trader, Mr Rusnak operated in the Foreign Currency Market, including the Euro Currency market (15). There is no physical location for the Foreign Currency Market; it exists as a virtual entity in dealing rooms. These dealing rooms are all connected via fax, telephone and computers and can be found in central banks as well as large banks and corporations. Rates of exchange for free-floating currencies are determined by the trading on the Foreign Exchange Market (FOREX). The Reuters agency provides an instantaneous feed of rate quotes to clients, at a cost. An important aspect of the Foreign Exchange Market is the fact that it has "…no regulation, no restrictions or overseeing board" and "…no mechanism to stop trading" (16). In the US, a set of 'best practice' guidelines is published by the Federal Reserve Bank of New York. These guidelines are not regulatory or legally binding and a contract between the buyer and seller provides the legal foundation for Foreign Exchange transactions.

Mr Rusnak essentially believed that the Japanese yen would strengthen against the USD. Based on this belief, the core of his trading strategy was designed to benefit in the event that this actually happened. According to court records, Mr Rusnak used three types of contracts to execute his transactions, namely "Spot", "Forward" and "Option" contracts (17).

Spot contracts identify two parties (a buyer and a seller), what currency they are buying or selling and what currency is accepted as payment as well as the ratio at which the transfer will take place. The ratio in this form of contract is the spot rate (the rate at which the currencies trade at the present moment). However, this rate is changing constantly, making it necessary for the two parties to agree on a rate that would probably differ from spot. Once this is done the contract is executed immediately, although funds between the parties normally only flow two days later. In reality, the administration departments of trading operations go through an administrative process that can be electronic or by phone or fax; it normally entails an exchange of the details of the transaction (18).

Mr Rusnak also made extensive use of "forward" contracts. When we look at the anatomy of a forward contract, it is easy to see why it was a 'weapon' of choice for him. A forward contract can be defined as "a cash market transaction in which a seller agrees to deliver a specific cash commodity to a buyer at some point in the future. Unlike futures contracts (which occur through a clearing firm), forward contracts are privately negotiated and are not standardized. Further, the two parties must bear each other's credit risk which is not the case with a futures contract. Also, since the contracts are not exchange traded, there is no marking to market requirement, which allows a buyer to avoid almost all capital outflows initially (though some counter-parties might set collateral requirements). Given the lack of standardization in these contracts, there is very little scope for a secondary market in forwards. The price specified in a forward contract, is for a specific commodity. If the value of the underlying commodity however changes, the value of the forward contract becomes positive or negative, depending on the position held.

Forwards are priced in a manner similar to futures. As in the case of a futures contract, the first step in pricing a forward is to add to the spot price the cost of carry (interest forgone, convenience yield, storage costs and interest/dividend on the underlying). Unlike a futures contract, though, the price may also include a premium for counter-party credit risk, and the fact that there is no daily marking to market process to minimize default risk. If there is no allowance for these credit risks, then the forward price will equal the futures price." (19).

Exchange traded forward contracts are called "futures" and are more regulated and more liquid than "forward" contracts (20). Forward contracts, on the other hand, are inherently private affairs. Unlike futures, they are not quoted on any exchanges and they are not standardized. These privately negotiated transactions are always 'Over The Counter' (OTC) transactions. The two parties will be exposed to one another's credit risk. All this suited Mr. Rusnak perfectly. Allied Irish Bank, the parent company of Allcorp, was a highly respected bank of substance. It is important to remember that Allied Irish Bank still managed to post a profit despite the nearly USD 700 million loss it suffered as a result of Mr Rusnak's activities. One of the fundamental differences between a futures contract and a forward contract is the fact that a futures contract makes provision for "margin" payments, commonly referred to as margin calls. Margin calls are defined as "…a call made upon a person with a futures contract … to deposit more cash with the broker if the market moves against the investor or if the margin requirements change" (21). Furthermore "…when the market turns against the buyer, the broker may call in substantially more margin…" (22). If Mr Rusnak had used this instrument, he would be running the danger that increasing margin calls, which would be inevitable if the market moved contrary to his view (against him), would undoubtedly force him to exceed his limits. This lack of marking to market allows a counter-party to enter into these transactions without any capital outlay for the term of the contract, other than the cost of the initial collateral requirement, which we know by now is relative to the perceived risk associated with the buyer of the forward. One of the inherent negative characteristics of forward contracts is the fact that there is little or no secondary market for these contracts. If you needed to counter-balance or hedge your position, you would be dependent on other instruments to accomplish that. On the positive side, from Rusnak's perspective, is the fact that he could take very large bets with little capital, allowing him to operate with little up-front cash. This; coupled with the fact that the forward transactions were 'Over The Counter' (OTC), non-quoted and non-standard transactions, created a recipe for disaster. These facts made the transactions more difficult than normal to monitor or, as Frank Partnoy ominously put it: "you might never be able to discover certain information about an OTC derivative unless you worked in the derivatives group at an investment bank" (23). It also implied that, if the market moved in the opposite direction to what Mr Rusnak expected, the sky was the limit to the potential losses sustained by the bank.

The third instrument used by Mr Rusnak was the Forex (FX) Option. The Forex Option "… involves the buying and selling of an opportunity to enter into an FX spot trade at an agreed-upon exchange rate, known as the 'strike price'." The buyer of an FX option has the ability to exercise the terms of the agreement to exchange currency at an agreed-upon price at a future date, known as the "expiration date" (24). An option differs from spot and forward transactions in a number of ways. These differences were pointed out in court papers:

a. "The buyer of an FX option is not required to exercise the option; he may or may not choose to exercise his right to exchange the currencies at the agreed-upon strike price on the expiration date of the option."
b. "… an FX option transaction requires the buyer to pay a cash premium to the seller for the rights given in the options contract."

In 2002 Colm Kearney, Professor of International Business at Trinity College Dublin, and Dr Elaine Hutson, a Finance Specialist from Dublin, tried to reconstruct some of the transactions that Mr Rusnak entered or allegedly entered into. One of the important facts about Mr Rusnak's trading is that he had actual as well as fake positions, the impact of which they explained (25).

They illustrated the positions that Mr Rusnak should have been holding compared to the actual positions that Mr Rusnak was holding (26). He believed that the USD would weaken against the Japanese YEN and, buying the appropriate forward at the ruling spot price, he would be able to generate a healthy profit, as the value of these forward contracts would increase as the USD weakened against the Japanese YEN. A skilled trader would, however, know that he could lose a lot of money if his view on the USD/YEN exchange rate was off the mark. In order to be prudent, the appropriate course of action would be to buy a put option on the Japanese YEN. A put option is "an option to sell a security at a specific price and at a specific date" (27). This activity is commonly referred to as "hedging". In this case, the put option would provide the buyer thereof with the right, but not the obligation, to sell his position if the JPY weakened against the USD past a certain point. This point is commonly referred to as the "strike price: The strike price is "the predetermined price at which the holder of an option may exercise his right to buy or sell securities from, or to, the writer of the option." (28).

If the Japanese YEN strengthened against the USD, the option would expire worthless and the loss would be equal to the cost of the option, called the option "premium". The option premium is "…a term applied to the deposit payable on a traded option in the stock and futures market" (29). Downside risk (risk of losing money) is eliminated for the cost of the option and potential upside (profit) is reduced by the cost of the option. However, as it turned out, Mr. Rusnak never bought the put option on the Japanese YEN. The reason for this was apparently that he could not afford to buy the appropriate hedge without exceeding his cash limits, because the collateral requirements from his forward counter-parties exceeded his cash limits as the USD/YEN exchange rate moved contrary to his hopes. This in itself may be an indication that his forward counter-parties grew nervous. As explained earlier in this chapter, the size of the collateral required is normally a reflection of the view the seller of the forward contract takes of the credit risk of the buyer. Forward contracts have inherent leverage (30). Leverage is: "in speculative terms, the opportunity for a large profit at a small cost. It implies high risk." (31). The first portion is exactly what Mr Rusnak needed. The second portion was a risk he had to take. Large banks that are dealing with one another normally require only a fraction of the value of the full forward contract. This amount, called collateral, could be as low as 5% of the value of the contract. In order to make a USD 100 million bet, Mr Rusnak had to provide collateral to the amount of USD 5 million. However, if the market moves contrary to your expectations, the leverage effect could bite you.

Prof Kearney and Dr Hutson went further and speculated that, in reality, things were slightly different. At the time Mr Rusnak was under tremendous pressure, as his losses were mounting. He also had to make back his losses with very little money, as his daily limits were curtailed. In order to generate the necessary capital, Mr Rusnak went for the proverbial double-or-nothing strategy (32).

He bought forward contracts by putting down, probably, 5% collateral. Then, instead of hedging his position, he went and doubled up his risk position by selling put options on the Japanese YEN. If the Japanese Yen strengthened against the USD, he would keep the option premium plus his profit. If the inverse happened, he would have double the negative exposure. However, by selling the puts, he would be earning a premium from the buyer of the put. It would have been possible for him to finance (at least in part) his forward with the premium he earned from selling the puts. If the USD strengthened against the Japanese Yen or even hold its 2001 levels, he would be in deep trouble. In reality, Mr. Rusnak raised nearly USD 300 million through the sale of deep in the money put options (33). Over and above the money he raised to finance his trading, he 'augmented' his directional long spot and forward positions, all betting on a strengthening of the Japanese YEN against the USD. Kearney and Hutson were dead on the money with their speculation. They clearly demonstrated that it is indeed possible for a trader like Mr Rusnak to enter into extremely large and risky transactions with very little initial outlay, a strategy that was central to most "rogue" trader events.

The USD however did not weaken against the Yen to the 73.77 to 96.75 levels needed for the options sold by Mr Rusnak to expire worthless. His firm was severely exposed and suffered massive losses.

The legal proceedings against Rusnak identified three elements to the motivation behind his actions. (1) According to the State (USA v John M. Rusnak) Mr Rusnak's actions were designed to create a false impression that he was trading profitably for Allied Irish Bank (AIB). (2) He did this in order to ensure that he would remain employed by the bank, which in turn would entitle him to all the benefits associated with that position. (3) This would include salary, bonuses, position, and status and maybe even (34) the lavish entertainment he received from the brokers he traded through.

In essence, the fraudulent activity can be divided into three phases or categories. The first phase of activities was designed to hide his losses derived from his actual currency trading. The second phase or group of activities was designed to allow Mr Rusnak to increase his trading volumes undetected. The third phase of activities was to raise capital for Mr Rusnak to continue trading after some of his other activities had been curtailed. According to the papers brought before United States District Court for the District of Maryland, the State argued that Mr Rusnak did the following:

In the first phase, Mr Rusnak was accused of entering "…false and fictitious foreign currency trades and trading information into the books and records of the Bank" (35). It was also claimed that he "…circumvented the confirmation process by creating fictitious telefaxes purportedly sent to the Bank by counter-parties to fictitious foreign currency trades and by causing these fictitious confirmations to be forwarded to personnel in the Bank's back office" and that he "...fraudulently convinced individuals in the Bank's back office that it was not necessary to confirm certain types of foreign currency trades."

Adding to this he also, according to court documents "... manipulated the calculation of his P&L (profit & loss) statements by entering false and fictitious trades and trading information into the Bank's Optics and DEVON systems, thereby concealing his actual trading losses. By manipulating his P&L statements in this manner, Rusnak ensured that he did not exceed his "stop loss" limit and thereby maintained his ability to continue trading on behalf of the Bank despite his large trading losses." Mr Rusnak also "...manipulated the calculation of his VaR (value at risk) by providing Bank personnel with a spreadsheet that contained false and fictitious information about 'holdover' trades, that is, transactions that the defendant falsely represented that he had entered into after the VaR closing time each day. These 'holdover' figures that Rusnak provided, together with the false and fictitious trades and trading information that he entered into the Bank's Optics and DEVON systems, allowed Rusnak to stay within his VAR limit and to maintain his ability to continue trading on behalf of the Bank despite the large risk inherent in his actual trading positions" (36). The Ludwig Report pointed out that, in a particular three-month period, Mr Rusnak used holdover positions on 52 days out of the 58 that were sampled. In some instances, the same holdover position was left for three straight days without anyone apparently noticing (37).

In an effort to cut the back office largely out of the loop, Mr Rusnak "...used Prime Brokerage Accounts (hereinafter PBAs) between the Bank and Citibank, Bank of America, and Merrill Lynch to conceal the details of his daily trading activity and to enter false and fictitious transactions into the books and records of the Bank. PBAs allowed Rusnak, on behalf of the Bank, to enter into foreign exchange transactions throughout a trading day with third parties without entering those transactions into the books and records of the Bank, and without the Bank confirming and settling each transaction; those functions were performed by the relevant prime broker. The Bank and each of the prime brokers typically had one net settlement of all of the PBA transactions on just one date each month. Rusnak entered false and fictitious prime brokerage transactions into the books and records of the Bank and then amended, cancelled or reversed those transactions before the monthly net settlement with a prime broker, thereby allowing Rusnak to conceal his trading losses and maintain his ability to continue trading on behalf of the Bank" (38).

After pressure was exerted on Mr Rusnak to reduce his use of the ABI balance sheet, he needed another source of funding. In order to raise money Mr Rusnak "...on behalf of the Bank, sold 'deep in the money' Japanese yen/US dollar option contracts, with five different counter-parties. These types of FX option contracts allowed Rusnak to generate large cash payments to the Bank from these counter-parties in exchange for similarly large liabilities to those counter-parties, which would come due a year after the cash payments. After entering into each of these five 'deep in the money' transactions, Rusnak entered false and fictitious option transactions into the books and records of the Bank to cancel out and to remove these large outstanding liabilities from the Bank's books and records, thereby improving Rusnak's P&L statements and his VaR calculations and concealing his actual trading losses." These five 'deep in the money' transactions are detailed in **Table 3**.

What Mr Rusnak did was to sell the right to these five counter-parties to sell agreed-to quantities of Japanese YEN to Allfirst at a prices ranging from 73.77 – 96.7500 Yen to the USD. The premium that the counter-party would pay to Mr Rusnak would largely be a reflection of the difference between the strike price of the option contract and the ruling price at the time of the transaction.

TABLE 3

Counter party	Trade Date	Expiration Date	Strike Price	Premium Paid
Citibank	Feb. 20, 2001	Feb. 20, 2002	73.7700	$125,052,000.00
Bank of America	Mar. 07, 2001	Mar. 07, 2002	75.0000	$74,878,340.00
Deutsche Bank	Dec. 06, 2001	Dec. 06, 2002	96.7500	$24,943,750.00
Merrill Lynch	Dec. 12, 2001	Dec. 12, 2002	92.0000	$25,015,000.00
Bank of New York	Dec. 24, 2001	Dec. 24, 2002	94.1900	$50,000,000.00

(39)

If the Japanese YEN strengthened against the USD, i.e. you would need less Yen to buy one USD, the value of the option would reduce.

However, if the value of the Japanese YEN declined against the USD and would you need more Yen to buy one USD; the value of the contract would increase. For this put to expire worthless, the Japanese Yen had to strengthen against the USD to a rates of less than 73.77- 96.75 Yen for every one USD. In actual fact, the USD would have to lose around 30% of its value against the Japanese Yen before these options would become worthless and would not be exercised (40).

In reality the yen traded as follows on the expiry dates:

TABLE 4

Expiration Date	Strike Price	Actual price
Feb. 20, 2002	73.7700	133.7600
Mar. 07, 2002	75.0000	127.0700
Dec. 06, 2002	96.7500	123.6900
Dec. 12, 2002	92.0000	122.7500
Dec. 24, 2002	94.1900	120.2700

(41)

In order to hide these put options, Mr Rusnak "…entered false and fictitious option transactions into the Bank's books and records in conjunction with these five 'deep in the money' transactions, thereby causing the Bank to have approximately $380 million in unrecorded but outstanding liabilities as of the end of 2001" (42).

According to court records, Mr Rusnak took a number of steps to conceal some of his transactions; he (43) "…rented a mailbox … to receive mail in the name of David Russel, a fictitious name, for the purpose of providing the Bank's independent auditors with a false confirmation of a fictitious option contract that the defendant had entered into the books and records of the Bank." He also "…provided to Bank personnel the fictitious name, 'Mr David Russel', with a fictitious counter-party, 'RBCDS FX', as the person who could confirm directly with the Bank's independent auditors a fictitious yen/US dollar option contract with a strike price of 84.1000 and an expiration date of January 8, 2001."

The bank duly sent off their request for confirmation and Mr Rusnak in turn "…(a) retrieved from the mailbox he had rented a letter sent by the bank to 'Mr David Russel' … asking 'David Russel' to confirm the fictitious option contract,

(b) signed a false confirmation of this fictitious option contract using the fictitious name 'David Russel' and the fictitious title 'VP', and (c) sent this false confirmation directly to the Bank's independent auditors, all for the purpose of concealing his fraudulent conduct from the Bank" (44).

By doing all the above, Mr Rusnak was able to incur and conceal losses totaling USD 691 204 113 up until the beginning of 2002. This amount was made up of (45) USD 291.6 million in nonexistent assets and USD 397.3 in liabilities that were fictitiously neutralized by nonexistent assets. An amount of USD 2.3 million in 'legitimate' trading losses was also identified. The USD 2.3 million was incurred in 2002. An interesting fact about Mr Rusnak's activities was that he compartmentalized his trading activities. An analysis of his transactions indicated that, of the 71 counter-parties transactions entered into, only 47 were legitimate. However, all the transactions he entered into with 19 Asian counter-parties were fictitious. The options explained in **Table 5** were entered into with only five counter-parties.

What is also very clear is that the losses incurred by Rusnak snowballed over a period of time. The total losses at 31 December 1999 totaled USD 89.8 million, consisting of real trading losses 'neutralized' with fictitious assets. This grew to USD 300.8 million by December 2000, once again made up of real trading losses covered up with fictitious assets. During 2001 the real options used to raise capital were added to the mix and the total losses more than doubled.

The question that immediately jumps to mind is how did Mr Rusnak manage to avoid detection for so long? It appears to be a fairly complex matter and I am doubtful if there is one factor that can be singled out as the cause of the incident. In my view, the climate at Allfirst was conducive to this event taking place. On the 8th of February 2002 the Board of Directors of Allied Irish Banks plc (AIB) authorized the Promontory

Financial Group LLC and the law firm of Wachtell, Lipton, Rosen & Katz to conduct an investigation into the events that led to the losses suffered by Allfirst Financial Inc and Allfirst Bank (46). The investigation was led by a former "Comptroller of the Currency" under the Clinton administration, Mr Eugene Ludwig. He purportedly had a strong banking regulation background and also provided a sense of impartiality to the investigation (47). The report became known as the "Ludwig Report" shortly after it was tabled on the 12th of March 2002. The findings of the Ludwig report can be grouped into a few categories.

In the first instance, the controls at AIB and Allfirst were hopelessly inadequate. The Ludwig Report (48) highlighted, among other things, the fact that:

"Senior management in Baltimore and Dublin did not focus sufficient attention on the Allfirst proprietary trading operation."

"Treasury management weaknesses at Allfirst also contributed to the environment that allowed Mr Rusnak's fraud to occur."

"Proprietary currency trading business was inadequately supervised."

"AIB Group Risk, and Allfirst senior management groups and the respective Boards, assumed that the control and audit structures governing the trading activities that were conducted at Allfirst were sufficiently robust."

There were numerous incidences where red lights should have gone on at both Allied Irish Bank and at Allfirst. Neither the departing trading manager, the treasury funds manager nor the treasurer ever conducted an in-depth analysis of Mr Rusnak's trading (49) or analyzed whether or not he was executing his stated strategy of "running a large option book hedged in the cash markets" (50). The 'deep in the money options', which expired unexercised, were never questioned, indicating that they were either never noticed or that they were not understood. Similarly, Mr Rusnak's profit-and-loss figures were never compared with the general ledger entries.

The prime brokerage accounts also provide their fair share of red lights. Over and above the fact that the initial motivation for using prime brokerage accounts was suspect, requests from Mr Rusnak in April of 1999 to withhold payments on trades raised alarm at the back office. In a Simultaneous Delivery versus Payment (SDvP) environment, an institution like STRATE, for example, in South Africa will match delivery from both parties before any transfers take place; this practice eliminates principle risk (51). In the absence of an SDvP system, payment can be withheld until the counter-party delivers. This practice is normally reserved for situations in which there is concern about the ability of a counter-party to settle. It does, however, provided time for Mr Rusnak to neutralize a fake transaction with another fake transaction. It is therefore no surprise that during that same period the back office found it difficult to confirm a number of transactions in these prime brokerage accounts (52). They subsequently raised concerns with Mr Cronin that intra-day off-market transactions could be executed with counter-parties that would be virtually impossible to confirm. This resulted in a meeting that included Mr Rusnak, his trading supervisor, Mr Ray, the heads of risk control and back office as well as the treasury funds manager. The outcome of the meeting was that Mr Cronin purportedly ordered a brief suspension of Mr Rusnak's use of these accounts, with the proviso that all future transactions entered into should be scrutinized. The aim would be to confirm the existence of an audit trail, as well as evaluating the motive for each transaction. However, all the parties failed to execute this instruction for various reasons, and the treasurer apparently never followed up to ensure his instructions were carried out. At the same time, numerous complaints were reportedly brought to the attention of the treasurer regarding Mr Rusnak's bullying of back office staff. Once again, Mr Cronin did little other than calling a meeting in which treasury staff were asked to respect one another (53). Difficulty in confirming trades executed by Mr Rusnak continued though 2000 and 2001 and he would often provide confirmations that did not match the transaction that was queried. No evidence exists that the possibility was ever considered that Mr Rusnak was only executing certain deals if confirmation for the existence of such transactions was sought.

One of the most fascinating facts about this whole incident is the extent of external red flags that should have alerted someone in a position of authority at either Allied Irish Banks (AIB) or at Allfirst. Between 2000 and 2002 at least five events took place that should have triggered some form of alert.

In March 2000 Citibank enquired from the Group Treasurer at Allied Irish Banks (AIB) if they would be able to cover a gross monthly settlement of more than USD 1 billion due at the beginning of April (54). Mr Ryan, the Group Treasurer, confirmed the ability of Allfirst to meet its commitments. Mr Ryan ordered a discreet enquiry by Allfirst risk-assessment staff. The explanation provided was that the Allfirst's liability was offset by a larger Citibank liability.

The question that immediately jumps to mind is twofold. In the first instance, why was Citibank not aware of its own obligation towards Allfirst?

Secondly, why were there such large trading volumes conducted by Allfirst? Evidence provided to the Ludwig investigation revealed conflicting reports regarding this incident. Claims by the Allfirst executive vice president of risk, Mr King, that he discussed this incident with the chairman of Allfirst was denied by the latter. Even if one ignores these discrepancies about who told what to whom, the senior management at Allied Irish Banks (AIB) should have been well aware of the extent to which Allfirst and, in particular, its FX options dealer was trading. Reports to the AIB Group treasurer dating back to 1997 indicated reporting on the fact that, of the USD 1 billion nominal FX options book, Mr Rusnak was responsible for 95% of the activity and of his 95%, 80% was speculative. Similarly, 10 K filings submitted by Allfirst to AIB for 1999 and 2000 clearly spelled out the fact that foreign exchange trading at Allfirst was running into billions of USD per year (55).

An anonymous source reportedly contacted Allied Irish Banks (AIB) to make them aware of the fact that Allfirst was engaged in "very heavy foreign exchange trading". Without relaying this enquiry to the Allfirst CEO or other executives, Mr Michael Buckley, the CEO of Allied Irish Banks (AIB), contacted Mr Cronin, the Allfirst Treasurer, directly for an explanation.

Mr. Cronin responded in writing as follows:

"To bring closure to our conversation earlier today about foreign exchange turnover, I confirm that we have had no unusual or extra large transactions in the last two weeks with counter-parties locally or in London. Our daily average turnover in this period was $159M."

Mr Cronin, in what could be interpreted as a slight reproof, went on to say:

"To the extent that someone who spoke to you has anxieties with respect to our activities, it could be explained by our concentration of turnover with two institutions, i.e. Citi and Bank of America. We transact 90% of our dealings via 'Prime' clearing accounts with these banks. This is done to minimize counter-party exposure through a monthly netting arrangement." (56).

This very forceful explanation from someone, whom the AIB CEO obviously trusted and respected, understandably put him at ease. There is, however, evidence to suggest that a little seed of doubt may have been planted with Mr Cronin. Halfway through June 2001, he started to receive daily reports of the extent of foreign exchange trading conducted by Allfirst. These reports clearly indicated that Mr Rusnak was trading hundreds of millions USD per day and, in some cases, his notional turnover reached nearly USD 4 billion.

Another matter that deserves attention is that of profitability. It appears, according to the bonus payments to Mr Rusnak discussed later, that although his 'turnover' increased dramatically, his profitability remained more or less the same. Surely this should have raised some eyebrows. The simple answer is that it did. In their efforts to prepare the financial results for 2000, staff at the financial reporting units at both Allied Irish Banks (AIB) and Allfirst detected the fact that Mr Rusnak's use of the balance sheet was disproportionate with the income that he generated. A meeting was subsequently held between the Allfirst Controller, its Director of Financial and Regulatory Reporting and the Head of Treasury Funds Management. Mr Rusnak's trading strategy was explained as a low-risk activity. This answer was apparently deemed to be satisfactory and relayed to Dublin, where it was also accepted (57). This event raises a serious question about how well everyone at AIB and Allfirst understood the transactions that Mr Rusnak entered into. Mr Cronin should, at least, have had a vague idea of what percentage of profit should normally be generated per USD million traded.

Foreign exchange trading per se is a largely unregulated activity. Most financial institutions however, especially banks, are regulated by a number of institutions. One of the topics raised in a comment letter by the Securities and Exchange Commission (SEC), the prime financial markets regulator in the United States of America, to Allfirst was the cash flows related to foreign exchange trading at the firm (58). Although the exact nature of the query is not known, it did at least prompt an internal investigation, which revealed the large "offsetting" foreign exchange positions held by Allfirst. It also raised sufficient concerns to warrant an instruction to the internal audit department to focus on trading in the next treasury audit.

In its reporting to the Central Bank of Ireland, Allied Irish Banks (AIB) included reports by Allfirst of its activities. One of these reports, destined for inclusion in its 2001 reporting to the Central Bank, reflected the existence of more than a USD 100 million in open foreign exchange positions held by Allfirst. The subsequent enquiry to the Allfirst treasurer Mr Cronin followed the same route as most others, and was passed on to Mr Rusnak. Mr Rusnak in turn explained the matter away by contending that it was merely a matter of incorrect reporting of prime account positions (59).

The trading structure in which Mr Rusnak operated facilitated his 'Lone Ranger' behavior. It appears that, as a proprietary trader, Mr Rusnak was trying to run something similar to a hedge fund, without the necessary risk management systems (60). As a lone trader, he was up against very sophisticated operations that had the competitive advantage over him in all respects. If one just looks at the strategy and tactics used by the derivative desks of major banks (61), one realizes that Mr Rusnak was playing out of his league. As a lone trader, he also had very little informal restraints to prevent him from engaging in his activities, (not that his counterparts at the major investment banks had any either). Mr Rusnak was, however, not working totally alone; there was a second trader who, looked after the external clients of Allfirst. Although they were physically sharing the same dealing desk, data feeds and even a telephone line, the institutional trader on the desk claimed that he was never aware of anything untoward going on (62). If this was indeed the case, Mr Rusnak was to all intents and purposes a one-man show. The fact that Mr Rusnak was provided with the necessary Bloomburg software to conduct trading from his home is another indicator that he probably didn't rely on his co-worker to execute transactions on his behalf when he was not at the office.

According to the Ludwig Report, the compensation package negotiated with Mr Rusnak was "questionable" from a risk point of view (63). The report also states that the structure of his remuneration package "…may have had the effect of encouraging greater risk taking on his behalf." It goes on to point out that such "aggressive" structures are not the best way to "attract" and "compensate" traders (64). Rusnak's salary was made up of two components; it had a basic salary component of +/- USD 100 000 (one hundred thousand) per year and a bonus component. His bonus component was calculated as 30% of the amount of net profit he generated after reaching a threshold of five times his basic salary (65). The remuneration and 'profits' generated by Mr Rusnak were as follows:

TABLE 5

YEAR	SALARY	BONUS	TOTAL	"NET PROFIT"
1997	$ 102 000	$ 0	$ 102 000	$ 520 000
1998	$ 104 000	$ 128 102	$ 232 102	$ 947 006
1999	$ 104 000	$ 122 441	$ 226 441	$ 928 136
2000	$ 108 000	$ 78 000	$ 186 000	$ 800 000
2001	$ 112 000	$ 220 456	$ 332456	$ 1 294 853

(Source: Ludwig Report) (65)

In 1997 Mr Rusnak made less than five times his annual salary in profits and therefore did not qualify for a bonus. It should also be noted that his 2001 'bonus' was never paid to him, for obvious reasons.

Perhaps the following summarizes Mr Rusnak's fraud. "Mr Rusnak was unusually clever and devious. He knew the banking system well from his experience at Chemical Bank, so he was able to circumvent their controls. However, given the fact that their controls were weak; this did not take so much cleverness as desperation" (66). As we will see later in this chapter, Mr Rusnak may have learned more from Chemical Bank's traders than we thought. At this point, however, it appears that Mr Rusnak's competitive advantage lay not in his skill as a currency trader, but rather in his understanding of the risk management and administration systems employed by his firm.

The aim of this paragraph is purely to determine if there were obvious signs of a possible gambling addiction and is exploratory at best. It is however relevant, as the incidence of gambling by those in certain financial markets is very high. Those in positions of responsibility and oversight should, therefore, at least be aware of this phenomenon. However, in most instances, those in positions of oversight are also gamblers, and participating in gambling is often seen as a necessary prerequisite and trademark for someone to be a good trader. This was clearly reflected in the role that gambling played among the top echelons of LTCM (67). In December of 1990 the "TASK FORCE ON GAMBLING ADDICTION IN MARYLAND" conveyed its findings to the Secretary of the Department of Health and Hygiene. It is ironic that, more than ten years before Mr Rusnak committed his offences; pathological gambling was regarded as a serious problem by the state of Maryland, where he lived. The report provided the following description of a pathological gambler: "The Pathological Gambler can be described as an individual who is above average in intelligence, honest, energetic, competitive, creative, athletic, hard working and motivated to achieve, a citizen with a solid set of values concerning law and order, health, family, job and country" (68). In describing the phases of pathological gambling, three phases are identified. The first phase is called the "winning phase": while he is winning, the gambler experiences a sense of "status, confidence, control and power". This phase is, unfortunately, more often than not followed by a losing phase. This phase is characterized by a marked increase in gambling and losses. This robs him of his self-esteem and, to get it back, he starts betting larger amounts. This losing streak is usually associated with personality changes. The gambler becomes "...restless, irritable, defensive and argumentative" (69). The report further states that the gambler can experience physical illness and that, without treatment for his addiction, criminal behavior is often the next step. Fraud and embezzlement are some of the trademark non-violent crimes committed by pathological gamblers.

When reading through this report, the similarities to behavior patterns described in the Ludwig Report are chilling (70). Reports of Mr Rusnak's "temper and bullying behavior" unfortunately drew little response from his superiors. It must, however, be emphasized that this type of behavior is typical of the trader and salesman behavior on Wall Street, as described by, among others, Michael Lewis in "Liar's Poker" and by Partnoy in "F.I.A.S.C.O.". For example, Lewis described the view of the Salomon Brothers Executives of their firm and its place in the market as: (they) "...began to treat it as an instrument of power and glory, a vast playground in which they could be the bullies" (71). If the executives at Allfirst had been alert to signs of addictive behavior, they could have intervened and possibly have averted the disaster.

One cannot over-emphasize the importance of values, norms and sanctions as key determinants of human behavior. If these social controls do not function optimally, we create the climate for extreme opportunism that may lead to severe personal and financial losses. Deviant role models can have an important influence on the behavior of financial market actors. Frank Partnoy, in his book F.I.A.S.C.O., described the corporate culture in the derivatives division of investment bank Morgan Stanley during the 1990s as one in which clients were seen as prey and marketing campaigns were viewed as hunting trips. The firm reportedly urged its derivative traders and salesmen to "rip a client's face off", "blow them up" or "blast a client to smithereens" (72). One of the senior managers at the derivative group of Morgan Stanley purportedly held the view that "... investment banking is like war, and derivative salesmen are the special forces..." (73). It was an era in which derivative traders and salesmen were making millions of dollars before reaching their early twenties. Investment banks were making hundreds of millions, if not billions, by selling derivatives. The buyers of these products included insurance companies and municipalities, as well as makers of soap and greeting cards. Why was everyone in the business of buying, selling or trading derivatives? The answer is simple: the lure of easy money. Derivative traders were regarded by many as 'rainmakers' and firms depended on them for phenomenal profits. These profits, in turn, funded and justified the payment of phenomenal bonuses. There were, however, those who lost a lot of money. One notable example was Niederhoffer, a very successful and highly respected hedge fund manager who was managing around USD 100 million in June of 1997. In the fifteen years before 1997, he built up a phenomenal track record, averaging returns of 30 % per annum (74). In 1996 he posted a return of 35%. In June of 1997 Niederhoffer made a wager on the Thai baht and lost nearly half his fund. In what Partnoy describes as a pattern of gambling behavior, Niederhoffer started increasing his bets in order to make his losses back. By October of 1997 Niederhoffer took the view that the Standard & Poor's top 500 shares would maintain their prices or go up. Accordingly, he started selling put options on the S&P 500 index. This put option gave the buyer the right to sell the underlying future at a specific date and price in the future. If the price went up, the options would expire worthless and the seller would keep the money he was paid for the options (premiums he received); however, if the price dropped, he would have to buy the futures from those holding the put options at the higher price. The magnitude of his losses would theoretically be the difference between the price he had to buy these futures at and zero, multiplied by the amount of options he had to buy. On Monday

27 October 1997 the USD 100 million hedge fund Niederhoffer was managing was wiped out, after a 7% drop in the US stock market that caused a severe collapse in the value of the S&P index futures that he had to now buy at a higher price. One can only speculate that Niederhoffer may have done this risky trade because he needed the option premiums to either enhance his returns or to make even larger bets. One of his chief investors was apparently the San Diego public employees' pension fund.

On page 196 of his book, F.I.A.S.C.O., Frank Partnoy mentions the fact that one of the companies that lost a lot of money on currency derivative transactions was a firm called Chemical Bank. An amount of USD 70 million was apparently lost on a Mexican peso transaction. Chemical bank claimed the transaction was unauthorized. Interestingly enough, Mr John Rusnak was previously employed by none other than Chemical Bank. In 1993 Allfirst recruited Mr Rusnak from Chemical Bank, where he had been a currency option trader since 1989 (75). On the 22nd of March and the 4th of April 1996 the New York Times reported that "a trader" from Chemical Bank has been indicted on charges of "…bank fraud and falsifying bank records", after it was found that he was hiding large unhedged bets on the Mexican peso from his superiors. He achieved this through the use of fictitious trades that had the appearance of offsetting his peso positions. Does this sound familiar? Court documents from the SECURITIES AND EXCHANGE COMMISSION v VICTOR R.GOMEZ, United District Court for the Southern District of New York, 96 Civ. No. 96-2056 tells us the full story.

Mr Gomez was the Vice President of the foreign exchange trading group at Chemical Bank. Primary responsibility for Mexican peso transactions rested on the shoulders of Mr Gomez. In November of 1994 Mr Gomez used forward contracts to take a position on the movement of the Mexican peso against the USD. Through fictitious entries he then created the impression that he had hedged his position by entering in offsetting positions in USD. The first leg of his trades was identical to the ones that Mr Rusnak entered into a few years later. The only difference was the currency. While Mr Rusnak wagered on the belief that the Japanese Yen would strengthen against the USD, Mr Gomez wagered on the belief that the Mexican peso would increase in value, or at least remain stable, against the USD.

Mr Gomez also failed to record some of his transactions (76). In particular, Mr Gomez sold a number of convertibility guarantees. These transactions were never recorded and, according to court documents, Mr Gomez kept the transaction papers "…in his desk drawer". Convertibility guarantees are, in essence, the same as the put options sold by Mr Rusnak. In this case, they gave the buyer the right to sell to Chemical Bank a specified amount of Mexican pesos at the market price on specified dates in the future. Mr Gomez, like Mr Rusnak, also received fees for selling these guarantees. In order to disguise these fees, Mr Gomez used false transactions to make the fees generated and interest earned on these transactions look like trading profits.

In Chapter 9 of his book, F.I.A.SC.O., Frank Partnoy provides us with a vivid account of the speculative abuses that eventually contributed to a severe financial crisis in Mexico. Of interest to us is the fact that Mr Gomez was the 'proud' owner of a number of Mexican Peso forward contracts, betting that the Peso would strengthen against the USD and, to make matters worse, for good measure he also was a counter-party to a number of really happy buyers of his convertibility options, which held a view contrary to his. Mr Gomez, as did many others, (77) at the time believed that the Mexican Central Bank would protect the Peso at all costs against devaluation against the USD. On Tuesday the 20th of December 1994 things went horribly wrong when the Mexican Central Bank decided to stop supporting the Peso. The result was a 40% devaluation in less than a month. The long forward positions on the Peso, as we explained previously forced Mr Gomez to buy Mexican Pesos at a price much higher than the market price, and the holders of the convertibility guarantees started to convert their Pesos into USD. The result, as we now know, amounted to a USD 66 million loss to Mr Gomez.

On the 5th of April 1997 'SFGate.com Business Briefs' reported that the 36-year-old Mr Victor Gomez, a former bank trader, had been sentenced to three years and one month in prison for concealing a USD 66 million loss while working for Chemical Bank. An interesting element of the judgment was the absence of a financial penalty, as Mr Gomez was apparently broke. The year of 1997 was, incidentally, the last year that Mr Rusnak did not earn a bonus. Of further importance is the fact that, at the very least, the sentencing of his former colleague was reported on Bloomberg, the financial news service monitored by virtually all trading rooms, making it highly unlikely that Mr Rusnak would not have been aware of it.

A further important clue in explaining this event is found in the Ludwig Report, commenting on how the back office staff perceived management priorities [78]. Back office staff perceived management as favoring traders because the traders are making the money and the back office staff, by implication, would be viewed as an expense. Irrespective of whether or not this perception was actually true, it would provide an explanation as to why the back office staff followed the path of least resistance and tried to avoid involvement in the process. The back office "…developed written policies under which it was *not* responsible for confirming the individual prime account trades…" [79]. It is, therefore, no surprise that determined back office action was only taken after Mr Rusnak's positions were closed down by Mr Cronin mid-January 2002. A purported instruction from the back office supervisor to confirm all Mr Rusnak's transactions was apparently only executed late in January of 2002, after the news that the closing down of Mr Rusnak's positions had been ordered [80]. This revealed 12 unconfirmed transactions; when the "counter-parties" were contacted that same evening, they denied any knowledge of the transactions. When Mr Rusnak was informed of the fact that difficulty was being experienced to confirm his trades, he provided the back office with "written" confirmations. Closer inspection, however, revealed that these transactions were fake and were generated by Mr Rusnak on his computer.

The treasurer of Allfirst, Mr Cronin, only requested and received detailed reports on Mr Rusnak's activities in mid-June of 2001, after Mr Buckley from AIB contacted him about concerns expressed by "a market source" regarding the extent of Forex trading conducted by Allfirst. None of the other executives at Allfirst, not even the CEO, was made aware of this enquiry. Mr Buckley explained this as his normal practice to directly contact the relevant executive. Although this may be true, I do believe the special relationship that existed between Mr Cronin and the AIB leadership structure is relevant. As I showed Mr Cronin was most definitely part of the inner circle at AIB. The Ludwig Report points out that Mr Cronin was initially viewed as an "AIB spy" and he was "...often excluded from senior management meetings and interactions" (81).

John M. Rusnak did not steal any money from Allied Irish Banks. He fraudulently and elaborately reported false profits and he fraudulently and elaborately concealed actual losses. There is definitive evidence suggesting that he was displaying signs of addictive behavior. His trading strategy was simple and directional and consistent, and so were his losses. John M. Rusnak was out of his depth and his trading counter-parties made nearly USD 700 million out of him. While the likes of Morgan Stanley were fielding "armies" of "special forces" (82) in what they viewed as "financial warfare" Mr Rusnak, like Mr Leeson, stood alone and we all know how the story about 'two against two thousand' ended. It is no wonder that he was wined, dined and entertained. There is also very strong evidence to suggest that Mr Rusnak was either exposed to the type of transactions he conducted while he was employed by Chemical Bank or, at least, that in 1995 he would have seen the method of hiding losses and creating false profits from the activities of Mr Gomez, who was also employed by Chemical Bank.

On a number of occasions the attention of executives at Allfirst and at Allied Irish Banks were drawn to the fact that their positions in the foreign exchange markets were raising eyebrows. Each and every time, they assured the market that everything was in order and that they were aware of the positions. I do believe one can interpret these enquiries as subtle tests by those who were dealing with Mr Rusnak, to determine if his dealing was authorized. These counter-parties had to know that Mr Rusnak was losing hand over fist, as they were making money at an equivalent rate.

One of the sad possibilities in this case is the fact that Mr Rusnak may "benefit" little from his incarceration. The report of the Task Force on Gambling Addiction in Maryland clearly states that "incarceration will not cure this mental illness, and no professional gambling treatment is available within any state, local or Federal penal institution" (83). Even more disconcerting is the comment made by the US attorney for Maryland after Mr. Rusnak was sentenced: "he'll be in with the bank robbers and drug dealers and other criminals because that is what he is", according to O'Donnell & Willing in a USA Today article of March 12, 2003. DiBiagio, the US attorney in question, argues that Rusnak's sentence is fitting because around 650 people lost their jobs, while others lost their bonuses or raises because of what Mr. Rusnak did. No mention is made about the bonuses and raises paid in previous years, based on Mr. Rusnak's fictitious profits, and the fact that job losses occurred only after Allfirst was sold. The transaction that led to the job losses was announced in September of 2002 (84) M&T Corporation, a US bank with Warren Buffet as its largest shareholder, merged with Allfirst. Allied Irish Banks (AIB) received USD 886 million in cash and also received 22.5% of the new company. The transaction pushed the shares of AIB up to EUR 12.96. After the nearly USD 700 million loss, the AIB share price dropped to around 10.50 Euros according to the Irish Examiner of March 26, 2002). The announcements of overcharging, tax evasion and fraud by executives in May of 2004 had little effect on the share price of AIB and, shortly after an initial dip; the shares were trading at EUR 13.81 (85).

There is no doubt that the job losses and loss of income mentioned by Mr DiBiagio is a very serious matter. However, if we locked up all those responsible for job and financial losses, our prisons would be filled with incompetent politicians and corporate executives. One example that immediately jumps to mind is the job losses that followed after the merger of Kidder Peabody with Paine Webber. As we earlier showed in the chapter dealing with Mr Jett more than 2 000 Kidder staff lost their jobs as a result of a decision by Kidder and General Electric shareholders to aggressively expand their MBS book. There is compelling evidence to suggest that a complete failure of formal and informal restraints was central to the creation of an environment in which Mr Rusnak could incur and hide his massive losses. The failure of these restraints was, however, a part of the culture at AIB. AIB made money to the detriment of its clients and the Irish State, the extent of which is very difficult to quantify, as is the impact on its clients and their families. Mr Rusnak made money for himself to the detriment of AIB. The lure of the big bonuses, the overseas holidays, lavish treatment by service providers and the obvious status, respect and sense of power that accompany such a lifestyle, were obviously an incentive for extreme opportunism. The competitive edge that Mr Rusnak had was twofold: he convinced his superiors that he could make money for his firm and he had a very good understanding of the bank's risk management and administrative systems. At the micro level this was only possible because his superiors never took the time to understand fully how Mr Rusnak was 'making' money for them. These superiors also created an environment in which there were little incentives for administrative personnel to question Mr Rusnak's activities. The mere fact that the expenditure of a few thousand dollars for an independent Reuters feed was frowned upon, as well as the relatively small basic salary that Mr Rusnak was paid, is a clear reflection of the AIB culture. A 2004 report by JP Morgan viewed AIB as "... the most profitable major bank in the 25-nation European Union, averaging nearly three times the level of profit per account versus the EU average" [86]. The powers at AIB attribute this to "extreme efficiency" and the favorable Irish tax regime; consumer groups tended to believe overcharging of customers was a more likely explanation.

Mr John Rusnak liked the status and benefits that came with his position. These, and the money he was paid in bonuses, were in all probability his primary motivators. As in the case of Mr Leeson, one cannot discard the possibility that an addictive personality had an influence. The balance between those factors that facilitated Mr Rusnak's activities and those that could have inhibited it was, however, severely skewed. Management failure can probably be singled out as one of the prime facilitators. Not only did a number of top AIB officials make themselves guilty of severe abuses, they also did very little to put effective risk management structures in place at Allfirst and to ensure rigorous enforcement thereof. Numerous internal and external warnings were also dismissed without proper assessment of their validity. This environment conducive to extreme opportunism, coupled with the fact that Mr Rusnak had a role model in the form of Mr Gomez, in all probability, lies at the root of the AIB losses.

On January the 5th 2009, after completing a drug treatment program, Mr Rusnak was finally released serving nearly six years of his seven and a half year sentence [87].

CHAPTER 7

THE NATIONAL AUSTRALIA BANK FOUR

On the 27th of May 2006 it was reported that two former National Australia Bank traders, David Bullen aged 34 and Vince Ficcara aged 27, were unanimously convicted of unauthorized trading by the Victoria County Court [1]. The two former traders were respectively found guilty on 17 and 12 charges of "gaining financial advantage for themselves and others" and one count each of "gaining financial advantage by deception". Both men had pleaded not guilty to all the charges brought against them. On the 4th of July 2006 Judge Geoffrey Chettle handed down sentence in the Victorian County Court. Mr Bullen was sentenced to three years and eight months in jail, of which he must serve a minimum of two and a half years [2]. Mr Vince Ficarra was sentenced to two years and four months in jail, of which he has to serve a minimum of 15 months. During June of 2005 Luke Duffy, who at the time of the unauthorized trading was head of the NAB foreign exchange trading desk, was sentenced to 29 months in prison after pleading guilty to three charges of "dishonestly using his position for personal gain". The presiding judge in the Bullen and Ficarra trial labeled Duffy as the ringleader of the quartet. In April of 2006 the fourth member of the quartet, Gianni Gray, was sentenced to 16 months in jail, of which he had to serve 8 months before he could be released on good behavior. When sentencing Mr Ficarra, Judge Geoffrey Chettle made two comments that are of the utmost importance to us. In the first instance, he said "I accept that your crimes took place in a culture where profit and loss distortion had occurred in the past and where risk taking was an inherent part of your occupational duties" and then went further by saying "I also accept that profit was perceived as being the be-all and end-all of business and that you somehow became swept up and carried along by the personality of Mr Duffy. You became enmeshed in the culture that saw you seeing yourself as invincible and somewhat arrogant" (3). The clear recognition of the influence that the NAB corporate culture had on these individuals, and the fact that the role of learned behavior was at least tacitly recognized by the judge, allows for a much clearer understanding of why such an event could take place. The effect of their behavior was a USD 277 million loss to NAB (4). Their demise was purportedly attributed to a single co-worker who reported "suspicious" transactions implicating the NAB Forex team (5).

The four traders involved in the event were all working on the currency options desk at NAB. Mr Gianni Gray manned the London desk and the other three were all stationed in Australia. They were authorized to conduct proprietary and agency business, transacting in a range of products that involved taking a view on essentially five different currencies (6). The products used ranged from non-exotic 'vanilla' type options that could be exercised during the life of the option (American) or on expiry of the option (European), to more intricate types like the 'butterfly spread', which we will look at in more detail. The sheer number of transactions executed over an extended period of time, rather than intricacy, provided the multiplying effect, very similar to Mr Iguchi's case.

The spot foreign exchange transaction entails "the purchase or sale of a foreign_currency or commodity for immediate delivery. Spot trades are settled 'on the spot', as opposed to at a set date in the future, and are also known as 'cash trades'" (7). Investopedia also tells us that "Futures transactions that expire in the current month are also known as spot trades because, in the case that goods are actually delivered, delivery time is reasonably expected to take one month."

Contrary to the spot foreign exchange transaction, the forward foreign exchange transaction is designed to lock in the price at which a firm like NAB "...can buy or sell a currency on a future date. It is also known as 'outright forward currency transaction', 'forward outright' or 'FX forward' [8].

It is also important to note that "in currency forward contracts, the contract holders are obligated to buy or sell the currency at a specified price, at a specified quantity and on a specified future date. These contracts cannot be transferred" [9]. In other words, if you read the market wrong your risk is real and could be substantial. As the name implies, this product allows for profits or losses to be settled with a cash payment and does not, as in the case of the spot foreign exchange or forward foreign exchange contracts, require physical delivery of the underlying currency (Investopedia). It is a "...short-term forward contract on a thinly traded or non-convertible foreign currency, where the profit or loss at the settlement date is calculated by taking the difference between the agreed-upon exchange rate and the spot rate at the time of settlement, for an agreed-upon notional amount of funds". These instruments are further characterized by a "...fixing date and a settlement date. The fixing date is the date at which the difference between the prevailing market exchange rate and the agreed-upon exchange rate is calculated. The settlement date is the date by which the payment of the difference is due to the party receiving payment. NDFs are commonly quoted for time periods of one month up to one year, and are normally quoted and settled in US dollars. They have become a popular instrument for corporations seeking to hedge exposure to foreign currencies that are not internationally traded" [10]. It is also an ideal instrument for speculation, as all transactions are cash settled and there is no physical settlement of underlying securities involved.

The APRA Report [11] also attributed some of the losses to the selling of "butterfly spreads". Consistent with the view of the NAB Four that the USD would remain strong against all the major currencies as well as the AUD and the NZD, they sold a combination of long out of the money volatility options and short at the money volatility options. The NAB position was a hedged version of the "short straddle" sold by Mr Leeson. The straddle has virtually unlimited downside potential when an exchange rate becomes volatile, while it only has limited upside potential if it remains stable. The "butterfly spread" has the same limited upside potential, but the downside potential is also limited if the exchange rate becomes volatile (12).

The product used by the NAB traders to generate cash has a lot less inherent risk than the ones used by Mr Leeson; however, their application of the cash they received as option premiums did expose them to further losses. The team also entered into a number of spot and option Forex transactions, all betting on the weakening of the US currency. The trading team of a bank like NAB can, for example, sell AUD to a client at a predetermined price at an arranged date in the future, without actually holding the underlying currency, AUD in this case. If the price of the sold AUD rises against their expectations, they have to buy in the AUD necessary to deliver to their client. The difference between what they received as a premium in the event of an option or future, or the price they negotiated in the event of a spot, and the price they have to pay, to secure the underlying currency for delivery, culminates in either a profit or a loss. If you believe a currency will depreciate, you can generate a profit by selling the currency without actually owning it (shorting it). If the currency depreciates in value, below the price you sold it at, you can buy it on the open market at the lower price and deliver to your client. The price difference will be your profit. If the price of the underlying currency actually appreciates, you have to buy the currency you need to deliver at the higher price, thereby incurring a loss. In this case, the losses they incurred on the weakening of the USD against the AUD were further exacerbated by similar transactions that presupposed a weakening of the Japanese Yen (JPY) and the British Pound (GBP) against the US Dollar (USD) (13). As we can see from the graph that follows *(Figure 3)*, the USD weakened substantially.

Most of the losses occurred in the latter part of 2003 (14). It is however important to note that the four traders manning and managing the currency options desk for NAB, were carrying a loss that they had been rolling with them from as far back as 2001. As we have seen in our other case studies, they were probably also looking for the 'Big Hit' to clean the books. An opportunity for the big hit presented itself in the form of a G-7 meeting that was scheduled for the 22nd of September 2003. The NAB traders held the view that the USD would remain strong and that the G-7 would promote a policy of tightly managed exchange rates that would, to an extent, ensure little volatility in especially the AUD and the NZD (two currencies that NAB must have had extensive research on). Over and above their expectation of little volatility in the USD's exchange rate in relation to major currencies, they also held the view that the USD would remain stable or strengthen in relation to other major currencies. On this they then wagered their futures. As we see clearly in *Figure 3*, the USD weakened sharply after the announcement and kept on weakening until their story broke and became public knowledge, where after it weakened substantially before gaining momentum again in the last quarter of 2004. It is not impossible that there were external party or parties who were aware of the positions of the NAB Four and made substantial profits from their positions. It is interesting to note that the behavior of the market around September 2003 was very similar to the behavior of the market around October 2002, when NAB traders sold deep in the money options in order to raise AUD 322 million. As in the AIB and other cases, these types of transactions alerted outside parties. The management of NAB received a number of enquiries that should have alerted them, similar to those received by the Barings and AIB management these enquiries were however also, dismissed without due investigation.

According to an investment dictionary, "...volatility refers to the amount of uncertainty or risk about the size of changes in a security's value.

FIG 3

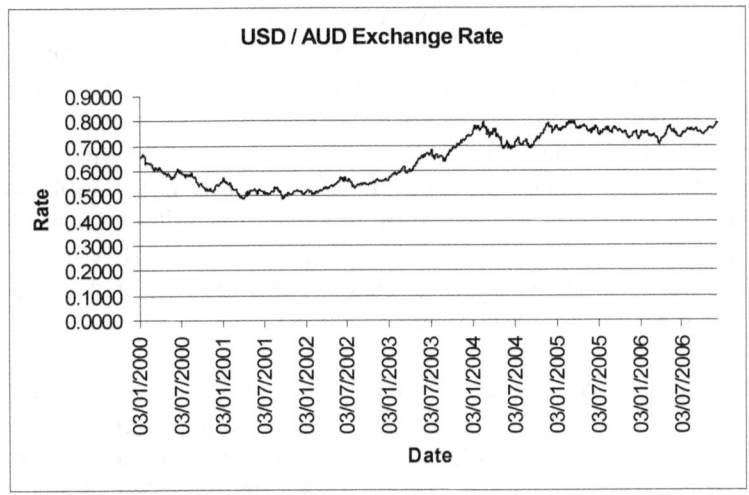

(Data Source US Treasury) (15)

A higher volatility means that a security's value can potentially be spread out over a larger range of values. Meaning that the price of the security can change dramatically over a short time period in either direction. Whereas a lower volatility would mean that a security's value does not fluctuate dramatically, but changes in value at a steady pace over a period of time" (16). Therefore, if you hold the view that the price of a stock, the exchange rate of a currency or the level of an index will not fluctuate a great deal over a certain period of time, you can make money by selling protection against such an event to those who either hold a view opposite to yours or have to hedge their portfolios because of risk management requirements. The buyer of an option for protection would normally only be exposed to the extent of his option premium, except for the case where the option seller cannot meet his obligations. The seller of protection against volatility is the one who potentially can incur substantial losses in the event of unexpected volatility that can often result from unpredictable events like earthquakes (Kobe) or acts of terrorism like 9/11.

"One measure of the relative volatility of a particular stock to the market is its beta. A beta approximates the overall volatility of securities' returns against the market returns. For example, a beta value of 1.1 means that the security will return 110% compared to what the market returns over a specified time period. Conversely, a beta of 0.9 will return 90% of the market's total return" [17]. An unnamed quantitative finance professor is also quoted as saying that "...short volatility trading is a high variance strategy: you win 99% of the time. You lose big 1% of the time." [18].

In order for us to understand how it was possible for the traders to hide their losses, it is first and foremost important to understand how the NAB administrative system for currency trading operated. Although currency trading was done from all the major trading rooms of the bank, everything was managed out of Melbourne and London [19]. All transactions were, however, recorded and administered centrally in Melbourne. If any of the trading rooms transacted with a counter-party, the transaction would be "cleared" from their books by the execution of an equal and opposite transaction with the global desk that would, for risk purposes, step into the shoes of the desk that executed the deal in the first place. The administrative system used by the dealers in the front office was called the "Horizon" system. This system was also used to perform daily profit and loss calculations (P&L) [20]. Once these P&L calculations were completed, reconciliation was initiated by the back office between 15 minutes and two hours after "end-of-day". This reconciliation was done only on those transactions that were still live, in other words, transactions that were not cancelled or neutralized by another trade entered into the system. A secondary system, called the "Kapiti" system, was used for ensuring that all transactions matched, i.e. have an equal and opposite leg. As we will show in more detail in the following paragraphs, this matching process was relying on corrupted data because of fictitious trades that "matched" other fictitious trades, or transactions that were simply cancelled during the "widow period" after the Horizon P&L calculations were completed.

In order to keep their mounting losses from being detected and to buy time to make back their losses, the traders used at least three different strategies. From the latter part of 2001 up until May 2003, spot FX transactions were used to manipulate the profit and loss account of NAB. By entering a spot FX transaction in a pair of currencies in which the traders were sitting with a loss, the opportunity to create a temporary false profit was developed. By entering an incorrect exchange rate, a fictitious profit was created from the transaction with an internal counter-party, similar to what Mr Leeson achieved with his 88888 account. This transaction was entered into the trading system (Horizon) and left until after the system closed for its end of day. The artificial profit negated the existing loss rolled over from the previous day. After the calculation of the daily P&L, the deal was amended with the correct exchange rate, the profit was deleted and the deal, in all probability, settled worthless. However, the spot FX transactions only affected daily P&L figures and a longer-term solution was needed. In order to achieve this, a change to the Horizon system was requested in May 2003 and completed before July of 2003, which allowed traders to amend or cancel their own deals. Who authorized this amendment is not clear, but it was most probably requested by the traders, as this allowed for a new level of manipulation. By the end of September 2003, losses of around AUD 45 million were covered up through the use of fictitious trades that were entered into the horizon system and later amended or removed all together. By entering fictitious unmatched trades between two portfolios on the Horizon system just before close of day, a profit could be created for one of the accounts. After the Horizon system had calculated the daily P&L, the fictitious trades were cancelled and, by the time the Kapiti system was matching trades, the two transactions together would have no impact and would, therefore, not reflect as an exception through being unmatched. These activities, once again, were very similar to the transactions used by Mr Leeson.

As the losses were mounting, the pressure on the four traders obviously mounted and the Head of Currency Options, Mr Luke Duffy, notified the back office that the reconciliation of internal transactions was no longer necessary. By the 10th of October 2003 the back office ceased their reconciliation of internal transactions. This now allowed for unmatched option trades to be entered into the system, which created false profits for the account the traders chose. The benefit of the fictitious option is that it will keep reflecting a profit up until its exercise date. By then it could be cancelled and replaced with another fictitious transaction. This activity is, once again, essentially the same as those used by Mr Leeson and Mr Rusnak. Over and above the fact that the use of fictitious transactions saved the traders a lot of work, it also allowed much larger "profits" to be created. This was essential as, by December 2003, the four traders had to cover up losses of around AUD 150 million. According to Mr Duffy, the decision to stop checking internal trades was the result of a cost-cutting exercise at NAB (21). After that he said that, when the risk section of NAB questioned him about profits or losses being too high or too low "…he'd tell [them]… anything that they would believe." This is a virtual replay of the SLK receivable incident at Barings. Were it not for the whistleblower at NAB who reported suspicious transactions, the firm could easily have followed the Barings route.

On the 23rd of March 2004 the Australian Prudential Regulation Authority released its findings regarding the events at NAB. Strikingly in line with our findings in all our other case studies, the report concludes that the cause of the event was undoubtedly the actions of the traders involved. This is unfortunately only half the story, and the report also states that this event can be attributed to the operating environment at NAB. Three key elements of the operating environment are highlighted: "lax and unquestioning oversight by line management; poor adherence to risk management systems and controls; and weaknesses in internal governance procedures" (22).

A key comment is, however, added to this "...the control failure in this case has more to do with poor implementation than poor design" (23). The report finds that, although the framework of control was not ideal, proper implementation and enforcement of what was available could, in all likelihood, have reduced the losses substantially and may have averted the event all together.

The APRA Report identified a number of internal and external warning signs that all, if heeded, could have initiated responses that may have reduced or prevented the event. Included were "critical internal audit reports" that were ignored; "prolonged limit excesses" that were allowed without any effort to either change the existing limits, if they were too low, or to enforce the existing limits, if proven to be appropriate. Added to this was a lack of urgency or the will to deal with "unreconciled reporting issues" (24). The PWC Report (25) provides us with a detailed analysis of warnings emanating from internal audit reports. As early as May 1999 the Internal Audit department at NAB identified at least two matters serious enough to justify the attention of the Managing Director and the Board Audit Committee. The most important problems regarding the currency operations at NAB were the "...inability to reconcile profit and loss between the front and back offices; no volatility smile included in revaluations; and no independent monitoring of risk concentrations". These shortcomings were brought to the attention of the Principle Board Audit Committee (PBAC) and, in a June 2000 quarterly audit report to PBAC, it is stated that "...substantial efforts to rectify..." the 1999 problems had been made by management. Although it is not clear what these efforts entailed, it appears that the implementation of the Horizon computer system seemed to be viewed as a solution. An instruction for quarterly updates on identified weaknesses was also issued, but the PWC Report could find no evidence of such updates. A subsequent September 2000 Internal Audit report covering the Horizon system's influence on the foreign exchange options area claimed that the system would solve some of the problems identified in 1999, but requested a post-implementation review to be conducted. Once again the PWC Report could find no evidence of such a review. A December 2001 Internal Audit review of the options area identified daily limit breaches by the foreign exchange area. In 61 out of 61 days these trading limits were breached and all were approved by the Global Head of Foreign Exchange. No explanation could, however, be found for these breaches and/or the reason why they were approved. The report also noted that revaluation rates used to revalue positions were only sourced from one broker. In response to this, the Group Internal Audit proposed that reports to the Principle Board Audit Committee should exclude matters of less than AUD 5 million. As we saw in the chapter on Barings where Mr Leeson was also requested not to advise London of all the errors made by Singapore; this led directly to the position where the 88888 account could be abused. In January of 2003 the Internal Audit report on Global Foreign Exchange apparently had no significant problems with the unit. The breaches of limits were, however, still occurring with impunity and the general perception appeared to be that the limits were inappropriate and the whole matter was downgraded as rather unimportant. I believe it is quite understandable that, if you raise a concern over a period of nearly five years and no-one does anything about it, it could get relegated to the back burner. The evidence in this section of the PWC Report proves that claims by Mr Bullen and the other traders that their superiors were aware of their limit breaches were correct.

There were also external warning signs that should have alerted management to possible problems. This included weaknesses in the NAB control systems that were identified by APRA during routine inspections and brought to the attention of management.

NAB management was alerted to "a lax approach to limit management; a culture of poor adherence to risk management policies; inadequate sourcing of revaluation rates; problems with interfaces to the Infinity risk engine; no formal validation or back-testing for NAB's approved VaR model; and inadequate stress testing" (26). The matter for concern is that, according to evidence led during Australian Senate Estimates Committee hearings, this routine inspection took place in August of 2001 (27). APRS however only raised their concerns with the bank in 2003. The time delay is, to this day, unexplained. The management of NAB obviously did not react to these warnings, even though they had ample time to do so. It is clear that the regulator, APRA, should also shoulder some of the blame. One can make the argument that, if they were so concerned with the risk issues at NAB, why did it take them more than a year to take these matters up with the bank? As we have seen in our other case studies, for example Barings, this is a classic replay of events. APRA also admitted that they were aware of the fact that NAB foreign exchange exposure was twice as large as the other three major Australian banks put together. There seemingly was an unwillingness or inability on the part of regulators to act swiftly and decisively against large financial institutions.

One of the most serious warnings that was present in virtually all our case studies was the fact that NAB counter-parties raised concerns about the nature and the extent of NAB foreign exchange positions (28), (29). According to the PWC Report (30) an unnamed Australian bank expressed concerns about the "size and risk profiles" of some transactions executed by NAB's currency options traders. These concerns were discussed during a visit to the "other" bank by Mr Dillon and a representative from Market Risk and Prudential Control (MR&PC) at NAB. The NAB response was one of aggression, and the other bank was accused of not "understanding" the NAB strategy. The "other" bank was also threatened by NAB to the extent that NAB would cease doing business with it and even some of the brokers used by the "other" bank. In October of 2002 the traders needed money, and they followed the tried and tested method used by, among others, Mr Rusnak and Mr Hamanaka – they sold two deep in the money options and raised AUD 322 million. The bank on the other side of the transaction probably read the AIB case study and duly queried the transaction with NAB. At NAB the matter was referred to the EGM Risk Management, but nothing else was done. This was notwithstanding the fact that Operations at NAB also queried one of the option sales and referred it to Market Risk and Prudential Control (MR&PC) who in turn sought an explanation from the traders. The explanation given was that it was more cost-effective to sell options to raise cash rather than to borrow the funds internationally. Those responsible for risk management at NAB were, therefore, not only aware of the transactions, they were also told that the traders entered into these transactions to raise cash. The important question is why no-one bothered to ask why the trading desk needed the money in the first place (31). It appears that the questionable trading practices such as Mr Leeson's massive positions were somewhat of an open secret. A former options trader was quoted saying "I can tell you that NAB have been doing dodgy trading stuff for much longer than a few months. The global options market has been waiting for them to blow up for years. No-one is surprised by this at all, except for the fact that it took so long" (32).

One of the most damning indictments against the NAB management was their arrogant response to the AIB incident (33). On the 6th and 7th of May 2002 the NAB board concluded that "A report concerning Allied Irish Bank's FX losses had been reviewed and it was noted that the Group had appropriate controls in place to identify control breakdowns on a timely basis to ensure that FX losses are minimized." Their view, it appears, was largely based on the findings of a meeting of the Principle Board Audit Committee, at which a seven-page memorandum that emanated from internal NAB workshops, comments by various NAB employees and two internal NAB documents regarding AIB and its relevance to NAB were tabled. Two of the more noteworthy comments made regarding the AIB incident's relevance to NAB come from the supervisor of the four traders and Joint Head of Global Foreign Exchange, Gary Dillon, who stated that "...I think the real test of our level of control is in the detail of the specific business structure in place. This is where I believe the NAB currency option business platform (sales/front office/back office/accounting); set up to accommodate the global currency option business, is far superior to others in the market and most others internally." In a similar vein Kevin Bakhurst from the Finance division of NAB viewed the use of daily profit and loss analysis as "not an effective tool", in spite of the fact that the AIB report viewed this report, as well as a thorough understanding of the reasons underlying daily profit and loss movements, as crucial. According to Bakhurst, a monthly analysis and reconciliation to the general ledger is a more appropriate system. One of the reasons provided by Bakhurst for his view is the fact that the use of different systems by front and back offices results in "significant profit and loss differences". What he is saying is that they do not have an accurate view of determining daily profit and loss movements, a view that on its own should have sounded the alarm bells.

A substantial number of other very crucial issues addressed by the AIB report were not even commented on in the NAB memorandum. These included the relevance of "the extent of proprietary trading and how to monitor and control it" and the crucial importance of and need for appropriate trading "limits to be in place". The AIB report also underlined the need for senior management "to understand the intricacies of proprietary trading before it is undertaken." and the need for the Chairman and the CEO to be actively involved in the "risk infrastructure and regular reporting to them to monitor the trading business". It also warns against "excessive reliance on VaR" and stresses the danger of "ignoring other risk information available" as well as the need for all transactions "...to be checked for reasonableness of market price and economic rationale". The need for serious attention to be given to supervisory reports was also stressed by the AIB report. It is quite clear that most of the AIB recommendations that were not addressed by the NAB memorandum were within the reach of the management and staff of NAB and, if these issues had been given the attention they deserved, the NAB FX losses would have been detected or even prevented. It is striking to note that most of the issues in the AIB report relate to senior and top management's active participation in and thorough understanding of the businesses they are supposed to manage. It appears that passing the buck and non-involvement was part of the culture at NAB.

When analyzing the culture at NAB we will, as we did in our other case studies, also use a much wider focus on the general culture of doing business that was prevalent at NAB. Was a lax culture the reason why numerous warning signs were ignored by NAB management and why there appears to be a lack of attention to detail and hands-on management regarding the FX unit? Was this culture also detectable in other dealings of NAB?

In October of 1997 NAB announced the purchase of a substantial stake in a US mortgage loan company, called HomeSide, for USD 1.7 billion (34). The Australian financial media were not all positive about the transaction and at least three commentators expressed serious reservations. One commented on the risk associated with new and untested technology that was still in the process of being implemented by HomeSide, while another underlined the fact that USD 1.1 billion of the USD 1.7 billion purchase price was goodwill. The high goodwill percentage was worrisome, as nearly 50% of HomeSide's clients were tied to the company for only three years. Anna Borzi, a banking analyst, also expressed concern about the fact that mortgage servicing was a new concept to Australian banking. In 2001 NAB announced to their shareholders losses of USD 4 billion at HomeSide. The losses were attributed to, among other things, "data entry errors; input of wrong assumptions; a modeling error discovered by external consultants; and a breakdown of the hedging model under extreme market conditions". A former NAB insider commented on the fact that the HomeSide losses were not detected and addressed earlier, and highlighted the fact that, if the NAB executives had implemented and enforced industry standard internal controls, the causes cited by NAB should never have happened. The NAB comment should also be seen against the backdrop of 1998 APRA guidelines regarding the use of risk models used by banks like NAB. According to these guidelines, users had to ensure that "the processes and models are conceptually sound; the bank has sufficient staff in the risk control, audit and back office areas who are skilled in the use of sophisticated models; the models have a proven track record; and they are regularly stress tested". A question that also jumps to mind is whether or not the inherent risks associated with Mortgage Service Rights (MSRs) were well known. In a 1998 10-K filing with the US Securities and Exchange Commission, HomeSide clearly states that "there is a substantial interest rate risk in MSRs. They go down in value when interest rates decline and up in value when rates increase. The risk management contracts used by HomeSide to hedge this exposure do the reverse, so hedge profits should be expected during periods of declining rates and hedge losses expected when rates are rising". It is therefore very difficult to comprehend how those involved in the due diligence of HomeSide did not realize the inherent danger posed by MSRs held by the firm it purchased. It is furthermore worrying (but not surprising) that KPMG, the auditors of NAB and HomeSide (since April 1998), never highlighted the inherent risk associated with MSRs. It is also noteworthy that in 2001 NAB employed Christopher Lewis as its "Executive General Manager Group Risk Management". This was the same individual who signed off the 2000 annual report without making any reference to the risks inherent in the MSR portion of NAB's business and the fact that the bank was about to announce a USD 3.6 billion loss. Lewis also headed the due diligence team that recommended the HomeSide transaction (35). As the auditors to NAB and HomeSide, KPMG should also have been acutely aware of the MSR risk, even if they only read the HomeSide 10-K filings to the US regulators.

The APRA Report is very similar to the Singapore Report, as it also highlighted and was equally critical of the culture that existed at NAB at the time. Efforts were made to cultivate a more enlightened (commercial) risk management approach at NAB and the relationship between risk management and operations appeared to be one of a partnership in the pursuit of profit rather than one of effective oversight and risk management. The culture in the Corporate and Institutional Banking division (CIB) of NAB was one of managing the constraints that management laid in their path to profit rather than solid boundaries for their actions. This is similar to a corporate culture wherein regulatory and other penalties are budgeted for as a legitimate and essential business expense rather than a deterrent against extreme opportunism. It should, however, always be remembered that the biggest risk facing any business is not making money. Because of this fact, the pressure on those responsible for managing risks could be immense, as the demise of their firm due to a lack of profits would also seal their own fate. Without strong support in word and deed for effective risk management on all levels including, and especially, board level, the work of risk managers will be an exercise in futility (36). The APRA report summarized the failure of NAB's internal risk management controls as follows: "... NAB's internal control systems failed at every level to detect and shut down the irregular currency options trading activity. NAB's internal governance model, which should have enabled timely identification and effective and quick escalation of serious risk issues on the currency options desk, simply did not function" (37). In other words, the main reason for the fact that the failure was complete and at all levels was the prevailing organizational culture.

In virtually every layer of the NAB structure, the APRA Report (38) identified contributing acts or omissions that created and maintained the culture necessary for an environment conducive to the activities that led to the event in 2004. There is an old saying in the financial world: "shit flows downhill" and from the evidence gathered by the APRA Report it is clear that, although risk was often talked about, there was little or no evidence to suggest that the Principle Board of directors of NAB took a proactive approach to managing the risks that come with the territory their divisions were operating in. The risk management committees that were established on an executive level were equally ineffective. One example highlighted was the fact that when, similar to the "Barings Event", an internal audit highlighted the existence of control weaknesses, the Risk Management Committee responsible for CIB either dismissed or ignored these warnings, underlining the total lack of importance attached to managing risk. The so-called Middle office that noted the irregularities emanating from the trading desks failed to clear up these anomalies with the trading desk and also failed to solicit adequate managerial response concerning the trading anomalies. The APRA report also probes the inability of the back office to identify the irregular and fictitious trades that were conducted and questions the skills of those employed, the resources allocated to them and the role of a culture that regarded back office activities as overheads that should be kept to a minimum. This lack of adequate resources was also emphasized as a crucial failing at Barings. Similarly, the APRA Report suggests that the back office/administrative function was indeed treated like second class citizens who were there to serve and not question the traders in their quest to generate profits, a culture we also identified at AIB. The CIB line management and staff had only one motto: "Profit is King" and as long as profits are generated everything must be fine. The equating of profitability with financial and operational wellness was an inherent culture identified in all the case studies we have analyzed up to now. This fundamental error is a partial explanation for the inability of anyone to identify the warning signs that, with hindsight, appear so clearly. Over and above the skewed profit/risk relationship, the APRA Report (39) also identifies the whole issue of "managing" bad news. Good news travels fast, the saying goes. Bad news, on the other hand, as we have seen in other case studies, is very often either repressed all together, or sanitized before it is fed through to boards of directors and even external organizations responsible for oversight. These actions do not absolve these organizations from blame and ultimate responsibility. It is their duty to put the necessary structures in place and to cultivate a culture that encourages openness and transparency. If traders know that they will lose their jobs if they do not reach the ridiculous profits that the board promised to shareholders, you will never get honesty and transparency.

A detailed analysis of the operations function revealed a number of crucial failures or omissions that, individually, could have prevented this incident (40). The APRA Report cited the reconciliation and validation functionality as one of the functions that was fatally flawed. It cited "failure to check or reconcile internal trades"; "failure to validate surrendered or amended trades" and "failure to extend validation procedures to close-out the processing 'window' between front and back office systems" as some of the most important. These failures were attributed to a number of causes. In the first instance, there was a lack of clarity about exactly who was responsible for what. Management delegated without ensuring that everyone fully understood what was expected of everyone and who was responsible to whom and for what. There was a lack of standard operating procedures, communicated clearly and implemented with the necessary training to ensure confident execution of tasks. Staff that is not confident can easily be steamrollered by traders with strong personalities. The operations area was also not consulted in decisions to change procedures that affected their ability to operate efficiently. One example was changes to the reconciliation process for currency options that were effected without consulting the Manager for Structured and Derivative Products. It also appears that the roles attributed to and enforced by role players in the operations department were too narrowly defined, allowing for gaps in oversight to develop (41). The APRA investigation also found evidence to suggest that some Global markets and operations staff, knowingly or unknowingly, assisted the 'quartet' by sharing information regarding the inner workings of the back office, allowing them to circumvent some of the procedures that could have detected their activities.

The operations area responsible for the foreign exchange and options team were primarily tasked with the timely processing of live transactions with external clients. They did however fail to apply the existing procedures diligently, when it came to internal transactions that were amended or revised. This failure in oversight allowed for non-matching trades to be entered into the system. Similarly, it appears that there were no effective procedures to flag very large or unusual trades. The back office system for foreign exchange had no effective exception report functionality, for off-market rates. The rate variance exception report that did exist was flagging so many exceptions that it was ignored – as the back office in London ignored Mr Leeson's error trade reports because there were so many (42). The system used by the front office did not have the capability to identify off-market rates.

The APRA Report (43) also identified major deficiencies in the calculation and management of the VaR model utilized at NAB. One of the most startling revelations was the fact that the application of the VaR model on the currency options business at NAB yielded results that were viewed as so inaccurate that, for a period of nearly two years before the event, the VaR excesses functionality was not used for currency options. This led to a situation where VaR was ignored for currency options and excesses were routinely signed off without any attention being paid to them. A further problem was the apparent uncertainty over whether or not the Global Markets division or the Market Risk & Prudential Control section had the ultimate responsibility for enforcing risk reductions. The APRA Report also criticized the Board of NAB and its senior management for not ensuring that the market risk monitoring functions was reviewed more frequently and that alternatives to the faulty VaR model were not pursued.

The monitoring of limits was essentially non-existent at NAB. During one particular month in the last quarter of 2003, the currency option limits were breached a record 750 times. Although this can, in part, be excused because of the unreliable VaR model, other commonly used risk measures like delta, gamma, theta, etc. (called the "Greek" risk measure parameters) were also exceeded with regularity. These excesses were signed off by the management of the front office and were known to the MR&PC. Even though market risk limits were exceeded with such regularity, no effort was made by management to either ensure that it didn't happen or to amend the set parameters if they were found to be inappropriate (44). As we have seen with the Barings and AIB events, failure to monitor and enforce limits was, in all the cases, a crucial failure that could have been easily enforced. According to comments made by Mr David Bullen during a television interview (45), management at NAB at least two levels above him were aware of the fact that they consistently and substantially exceeded their limits. Neither they nor the risk management committee, on which the CEO of NAB sat, did anything to curb this behavior.

Before we look at the financial incentives of the four traders, we should put their contribution to the bank's profits into perspective. According to Mr. Duffy (46) "his" group was set a profit target of AUD 37 million for the 2002/03 year. Was it this excessive target that set the scene for a disaster? Was this target reachable with the AUD 3.5 million the traders were allowed to risk on a daily basis? If not, is this the reason why the regular trading outside the limits was allowed? Is the fundamental cause of the "rogue" effect unrealistic profit expectations coupled with insufficient quality staff, systems and other resources? (47).

It is highly likely that the remuneration system used by NAB was the principle incentive for these four traders to hide their losses. In the same vein, financial incentives for those who were supposed to oversee and manage them is in all probability also a strong contributing motivator for allowing the four traders to conduct their activities unchecked and unhindered. Where the four currency traders received nearly double their annual salaries in bonuses of between AUD 120 000 and AUD 265 000 for the 2002/03 year (48), the global head of foreign exchange, Mr. Gary Dillon, received a bonus of AUD 500 000 (49) at the end of 2003. As we found in the case of Allfirst's treasurer, Mr Cronin, and Mr John Rusnak, we also find that Mr Dillon was a close friend of Mr Duffy.

As we have seen from the other case studies, this was in no sense an isolated event. What is of extreme concern is the fact that, research conducted by Dr Stephen Brown (professor of finance at the Stern School of Business at New York University) on the trading practices of Australian equity trading firms reveals that what happened at NAB is not unique, as there are traders who "on a regular basis" behave like Nick Leeson (50). He further says that "...if they are given a sizeable chunk of money to behave with in this way, they are going to look like winners until the ruin event occurs."

By now we have seen that money and status are principle motivators for extreme opportunistic behavior. The NAB event does, however, confirm our suspicions of why these events occur. On page 6 of the APRA report "Line management", "Operations (back office)", "Market Risk (middle office)", "Executive Risk Committees", and the "Principal Board" are all implicated as facilitators to the NAB event. In its conclusion, the Australian Prudential Regulatory Authority (APRA) identifies "cultural issues" as the heart of the problem. In the world of sophisticated exotic derivative structures, where a PhD in mathematics or an MBA are normally the yardstick for admittance, this was a first. The acknowledgement of the importance of cultural issues is key to a better understanding of opportunistic behavior.

The failures at NAB were complete and on all levels. It is fairly clear that this event was not only detectable but also preventable. All that was necessary was for the most basic risk management principles to be enforced rigorously from the board level downwards. Then why was it not done? The culture at NAB was one in which profit was the ultimate pursuit and everything else was secondary. The risk of not making the desired profit weighed so heavily that every other consideration was cast aside as if they were unnecessary stumbling blocks inhibiting the ability to make profit. The end result was the resignation of both the chairmen, Charles Allen, and Frank Cicutto, the CEO of NAB. The new chairman, Mr. Graham Kraehe, was a member of both the audit and risk management committees that failed (51). It is therefore not surprising that, when asked if NAB would learn from this incident, one of the traders (David Bullen) responded "not a chance". The whole institution will have to change. They would have to accept what they were doing; managers would have to stop playing political games" (52).

A culture of opportunism was undeniably in existence, not only while the Forex traders were racking up their losses, but well before their time. This fact was so obvious that even the sentencing judge acknowledged it. I do not believe the extreme opportunism displayed by management at NAB is any different from that exhibited by the traders. The losses due to the HomeSide fiasco and the Forex losses were both incurred due to the pursuit of profits through questionable means. There is little difference between management exposing shareholders' funds to risky investments and traders doing it through risky Forex transactions. In both cases, it was nothing short of gambling. The role of learned behavior is also clear in this case. The court proceedings show that Mr Duffy was setting an example to some of the other traders. From his perspective, he claimed that he took his cue from senior management, who allowed him to regularly break daily limits in his efforts to achieve the profit targets they set for him and his team. In this case, there is also evidence that the traders were assisted by management and back office staff in their efforts to hide their losses. Like most of the other cases of extreme opportunism, the activities of the traders went on for many years and were clearly visible to outsiders, who even alerted NAB management. The Australian regulators were also implicated in this event. Their very slow response to clear risk management failures at NAB is a reflection of severe shortcomings in the enforcement of regulations. The same applies to the NAB auditors in both the HomeSide affair and the Forex scandal. It is a recurring theme through virtually every incident of extreme opportunism that the auditors made little or no contribution in detecting opportunistic conduct.

Non-existent or poorly enforced formal restraints, a corporate culture of opportunism that acted as a catalyst for individual opportunism rather than a source of informal restraint, coupled with a total absence/failure of basic risk management procedures provided the opportunity for an extremely opportunistic pursuit of money. Evidence of a gambling culture and access to very volatile products and funding methods obviously did little to restrain opportunistic behavior. There is ample evidence to suggest that the group of traders was strongly motivated by the financial incentives offered by NAB. The required balance between facilitators and inhibitors of opportunistic behavior was, however, nearly non-existent. The NAB event is one of the clearest examples of a total absence or breakdown of inhibiting factors, and it is fitting that substantial blame was apportioned to the NAB management and even the regulatory authority in Australia. In January of 2004 AFP Sydney reported, that the NAB losses had ballooned to USD 277 million, nearly twice the initial expectations (53).

This was however not the end of NAB's troubles, in July 2005 its chief executive had to admit that they overcharged 200 000 of their clients from as far back as 1982. The amount involved is an estimated AUD 80 million (54). There is a striking resemblance between this discovery and the activities of AIB described in Chapter 6. It seems the two banks shared more than a 'rogue' incident.

CHAPTER 8

MIKE MILKEN & THE US SAVINGS & LOANS CRISIS: IN PERSPECTIVE

As we have seen throughout this book, extreme opportunism in virtually all the case studies involved the concealment of profits and losses and or the creation of fictitious profits and losses. These activities were, however, not limited to individual 'rogue traders' or 'maverick executives' of large firms. This exact same behavior can be identified during the events that are commonly referred to as the US Savings and Loans crisis. Although blame has often been apportioned to the likes of Mike Milken and his 'junk bonds' as the root cause of the disaster, the facts show us that politicians and regulatory institutions often displayed behavior similar to those of the so-called 'rogue traders'. I would also like to emphasize that the analysis of Mr Milken's case is not aimed at determining his guilt or otherwise. It is aimed at determining the rationality or lack thereof displayed by regulators, the legal system and society at large. Throughout this journey we have seen the practice of and apparent need, to bestow the cause of all evil on 'immoral' individuals. This may be our nature, but it is in all probability also our biggest hurdle in determining the true causes of so-called 'rogue' events and/or actions displayed by institutions and individuals alike.

According to Professor Niel Fligstein a respected economic sociologist: "state actors are constantly attending to some form of market crisis or another. This is because markets are always being organized or destabilized, and firms are lobbying for state intervention" (1). Rules are the embodiment of the interests of dominant groups and transformation of such rules will, in the normal course of events, only be implemented if such a dominant group is in crisis. Fligstein also points out that stable rules are often more important than their content. One trademark of the Savings and Loans industry during 1980 and 1989 was rapid and frequent deregulation followed by rapid and frequent re-regulation. Another interesting point of interest regarding the Savings and Loans industry was that operators could operate under either a Federal charter or a State charter. This allowed for a duality in regulatory controls and guidelines, creating a system in which the rules most advantageous to the operators, and not the depositor, were often the most popular.

At the end of the nineteen seventies and early in the eighties the Federal Reserve Board of the United States raised interest rates in an effort to control inflation. The method employed was to raise the rate that the government, as lender of last resort, charges to the banks of the country. The effect of such a decision was that the rates companies paid on their debt (corporate bonds) exceeded 15% during 81/82 (2). Within a mere three years the Federal Reserve managed to bring down inflation from 13.5% to 3.2%. This monumental achievement was, however, not without a price. One of the most immediate casualties was the level of unemployment in the United States, which rose to levels reminiscent of the Great Depression. This was unfortunately only the beginning. With higher interest rates, one of the most vulnerable sectors was the banking sector and, within its ranks, none were more vulnerable than the "thrifts" or Savings and Loans companies that specialized in providing home loan finance to individuals. The basic operational methodology employed by these firms was to collect funds from depositors and lend this money out to those who needed home loan finance. Although this form of banking is perceived by many as low risk, one element of their business model had a hidden risk potential. The interest rates charged on existing mortgages were fixed, while the interest they paid their depositors fluctuated with the ruling market-related rates. The result is simple: if you pay out more than you get paid, you will go under. The reality of what the high interest rate environment did to the viability of the Savings and Loans operators was, however, not clear to everyone involved. This was due to a little creative accounting that was initiated, not by a 'rogue trader' or greedy corporate executive, but by none other than Uncle Sam himself (although the greedy executives probably paid for a lot of lobbying). As we have seen in numerous corporate collapses, for example AT&T and ENRON, future profits came into play. Towards the end of 1982 the Federal Government of the United States of America allowed the ailing Savings and Loans companies to revamp their balance sheets by reflecting expected future earnings as a valuable asset in the form of goodwill, which created a false impression of financial soundness. Although their balance sheets were bulging they were still losing money hand over fist, as they were paying out more than they were getting in. However, this problem was also not insurmountable to the US Federal Reserve. As governments have the power to regulate, they also have the power to deregulate, and it was this arrow that was now pulled out of the proverbial quiver.

The preferred strategy of the Federal Government was to allow the Savings and Loans firms to trade themselves out of the hole they found themselves in (just like any self-respecting 'rogue trader'). This was achieved through deregulation of the industry. This strategy had already been employed from 1967 at state level by Texas, which allowed its Savings and Loans firms to invest up to 50% of their net worth in property development loans. With their newfound freedom, the "thrifts" embarked on a three-pronged strategy commensurate with those followed by our rogues. They started lending out to higher risk borrowers (like real estate developers) at higher interest rates, reflective of the risk. They also started to invest in riskier investments like high yield bonds or, as they were more commonly referred to after the collapse of Drexel Burnham, 'junk bonds'. The only other thing they had to do was to hide the risk associated with their investments. This they could easily do, as they were not as closely regulated as normal commercial banks, which had to make provision in accordance with the risk they were taking on board. In fact, the Federal Home Loan Board (3) reduced the net worth requirement for insured Savings And Loans operators from 5% to 4% of total deposits in 1980 and then to 3% in 1982, with the added bonus that they could use the liberal Regulatory Accounting Principles system instead of the more restrictive Generally Accepted Accounting Principles (GAAP). However, in 1986 the US Government came under pressure for the generous tax policy towards real estate investments that it introduced in 1981. When the tax breaks evaporated so did the profits, and the next step for real estate investors and developers was to default on their obligations to the "thrifts" they borrowed money from. The increase in bad debts seriously threatened the solvency of the S&L firms.

Another contributing factor to the whole crisis was reductions in regulatory and supervisory staff, as well as the use of underpaid and inexperienced staff – a problem highlighted by Mr. Leeson as a major contributing factor in the Barings Collapse. The average Savings and Loans examiner had only two years' experience and started with a measly USD 14 000 per annum according to the FDIC. In the period between 1982 and 1985, while the Federal Home Loan Board was cutting back on staff, the assets in the overall industry grew by 56%, while some states like California and Texas experienced 100% growth per year. Ironically, in 1987, the state that first started to deregulate in 1967 also led the way when losses in the state of Texas accounted for over 50% of all the Savings and Loans losses in the US. In typical Texas style, 14 of the largest losses also came from Texas. However, in the defense of Texas, it must be added that the state's major source of revenue – oil – took a major dip at the time, causing office rentals demand to decline and adding to the real estate collapse.

Economist and Nobel laureate, Professor Joseph Stiglitz, sums up the Savings and Loans crisis in the United States by underlining the role of a skewed incentive package which, among other things, promoted creative accounting through the implementation of poorly designed deregulation (4). When under pressure for their survival, these Savings and Loans companies took large risks, not unlike those undertaken by the so-called 'rogue traders'. The fact that these firms felt that the Federal and state governments were condoning their risky strategies through deregulation and increases in insurance offered to depositors, was a structural factor that created the environment for extreme opportunistic behavior. The question that must be asked is: is there really a difference between the opportunism displayed by politicians and that displayed by business executives and traders, or is it merely a question of incentives that are large enough and countervailing mechanisms that are too weak or non-existent? Stiglitz also points out that the thin line between ethical and unethical behavior eases the way for moral restraints to be swept aside with relative ease by the business community.

The cost of the US Savings and Loans collapse was substantial. The cost to the public sector, i.e. the United States taxpayers, is estimated at USD 123.8 billion and to the private sector USD 29.1 billion (5). It is no wonder that the US Government was looking for scapegoats, and Mike Milken was an easy target. His salary of USD 500 million per annum made even the likes of Rockefeller and Donald Trump envious, and the hostile takeovers funded by his high yield or 'junk bonds' made even the most generous of campaign contributing corporate captains nervous. During the sentencing of Mr Milken, the judge made reference to the existence of a perception that he was responsible for the Savings and Loans crisis and the job and financial losses associated with the collapse. However, she did point out that, in order for the state to prosecute Mr Milken for such losses, it had to separate his actions from all the other factors that may or may not have influenced the Savings and Loans industry (6). What the judge omitted to say was the fact that the US Government probably was the biggest contributor to the disastrous final years of the Savings and Loans industry.

There are, however, a number of problems with blaming Mr Milken for the Savings and Loans collapse; first is the fact that there were problems that were inherent in the Savings and Loans industry long before Mike Milken ever sold 'junk bonds' to them or they were allowed to hold them. Secondly, between March of 1985 and December of 1991, Savings and Loans companies never held more than 1% of their assets in the form of 'junk bonds' (7). The reason why Savings and Loans were allowed to invest in higher yielding, and therefore riskier investments, were precisely because they were in great financial distress. One of the most important findings regarding the role of 'junk bonds' in the Savings and Loans was made in 1989 by the US General Accounting Office (GAO) following an instruction by the US Congress in 1987 (8). The report released in March stated unequivocally that "A review of FHLBB data and discussions with its officials showed only one case in 1985 in which high yield bond investments appeared to have been a factor in a thrift failure. However, in that case, mismanagement of the institution's high yield bond portfolio was only one part of a broader pattern of unsafe lending and investment practices leading to the institution's collapse." It should also be borne in mind that, although Drexel was the largest operator in the high yield bond market, it was most certainly not alone.

Daniel Fischel analyzed the crimes that Mike Milken pleaded guilty to and came to the conclusion that the "crimes" were "trivial" at best (9). The sixth charge Mr Milken pleaded guilty to, was related to assisting David Solomon to reduce his taxable income through a transaction wherein Solomon would purchase illiquid securities from Drexel, which he subsequently sold at a loss that it claimed from his taxable income. The upside to Solomon was an "undertaking' from Mr. Milken that he would make up for their loss by finding them profitable transactions in future. (David Solomon was not associated with Salomon Brothers).

Fischell contends that Mr Solomon made a real loss, which he was legally entitled to deduct from his taxable income. The fact that Mr Milken undertook to find him profitable investments in future to offset his losses was an undertaking and nothing more; it could not be regarded as an asset as the prosecution contended. However, it can be argued that the sole purpose of the transaction was to reduce taxable income, an action that most businesses enter into on a daily basis.

The fifth charge also involved Mr David Solomon and related to the adjustment of bid-ask spreads offered by Solomon's Finsbury Fund in their transactions with Drexel. Drexel charged Mr Milken's department a 1% fee for promoting and selling the shares of the Finsbury money market fund, which invested in Mr Milken's high yield bonds in order to get a higher return for their investors. In order to recoup the fee, Solomon agreed to adjust the bid-ask spread in favor of Drexel in securities transactions with it. According to Daniel Fischel, the adjustment was so minor that Drexel always remained competitive and the fact that Drexel promoted the fund and invested in the high yield bonds of Mr Milken could well have made money for investors in the Finsbury Fund, rather than losing them money.

The first four charges that Mr Milken pleaded guilty to all related to the failure by Mr Milken to accurately record the true ownership of securities in their books, records and regulatory public filings. This activity, commonly referred to as "stock parking", essentially allows the owner of a stock to keep his ownership of a particular security secret. This was and still is a common practice that can be achieved in a number of ways. Large firms would use nominee accounts and a myriad of broker dealers to prevent market participants from detecting their interest in a particular security. As Mr Leeson pointed out, the market would react once participants detected that Barings were buyers of a particular security. Very often the price of the security in question would rise merely because of the fact that a large institution expressed interest in it. This effect could be detrimental to the members of a pension fund, for instance, which would now have to pay more for the securities it is interested in. The question immediately comes to mind: why was this practice such a big issue? The answer lies at the bottom of the whole Milken incident. The largest users of Mr Milken's services were firms that specialized in doing what is commonly referred to as hostile takeovers. This practice, described vividly in the best-selling book "Barbarians At The Gate", redesigned the face of corporate America.

In order to put these charges into perspective, one has to look at the environment in which Mr Milken operated. One example is the revelation that Salomon Brothers manipulated the bond market during the late 1980s and early 1990s, and the fact that the firm's chairman, John Gutfreund, was aware of the false bids made by Paul Mozer at treasury auctions to achieve this manipulation (10). According to Frank Partnoy (11), Gutfreund's hands-off management style encouraged his traders to skirt the rules. One example of such trading involved the buying and selling of bonds at artificial prices to create artificial losses for Salomon in order for the firm to reduce its taxable income. As we now know, this same strategy was also employed by the likes of ENRON and Global Crossing a number of years later, when transactions involving billions of dollars were executed. The use of these transactions was, however, widespread and by no means isolated to the firms mentioned. Tax fraud was also not the only brilliance displayed by Salomon's traders. Around 1990 Paul Mozer hatched a plan to corner the treasury market in the US. At auctions of Government bonds by the US treasury to Prime Brokers, an unspoken rule existed that no one broker was allowed to bid or be allocated more than 35% of a particular issue. During 1989 and 1990 Paul Mozer tried, on a number of occasions, to breach this rule and when cautioned by a treasury official about his conduct, threatened the official that the chairman of Salomon would contact the secretary of the

Treasury (12). On the 10th of July 1990, this unwritten rule was formalized by the US Treasury, leading to a public outburst by Mozer against the Treasury. After being forced to apologize by the second-in-command of Salomon and a break to London, Mozer came back with a vengeance. Instead of accepting the rule, Mozer simply designed a strategy to circumvent it. On the 21st of February 1991, Paul Mozer submitted a bid on behalf of Salomon for 35% of the auctioned stock and submitted similar bids on behalf of a Salomon client, Mercury Asset Management, and S. G. Warburg & Co., a subsidiary and a hedge fund managed by George Soros. The clients were blissfully unaware of these bids. After the transaction the bonds were booked over to Salomon through a fictitious transaction, through which Salomon bought the bonds from their clients at below market value. Through this strategy, it was possible for Mozer to control more than 50% of a particular auction. The problem, however, was that Mercury also entered a small USD 100 million bid of their own, pushing them over the 35% limit. The US Treasury questioned Mercury and also Mozer, who they knew submitted a bid on behalf of Mercury. Mozer called Mercury and told them it was an administrative error and asked them to keep the matter confidential. Mozer also notified John Meriwether, who in turn called Thomas Straus and Salomons's legal council, Donald Feuerstein. A decision was taken to advise Gutfreund, but no action was taken to curtail Mozer's activities. At this time Mozer managed to acquire an additional USD 1 billion worth of notes at the April auction by bidding unauthorized on behalf of another hedge fund, Tudor Investment Corporation. When Gutfreund returned from out of town, he was advised by Meriwether, Straus and Feuerstein of Mozer's actions. Although Feuerstein pointed out to the group that Mozer's actions were illegal, there was no obligation on Salomon to advise the authorities of what occurred. Once again, no decision was taken to curtail Mozer's actions. At the May auction Mozer managed to corner 86% of the market and was in a strong position to manipulate the price of the securities he bought. However, Mozer's trading was not a secret, and other hedge fund managers like Caxton Group, Steinhardt Partners and Tiger Management were actively vying to participate with Salomon in manipulating the market in auctioned securities.

In June 1991 Gutfreund finally decided to rein in Mozer by telling him to stay within the regulations for the June auction while he (Gutfreund) met with Treasury officials, claiming innocence on the side of Salomon. Salomon hired the firm of Wachtell, Lipton, Rosen & Katz on a limited mandate when regulators started asking for documents. Although their initial brief was only to investigate the May auction, they soon realized the extent of the manipulation and, when they provided their findings to Gutfreund, Straus, Meriwether and Feuerstein, the four were forced to issue a press statement regarding the irregularities. During August of 1991, under pressure from the Chairman of the New York Federal Reserve, E. Gerald Corrigan (a personal friend of Straus), the four Salomon officials resigned.

Paul Mozer, the trader that he was, entered into a process of negotiations with prosecutors, holding as his trump card his in-depth knowledge of the schemes used by Salomon to avoid more than USD 100 million in taxes. He finally pleaded guilty to submitting false bids on behalf of Warburg and Quantum at the February 1991 auction, a crime with a specified maximum sentence of ten years. Judge Leval obviously took Mr. Mozer's assistance to the prosecutors into consideration when sentencing him to a fine of USD 30 000 and a four-month jail term in a Florida minimum security prison for a crime the Judge described as "extremely foolish, arrogant" and "insouciant" (13). The judge also concluded by underlining the importance of deterrence of others as a motivation for his sentence. Gutfreund, Straus and Meriwether were respectively fined USD 100 000, USD 75 000 and USD 50 000 each and Gutfreund was also banned for life from being in charge of an investment bank. Straus and Meriwether were also suspended from the industry for six and three months, respectively. As a going-away present,

Meriwether managed to successfully settle with Salomon for USD 18 million, as compensation for his loss of income (14).

Were the actions of Mozer, at Salomon's, those of an isolated 'rogue' in a reputable firm and can we glibly classify the actions of Mr Milken as a lone 'rogue' within Drexel? Joseph Stiglitz commented on the effects of deregulation in the 1990s that led to, opportunistic conduct by among other Citigroup, Salomon Smith Barney and Merrill Lynch (15). Their activities included among other things, systematic stock manipulation (commonly referred to as pump and dump) and the allocation of IPO stock from some clients, at discount prices to other favorite clients, to elicit other business. One of the most infamous proponents of such manipulative activities was Jack B. Grubman, the telecommunication analyst for none other than Salomon Smith Barney. Grubman a close friend of the CEO of WorldCom Bernie Ebbers, recommended WorldCom shares as a buy since 1999 and maintained this recommendation up until April 2002 a mere three months before the firm filed for bankruptcy (16). According to Stiglitz, "each bank knew that its competitors were engaging in similar practices, and if it didn't compete, it would be left behind; each banking officer knew what that meant: smaller bonuses, perhaps even being fired" (17). Grubman's resignation statement contained these chilling words: "I did my work as an analyst within a widely understood framework consistent with industry practice that is now being extensively second guessed." (18). Would it be preposterous to suggest that, if Mr Milken didn't offer this service to David Solomon, in all probability he would have found it somewhere else? This proposition in itself would suggest that it is quite plausible that what Mr Milken did was not the actions of a 'rogue' but rather a standard service offered by Drexel and its competitors. Was Mr Milken any different from the traders at Salomon who were paid millions of dollars for designing transactions through which legal rules could be circumvented (19) or their analysts that recommended failing companies (20)? I believe a large body of evidence suggests otherwise.

During sentencing of Mike Milken, Judge Kimba Wood outlined her guidelines for determining an appropriate sentence for Mr Milken. According to the judge, the purpose of sentencing a convicted felon is essentially "…individual deterrence, general deterrence, punishment or just deserts, retribution and rehabilitation" [21]. The judge went on to say that the fact that Mr Milken was barred from working in the securities industry for life; his USD 200 million fine and USD 400 million restitution fund (to compensate "victims" of 'junk bonds'), as well as possible further civil law suits, coupled with the emotional stress he and his family endured, served as a more than adequate individual deterrent. In the final analysis, Judge Wood confirmed that Mr Milken had to serve a jail term for the purposes of acting as a "general deterrence" to others who were contemplating similar crimes. In other words, the principle aim was to ensure that other similar actions would be discouraged through sending Mr Milken to jail for an extended period of time. Mr Milken was sentenced to a jail term of ten years and two months, which was subsequently reduced to two years before he was released on parole. The reasons cited for the reduced sentence were his "exemplary" behavior in prison and the assistance he provided to Federal prosecutors in other cases that involved 'junk bonds'. The reduction of Mr Milken's sentence should, however, not detract from the fact that the overall sanction he endured must have had a severe impact on him and his family, as it undoubtedly had on others like Messrs Blank, Leeson, Iguchi, etc., none of whom were hardened criminals or, as far as we know, had criminal intent.

If one justifies the use of jail sentences as a general deterrent, one obviously views the conduct/behavior to be discouraged in a very serious light and one would expect that all such behavior should be treated in the same fashion. It is here, unfortunately, where cracks in the criminalization of Mr Milken and many other 'rogue' trading incidents appear.

Judge Wood summed up the essential motivations for Mr Milken's crimes as actions aimed at increasing his clients' loyalty to him, increasing the likelihood that said clients would in future use and pay for his services (22). This Mr Milken achieved through "…skirting the law, stepping just over the wrong side of the law in an apparent effort to get some of the benefits from violating the law without running a substantial risk of being caught" according to Judge Wood. However, if we have to measure the financial services industry and maybe even business at large across the globe, against this set of immoral actions and motivations, I doubt if many would escape the wrath of Judge Wood. It is also important to determine if the laws that were purportedly being skirted were clearly defined and consistently enforced, otherwise skirting might not be the appropriate term, as it is not possible to skirt an imaginary line. What is of special concern when the two cases are compared is, in the first instance, the apparent 'fuzziness' of the charges that Mr Milken pleaded guilty to and the 10-year sentence plus the massive fines the judge deemed appropriate compared to the clear-cut transgressions by Mr Mozer (not even taking into consideration his participation in the tax evasion activities of Salomon) and the relative slap on the wrist he received as a sentence.

We can also compare the action taken against the Salomon officials with Mr Milken's punishment. The Salomon officials were well aware of Mr Mozer's market manipulation transgressions and also intimately involved in efforts to evade more than USD 100 million in taxes. Mr Milken on the other hand was accused of assisting a client to evade tax. When we make this comparison, there appears to be a lack of consistency, even taking into consideration that Mr Milken's term of incarceration was reduced to just over two years, for his cooperation with the state. In an effort to underline the schizophrenic character of those sanctions purportedly employed as a deterrent against conduct of an extreme opportunistic nature, I will make a condensed analysis of events at one of the largest and most prominent global firms, Royal Dutch Shell Petroleum Company, more commonly known as Shell.

The misstatement of reserves sound a lot less ominous than having yourself likened to the "head of the Mafia" (23) or having the demise of your firm, Drexel, compared with the "fall of Nazi Germany". The essence of the charges leveled against Mr Milken and most of the so-called 'rogue traders' was the fact that they misled their clients and/or superiors and, in some instances, the receiver of revenues. They misstated the extent of their profits and losses to keep their jobs and/or to receive large bonuses or, in the case of Mr Milken, misled investors in his 'junk' bonds. Their actions are not dissimilar to corporate executives who misstate their profits and/or losses to either pay less tax, or to mislead investors by showing fictitious profits, or to ensure that the share price of their company rises, allowing them to exercise their lucrative share options. Are we consistent in our treatment of white collar crime, or are we merely an unruly crowd with pitchforks baying for the life of a 'pacifist' Count in Transylvania because we believe he drinks blood?

In April of 2004 the BBC reported that information had emerged confirming the fact that executives of Shell had been lying about the extent of the firm's oil and gas reserves since 1991 (24). The report stated that the Head of Oil and Gas at Shell, Walter van de Vijver, in an internal memo claimed that he was "sick and tired about lying about the extent of our reserves issues" and the fact that they may not be able to fool their investors forever. It is clear that Mr van de Vijver was aware of the purpose of the lies. Shell was misleading their investors, as it was charged but never proved that Mr Milken was lying to his. It was, however, also reported that Mr van de Vijver instructed staff to destroy an incriminating document he labeled as "dynamite", an action that also occurred in the ENRON case. The defense raised by Mr van de Vijver was the fact that he viewed the matter as a "business problem" and not a "regulatory and disclosure" problem. In other words, lying is fine as long as you do not breach a regulation.

What Shell did was to lie about their reserves until they could "trade" themselves out of their position and disclose their shortfall at more appropriate levels. The shortfall in 1992 was 4.5 billion barrels lower than declared, while the shortfall in 1993 was a mere 500 million barrels. How does this differ from the actions of Mr Leeson or Mr Iguchi and most of the others we analyzed up to now? Their strategy obviously worked perfectly, as the price of Shell overall dipped a mere 0.76% on the London exchange following the disclosure. The result of the deceit was the resignation of the chairman, Sir Philip Watts, Mr van de Vijver and Judy Boyton, the finance officer who was never accused of any wrongdoing. The rest of the board of Shell was cleared of "material responsibility" notwithstanding the fact that a review found that "many executives had been aware of the problem". Shell was also investigated by the US Justice Department and the SEC and in August of 2004 a settlement was reached.

The SEC release no. 116 of 2004 was very blunt about their view of the essence of Shell's conduct. The document they released announcing the settlement states clearly in its heading that the case settled was one of "Fraud" through the "Massive Overstatement of Proven Hydrocarbon Reserves". In the settlement announcement, the SEC also clarifies the reason for these illegal actions by stating that "...the Commission also found and alleges that Shell's overstatement of proved reserves, and its delay in correcting the overstatement, resulted from, (i) its desire to create and maintain the appearance of a strong RRR, (ii) the failure of its internal reserves estimation and reporting guidelines to conform to SEC requirements, and (iii) the lack of effective internal controls over the reserves estimation and reporting process. These failures led Shell to record and maintain proved reserves it knew (or was reckless in not knowing) did not satisfy SEC requirements, and to report for certain years a stronger RRR than it actually had achieved" (25). One of the most damning claims made by the SEC is the fact that Shell was undeterred and resolute in its persistence with the fraudulent actions. The SEC report states that "...Shell was warned on several occasions prior to the fall of 2003 that reported proved reserves potentially were overstated and, in such critical operating areas as Nigeria and Oman, depended upon unrealistic production forecasts. In each case, Shell either rejected the warnings as immaterial or unduly pessimistic, or attempted to 'manage' the potential exposure by, for example, delaying de-booking of improperly recorded proved reserves until new, offsetting proved reserves bookings materialized." There can be absolutely no doubt that Shell was trying to trade themselves out of a hole in an extremely opportunistic fashion that was no different from the actions of many of the so-called 'rogue traders' we have analyzed thus far. Similarly, we find that a generally corrupt environment was also allowed to develop and persist as management failed to implement effective controls and oversight. There can be little doubt that the lack of oversight and control mechanisms and systems were by design and not by accident, as it would have been impossible for the executives of Shell to commit their fraud over such an extensive period in a system with effective checks and balances and a company culture committed to honesty and transparency.

One noteworthy example was the fact that the Group Reserves Auditor was not given either the training nor resources or the authority to conduct his work with any measure of success (26). The Group Reserves Auditor also had to report to the Exploration and Production (EP) Division, exactly the same people he was suppose to audit. It was, therefore, not surprising that, over a five-year period, he never attributed an unsatisfactory rating to any of the units he audited. The frequency of his visits to units he audited was only around every four to five years. There were also clear indications that the Group Reserves Auditor was not objective in his approach, as he allowed questionable proved reserves to remain booked, even if the local management felt they should be de-booked. Furthermore, he also assisted local management to submit plans for development that he knew had little or no chance of becoming a reality, solely in order to support questionable proved reserves.

The settlement followed a number of charges that were brought against the Royal Dutch Petroleum Company and 'Shell' Transport and Trading Company plc earlier. In the Houston Division of the United States District Court for Texas, the SEC allegations provide us with a window on the culture at Shell. In the first instance, the fraud was conducted over a number of years. The following table shows clearly the extent and the impact of the fraud and the level of distortion achieved by it.

TABLE 6

Year	Proved Reserves Over-statement	% Over-statement	Standardized Measure Over-statement	% Over-statement
1997	3.13 boe	16%	N/A	N/A
1998	3.78 boe	18%	N/A	N/A
1999	4.58 boe	23%	$7.0 billion	11%
2000	4.84 boe	25%	$7.2 billion	10%
2001	4.53 boe	24%	$6.5 billion	13%
2002	4.47 boe	23%	$6.6 billion	9%

(27)

It is quite clear that this is no random act; the executives are consistently overstating their reserves by around 20% and potential future income by around 10%. Furthermore, Shell also overstated their reserves replacement ratio, commonly referred to as RRR, in order to enhance the perceived longer term viability of the firm. This overstatement would have had a material affect on the potential future earnings of Shell and its ability to maintain its revenue streams in future. These misstatements had no other purpose than to mislead investors in the shares of Shell.

The SEC brought four charges against the firm. The charges related to "... directly or indirectly, falsified or caused to be falsified, their books, records and accounts" [28]; failure by Shell to "... make and keep books, records, and accounts, which, in reasonable detail, accurately and fairly reflect the transactions and dispositions of its assets" and to "...devise and maintain a system of internal accounting controls sufficient to provide reasonable assurances..." on a number of issues, among others to ensure that "...preparation of financial statements..." conform with acceptable standards and to "...maintain accountability for assets...". Shell was also charged with failing to ensure that, at regular intervals, comparisons were made between what assets were reflected in its records and reality, and to ensure that "...appropriate action is taken with respect to differences".

In a similar vein, Shell was also charged with failing to file prescribed reports in line with SEC regulations and ensuring that these reports contained all necessary information to prevent it from being misleading. The primary charge leveled against Shell was that "as a result of the Defendant's knowing or reckless overstatement of their oil and gas reserves in their financial statements, the Defendant's commission filings ... as well as other public statements, contained materially false and misleading statements and disclosures. These filings contained untrue statements of material fact concerning the company's reported proved reserves and omitted to state facts necessary to make the statements made, in light of the circumstances they were made, not misleading". In the light of these charges and the other evidence available, one has to ask the question: at what point could a case have been made for a charge of conspiracy to commit fraud on an unprecedented scale?

There can be no question that the executives of Shell who were forced to resign did endure some level of humiliation and even financial loss. The Administrator of the SEC Fort Worth Office, Harold F. Degenhardt, commented on the penalties imposed on this massive institution by underlining the fact that the fraud was conducted over an extended period. Unfortunately, he omitted to mention the fact that the fraud was committed and maintained with the knowledge and active participation of its most senior executives, notwithstanding the fact that they were warned on several occasions. Degenhardt did, however, conclude that the actions of Shell warranted a "...strong enforcement response, including imposition of significant civil penalties..." (29). He further motivated the penalties imposed in much the same way as Judge Kimba Wood did when sentencing Mr. Milken, by saying that their aim is to "... deter Shell and others from engaging in similar misconduct". He did, however, mention that the investigation was ongoing and that those responsible for the failures at Shell would come under additional scrutiny.

Without admitting or denying any of the findings of the commission, Shell "...consented to a cease-and-desist order finding violations of the antifraud and other provisions of the federal securities laws, and by paying $1 million disgorgement and a $120 million penalty in a related civil action the Commission filed in US District Court." Shell also agreed to spend USD 5 million internally under guidance of their own legal director to upgrade their compliance. A case of market abuse brought against Shell by the Financial Service Authority in the UK (the FSA) was also settled with a GBP payment of USD 17 million. To put these penalties into perspective, we need to take a look at how these penalties would have affected a company like Shell if weighed up against the benefit that could be derived from committing fraud. When we analyze Shell as an entity, we find that in 2005 it ranked as the third largest corporation in the world when measured by its turnover of USD 306.73 billion and will rank second if ranked by its gross profit of USD 25 billion in the same year (30). Even if Shell was fined USD 200 million, that would still only represent 0.8% of their annual gross profit and 0.065% of their annual turnover, hardly figures that would strike fear into the hearts of its corporate executives and shareholders.

On the 31st of August 2006 the SEC announced that they would take no action against Sir Philip Watts, the Group Chairman of Shell at the time of the overbooking of oil reserves (31). The two other officials who resigned due to the scandal, Judy Boynton and Walter van de Vijver (32), were also cleared by the SEC notwithstanding the fact that Watts and Van de Vijver, according to evidence led before the SEC hearing, were well aware of the fact that investors and the authorities were being deliberately misled (33). One should also ask the following question: were Watts and Van de Vijver owners of Shell shares or did they trade in Shell shares during the period of fraudulent reporting, and did they receive any bonuses or share allocations based on the share price of Shell? If the answer to any of these questions was yes, a criminal case appears to be fairly clear-cut. One also has to ask the question: why were any penalties paid in the first place if no-one was guilty of any wrongdoing? If we compare the sentences meted out to ENRON executives, there appears to be a glaring discrepancy. Mr. David Delaney, former CEO of ENRON North America, was sentenced to two and a half years in prison and previously paid a USD 8 million penalty to the SEC to settle fraud charges; the founder of ENRON died of a heart attack after being convicted of six counts of conspiracy, securities fraud and wire fraud (34). The CEO of ENRON, Mr. Jeffrey Skilling, was convicted of 19 counts of conspiracy, securities fraud and insider trading and was sentenced to a jail term of 24 years in prison and his assets of USD 45 million were to be seized and distributed among

former ENRON employees (35). Although evidence existed that
ENRON manipulated the energy price of the California
electricity market and forced its staff pension fund to invest
heavily in ENRON stock (leading to the bankruptcy of many
pensioners), the essence of the charges against Mr. Skilling, as
per the final indictment against him, was that he was "...
providing investors with false and misleading financial
information from 1999 up until ENRON filed bankruptcy in late
2001" (36). The difference between overstating your profits and
overstating your proven reserves unfortunately escapes me.
Another interesting phenomenon we observe in the Shell
incident is the fact that autonomous executive properties are
bestowed on companies. It appears that the reality of what
constitutes a company, i.e. groups of individuals and
relationships between such individuals and groupings, has
escaped the majority of modern observers. If the SEC found
that Shell had overstated its proven reserve over an extended
period of time and that its senior executives were aware of and
participated in such fraud in order to mislead investors, how is
it possible that no-one was found to be responsible for the fraud
individually or collectively?

This was by no means the first time that Shell was a party to
opportunistic behavior that was concealed. In 1993 Showa Shell
Sekiyu, 50% owned by Royal Dutch Shell, announced that it
suffered a loss of around USD 1 billion due to losses from a
USD 6.4 billion foreign exchange position (37). The group
managing director of Shell blamed it on "...a gross
contravention of established rules and practices, which was
deliberately concealed." The result of this incident was the
resignation of four top officials of Showa Shell Sekiyu and the
dismissal of a fifth (in all probability the trader involved). No
evidence could be found of any legal action taken against those
involved. What is also of importance to us is the fact that the
losses were only announced a few days before Royal Dutch
Shell announced an 8% increase in net income for 1992,
causing an increase in the share price of Shell despite losing a

USD billion. It appears that the investment community is not put off by losses of even a billion, as long as overall profits increase. One must also comment on the timing of the Showa Shell announcement – were the losses made public as soon as they were discovered or were they concealed, like the overstatement of reserves, until the financial climate was appropriate to allow for a low-impact announcement?

It is of interest to note that Shell Chemical Company also settled charges related to dishonesty and misleading others in 1999 (38). In essence, Shell was charged with providing "...the means for its trade customers to deceive the public, in violation of the law". The case against Shell related to the fact that Shell provided its trade customers with "...allegedly false or misleading representations about tests it conducted..." relating to some of its chemical products, in this case an oil additive. The moral issue at hand is: what is the difference between lying about the effectiveness of your products, your proven reserves, the profitability of your company or the extent of your losses?

In this chapter we have provided clear evidence of discrepancies in the criminalization of opportunistic behavior, as well as the prosecution of extreme opportunists. In spite of all the evidence presented thus far, there may still be some that argue that opportunistic behavior may be limited to a handful of 'rogue' employees. Any doubt about the extent of opportunistic behavior associated with financial markets was, however, dispelled in 2006 when Erik Lie announced the findings of his research into the possible manipulation of the price levels at which executives of companies are granted stock options. A stock option, in essence, gives the recipient the right to purchase the stock of the company in the future (39). Normally such options expire after 10 years. The price at which the executive can exercise his options is called the 'exercise' or 'strike' price. The strike price of stock options is divided into three categories based on its relation to the ruling price of the underlying share: 'out of the money' (lower than the ruling price), 'at the money' (at the ruling price) and 'in the money (higher than the ruling price). These options can be granted any time during the year and the grant date may vary from year to year. For a variety of tax and reporting reasons, most executive option grants are at the money options.

The incentive to grant the stock options at a particular time during the year is therefore clear. If you receive your options on the lowest price during the year, any rise over that price is to the benefit of the option recipient. The problem is that the executives of companies are not psychic and do not know for certain what the share price of their company will be in the future. However, this is not an insurmountable problem if you are an opportunist. All you need is the benefit of hindsight, i.e. backdate the option, or grant your option before you make an announcement that you know will push up the value of the underlying shares or after an announcement that will adversely affect the share price. The practice of timing option grants to occur before the announcement of good news is referred to as "spring loading" and the timing to fall after bad news is referred to as "bullet dodging".

Lie provides clear evidence in line with what one would expect when the granting of options was manipulated. In one example (see *Figure 4*) he shows that the probability of an official grant date being set retroactively was virtually 100%, "…unless executives have an informational advantage that allows them to develop superior forecasts regarding the future market movements…" of their company's future share price. If this was indeed the case, the conduct is tantamount to insider trading.

Research conducted by David Yermack and published in 1997, investigated the relationship between company announcements and the issuing of stock options in the US between 1992 and1994. He concluded that "…grants are timed to occur before anticipated stock price increases" (i.e. spring-loading).

FIG. 4

(40)

A similar study conducted by David Aboody and Ron Kasznik, published in 2000, investigated this relationship between 1992 and 1996 and also concluded that "…information flow around grants is manipulated." (41). Research conducted by Lie and Randy Heron used a sample of 39 888 grants to executives from 7 774 US firms between 1996 and 2005. Their findings showed that an estimated 29% of the firms investigated, in some form or other, manipulated options granted to their top executives (42). Lie also contends that backdating can be very difficult to identify, as many grants are never filed with the SEC and companies employ a range of strategies to obscure the activity.

In 2002, legislation under the Sarbannes Oxley banner was introduced to force executives to report their new option dates within two days, compared to the period of months that was allowed before. The effect of this new legislation is clearly demonstrated by Lie. In *Figure 5* he shows that legislation to tighten the reporting regime applicable to the granting of stock options to executives in the United States will at least curb the practice of backdating stock options.

FIG. 5

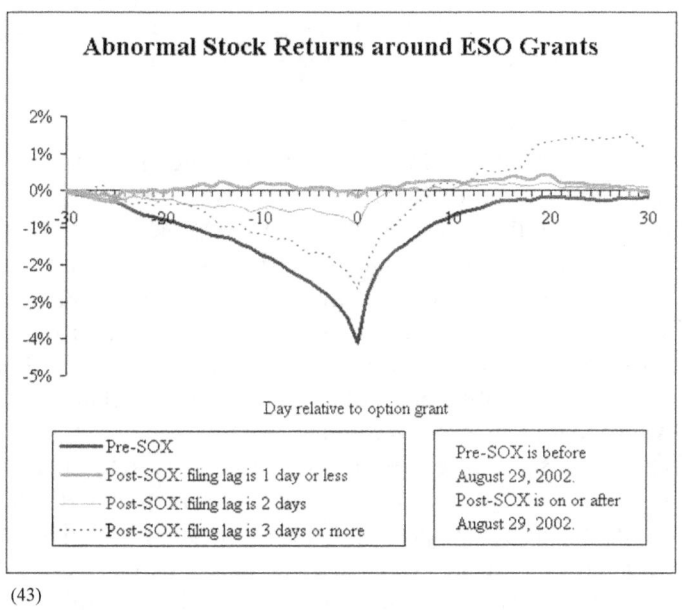

(43)

Other practices, like timing stock option grants, to occur after bad news was disseminated, or before good news is reported, remain a problem. Similarly, the manipulation of information flow to influence share price movements before or after selected option granting dates still remains a problem.

In this chapter we have seen that the US Savings & Loans crisis can largely be attributed to erratic spurts of regulation and deregulation, followed by re-regulation. The reason for this erratic behavior can most probably be found in the interrelationships between politicians and pressure groups. The impact of this erratic behavior was massive and resulted in a cost to taxpayers running into billions of USD. No action was, however, contemplated against those responsible for the crisis. We do find that a perception was created that Mike Milken was responsible for the crisis, and we find that substantial sanctions were exercised against him for charges that appeared to be trivial. Although one can argue that, during plea bargains, defendants are often allowed to plead guilty to lesser charges, the case against Mr Milken was viewed by legal commentators as shaky at best.

What is important for the reader is to note the discrepancy between the way Mr Milken's case was handled by the authorities and the way in which Mr Abel Mozer and other Salomon executives were treated in what appears to be a clear-cut case of deliberate market manipulation and fraud over a period of time. We also saw massive discrepancies in the way ENRON executives were treated for essentially manipulating the company's profits and losses and lying to shareholders, when compared to the treatment meted out to Shell for inherently the same offences. There can be little doubt that such inconsistencies by regulators and enforcement agencies contribute to the development of an environment conducive to extreme opportunism. One partial explanation for some elements of this type of behavior is offered by Ari Adut when he argues that the secrecy of these opportunistic behaviors contributes to the erratic enforcement of the norm [44]. According to Adut: "the norm will then be under enforced as long as its transgressions are committed in, or remain private. Once a scandal breaks, however, the externalities that are put in motion by the publicity of the transgression may prod polluted or provoked third parties into showing extraordinary zeal vis-à-vis the offender, to signal rectitude or resolve" [45].

In this chapter I presented compelling evidence regarding the extent of opportunistic behavior displayed by company executives in the United States. These same types of executives would have been the clients Mr Milken dealt with and was found guilty of assisting to avoid taxes. One of the uses of executive stock options, according to Lie, is to "cheat on corporate taxes" (46). Similarly, the abuse of insider information to ensure stock options are always granted at a very favorable price is also applicable to the manipulation of strategic insider information by Shell executives. In the Shell case, the concealment of strategic negative information would have allowed option holders to exercise their existing options at a price above the issue price, something that would in all probability not have been the case if they did not manipulate their proven reserve figures upwards.

The information provided in this chapter underlines the dire need for well directed, efficient and consistent regulation. In any environment where incentives are massive and countervailing mechanisms are weak, such regulation is a must even though it might be unpopular.

222

CHAPTER 9

THE SUB PRIME COLLAPSE

According to an article by Yalman Onaran published by Bloomberg.com in August of 2008 write downs and losses to banks attributable to sub prime losses exceeded USD 500 million. In the same article Nouriel Roubine an economist from New York University is quoted as estimating potential losses overall, to exceed USD 2 trillion [1]. This is 1,000,000,000,000 or 10 to the power of 12, times 2. Any losses attributable to 'rogue traders' shrinks into insignificance, compared to this mammoth figure. But what is this 'sub prime' phenomena that caused so much misery?

Our handy online investment dictionary provides us with the following insights into what this term represents [2]. It explains sub prime as "A type of mortgage that is normally made out to borrowers with lower credit ratings. As a result of the borrower's lowered credit rating, a conventional mortgage is not offered because the lender views the borrower as having a larger-than-average risk of defaulting on the loan extended to them. Lending institutions often charge interest on sub-prime mortgages at a rate that is higher than a conventional mortgage in order to compensate themselves for carrying more risk." It elaborates on the initial explanation and adds the following, "Borrowers with credit ratings below 600 often will be stuck with subprime mortgages and the higher interest rates that go with those mortgages. Making late bill payments or declaring personal bankruptcy could very well land borrowers in a situation where they can only qualify for a subprime mortgage. Therefore, it is often useful for people with low credit scores to wait for a period of time and build up their scores before applying for mortgages to ensure they are eligible for a conventional mortgage." This information is not hidden or hard to come by and would have been available to anyone that wanted to find out more about this investment. One needn't be an investment guru or a 'quants' expert to deduce from the mere description that this is a risky type of investment.

This investment sounds vaguely familiar, high yield, high risk of default, sounds like 'junk bond'. If we go to Investopedia again we find that a 'junk' bond is an "A bond rated 'BB' or lower because of its high default risk. Also known as a "high-yield bond" or "speculative bond" (3). These are usually purchased for speculative purposes. "Junk bonds typically offer interest rates three to four percentage points higher than safer government issues." 'Junk bond' issuers are normally companies with a less than stellar track record and have to pay higher interest rate to bond holders to compensate these lenders for the higher (real or perceive) risk of default by the issuer on its payment commitments (4). Similarly sub-prime borrowers also have less than perfect credit records and have to pay the banks they borrow from a higher interest rate in order to be granted a home loan as they are also regarded as having a higher potential default risk. In both cases a higher return is due to higher risk. If these were high risk investments how did they end up in the portfolios of municipalities and pension funds?

The answer is that many of them had investment grade rating from one or more of the rating agencies. If these things are indeed risky how is that possible? Apparently you need to add a bit of mathematical sauce to it with a sprinkle of statistics and 'voila', manure is gold. The ancient alchemists would have been proud. Mike Milken based his trust in 'junk' bonds on a statistical analysis that proved that the risk of default posed by the so-called fallen Angels (former investment grade companies that hit on hard times) were a lot less than what was generally believed. According to an article in the International Herald Tribune of 29 April 2008 (5), Mike Milken is quoted as questioning the insight in to the mechanisms of the financial markets of those that wants to draw a parallel between the Sub-prime collapse and the hardships that befell the 'junk bond' market a mere twenty odd years ago. According to Milken "the disastrous lowering of underwriting standards and other unfortunate practices" is at the root of the sub-prime problem. The use of securitization per se is not the problem, those that abused the "tool" is at fault, not the tool itself, summarizes Mr. Milken's argument.

We therefore have to focus some of our attention on those that wielded the tool i.e. the bankers. According to Satyajit Das author of among other "Traders, Guns and Money: Knowns and Unknowns in the Dazzling World of Derivatives", the root of the problem can be found with a change in business model utilized by banks. In an article published in the "in Finance" magazine of the Financial Services Institute of Australasia this change was necessitated by the advent of risk adjusted returns as the new performance measurement yardstick, introduced in the 1990's by the likes of JPMorgan and Bankers Trust (6). 'Risk Adjusted Returns' refers to "A concept that refines an investment's return by measuring how much risk is involved in producing that return, which is generally expressed as a number or rating. Risk-adjusted returns are applied to individual securities and investment funds and portfolios." (7). Through the use of mathematical modeling or 'quants' as it is commonly referred to, the risk associated with a particular business practice could therefore be calculated. The problem is however that depending on the assumptions used by the modeler the risk associated with a particular practice as well as the risk adjusted return could be 'adjusted' upwards or downwards i.e. manipulated. The usefulness of this little toolkit will reveal itself later. A great deal of blame has also been shifted onto the shoulders of Federal Authorities including Alan Greenspan. It is with him that I will start my analysis.

In an article published in the New York Times of February the

10th 1991 the chairman of the US Federal Reserve, Alan Greenspan is quoted as making a number of comments, which with hindsight is crucial in our quest of reaching an understanding of the origins of the sub prime crises (8). According to Louis Uchitelle, Alan Greenspan, chairman of the Federal Reserve at the time, expressed concerns about the fact that Federal bank examiners that were tasked with supervising lending practices at commercial banks, lost track of banking's true nature, thereby contributing to the reluctance of banks to lend. Mr Greenspan is quoted as calling the system in place at the time "archaic". He emphasized the fact that banks have a very important, "special", role in society. He expressed concern about the lack of demand for new loans in the latter half of 1990, from consumers and companies alike. This fact is exacerbating the economic downturn as there is a lack of appetite for credit for spending and investment. He acknowledges the fact that Federal Reserves were reducing interest rates in order to encouraging lending, and will continue to do that in order to stimulate lending. Mr Greenspan contributes the lack of real estate expenditure in part to the way Federal loan examiners are encouraging banks to appraise their loans, not taking into consideration that banks should be providing a service to society.

Mr Greenspan is further quoted as criticizing the short term view employed for valuing among other real estate portfolios. "There is an increasing tendency to look at deposit institutions and say we should mark to market the loan portfolios, meaning trying to regain the values in real estate, for example that the loans represent if we sold them in the market tomorrow," Mr Greenspan blames this for the fact that banks are offering "inadequate loans" for property buyers, because they believe that property prices will continue to fall. This valuation methodology shortcoming he claims was on the flip side also responsible for the overvaluation of property in the 1980's.

Mr Greenspan reiterates his emphasis on the fact that the

"nature" of banking is long term and that its portfolio's should be treated as such. "Commercial banking is the practice by which you make illiquid loans." The article then strikes at the heart of the way in which bankers should operate their business. I highlight this extract from the article as it is fundamental to the underlying causes of the sub prime crises.

"Bankers should determine the profitability of a loan over its lifetime, even 20 years, and not the day-to-day value of the underlying real estate and, when borrowers get into trouble, the banks should work with them to solve the problem, Mr Greenspan said. The bank examination process should reflect this role of banking."

"The basic process is not to get paid back immediately or to sell the loan," but to carry the loan for its full life, Mr Greenspan said. Accounting practices, as well as the examination process, should reflect this, he added." (9)

The article also notes that Mr Greenspan indicated that changes to the regulatory environment are envisaged, in order to remedy these shortcomings. Mr Greenspan is clearly unhappy with the short term mindset that is overshadowing banks and their ability to execute their role in society. Mr Greenspan sees banks as much more than just entities designed to maximize shareholders interest. Mr Greenspan sees them as having a "special role in society". These are very powerful words; on the one hand it indicates that banks have what one might call a "moral" obligation, towards society. This 'moral' obligation would be the extension of credit to society, the question would however be, would society have a moral obligation towards banks in the event that banks may one day need credit, if they fell on hard times, due to the execution of their 'social responsibility'. The answer to this would be a qualified yes. If the bankers executed their social obligation in a responsible manner, they undoubtedly deserve to be bailed out. One can however also argue that a moral responsibility rests on the shoulders of society that borrowed the money from them, to be responsible in the way they handled credit extended to them. In a perfect world where bankers and borrowers always act responsibly, the noble aim of the chairman of the Federal Reserve were probably realistic and attainable. We unfortunately find it hard to shake the effects of the incident in the garden with the apple and the snake.

The problem was that the Bankers only heard half the plea from Greenspan. He implored them not sell off these new 'sub-prime' loans. Unfortunately selling of these sub-prime loans was part and parcel of the risk management strategy of these banks. The rationale was that the bank would only be exposed to this high risk debt for the period it took them to securitize the debt, get it rated investment grade by a rating agency and sell it off to some unsuspecting municipality in Norway. They again as in 1980's believed that as the value of collateral (value of the property) would keep on rising providing ample protection to the bank in the event of a default. It appears that the only moral obligation the banks viewed as 'important' was to make as much money as possible for themselves by being merchants of risk in stead of being managers of risk.

In order to achieve their objectives bankers employed what Sayajit Das refers to as "Voodoo Banking". According to Das the origins of the present extreme financial difficulty, may be found in the business model of banks (10). The model was quite simple; make more money by doing more business; more risky business means more profit. Increase your leverage and optimize your capital management/utilization. Exploit favorable regulatory rules to the maximum. This sounds like good business sense, where did things go wrong?

The idea of lending more money to more people is fairly straightforward, the problem is that with the new concept of selling your loan book off and thereby realizing the potential future income immediately, one constantly have to find new borrowers to bundle, securitize and sell off. Initially credit worthy clients was enticed into taking up easy credit, the property and stock markets were booming.   As everyone targeted the most secure groups of potential borrowers first it was not very long before the pool of potential creditworthy prime borrowers was exhausted. The profits associated with this new way of banking were however booming and in an effort to find new borrowers bankers had to 'lower their standards'. Banks also increased their reach by using loan brokers or loan originators to find more borrowers. These agents were motivated, with substantial upfront commissions, to find more borrowers. The emphasis was on quantity and not quality. With banks now actively pursuing people who could never dream of getting credit, through agents that had little vested interest in the quality of borrowers they targeted, the seeds of a disaster was planted.

The major problem for the banks was how to 'manage' the risk associated with their newfound 'clients'. This problem was not insurmountable, as banks utilized very sophisticated quantitative models to asses the risk associated with their new clients. They also took collateral as a safeguard against default by borrowers. This model allowed the banks to increase the size of their loans and allowed them to give loans to borrowers that could not be regarded as prime borrowers. These non-prime borrowers that would not have qualified previously became the backbone of profitable banking. This new approach was not only very profitable it was also in support of government policy, a truly win-win situation, or was it.

These toxic assets found their way into investment portfolio's designed to provide pensions to widows, orphans, and the elderly, due to the fact that when they were sold to these Funds they were not seen as toxic but as investment grade. In the same way as Mexican debt found its way into portfolios by being packaged and rated these debt we refer to today as toxic had the stamp of approval of the rating agencies deeming it investment grade. In a document first published in the New York Times of April 27 2008, very aptly titled "Triple-A Failure", Roger Lowenstein cast some light on how this happened (11). In the first instance one must recognize the fact that rating agencies charge substantial fees to financial institutions, to rate their securities. The extent of their fees are reflected in the fact that one of the rating agencies, Moody's, saw a 900% earnings increase in recent years. The rating of securitized sub-prime mortgages played no small part in the surge in rating agency earnings.

The fact that the rating agencies may not have been as objective as they should have been is extremely likely. There were however other methodological problems as well. These shortcomings are abundantly clear from the following. In the first instance Moody's used a model in 2007 that they started using in 2002. By their own admission, the mortgage market has "evolved considerably" during that period. Secondly raters from Moody's admitted that their expertise did not lay in assessing the underlying assets of the securities they were evaluating. All they were doing was ensuring that the mathematical calculations were correct. The problem with using mathematics to predict financial market behavior is that assumptions need to be made. This is unfortunately where most mathematicians and actuaries come unstuck. Their mathematics is technically correct, their assumptions are often flawed. This weakness is illustrated by the Monte Carlo simulation used by the Moody's raters. In order for this simulation to be useful for Moody's purposes the underlying bonds of the collateralized debt obligations valued, had to perform like bonds drawn at random from a collection of historical bonds. The assumption was therefore that a bondholder in 2007 would behave exactly the same as bondholders have behaved up until 2002.

Changes in the reasons why people applied for mortgage bonds and changes in the underwriting standards used by those that approved these applications, were not taken into consideration.

The utilization of housing loans as finance to speculate in the property market and lowering of vetting standards due to the fact that banks would only hold these loans on their books until they can securitize and sell them off, has apparently passed the maths 'boffins' at the rating agencies by. As early as 2005 some money managers like James Kragenbring however detected the pricing anomaly of these sub prime underpinned debt and started betting that this market would collapse (12). Even when the rating agencies became aware of the lowering of standards used to evaluate new borrowers they believed in their models that told them that house prices would keep rising. Only in 2007 after they looked away from their models at the realities on the ground, did the raters at Moody's realize that their models were not as infallible as they thought. By then it was already too late and when the rating agencies started down rating these previously investment grade sub-prime underpinned paper to non-investment grade sub prime underpinned paper, the price collapse was inevitable. In an article entitled "The Financial Modelers Manifesto" Professor Emanuel Derman and Dr Paul Wilmot, two quants specialists, cautions the users of financial models, "Our experience in the financial arena has taught us to be humble in applying mathematics to markets, and to be extremely wary of ambitious theories, which are in the end trying to model human behavior. We like simplicity, but we like to remember that it is our models that are simple, not the world." (13).

It appears from the above that the rating agencies must shoulder some of the blame for this sub prime related collapse. Some observers however tend to disagree. In an article entitled "Stop persecuting rating agencies" published in the International Financial Law Review of May 2008 an unnamed commentator places the blame on the shoulders of the investors (14). According to the commentator "Disingenuous banking and lazy investors are the problem." Investors did not read the accompanying documentation that accompanied the CDO's they were buying and did not question the claims made by the rating agencies and the intermediaries selling these triple-A (AAA) rated securities. Technically speaking this commentator does have a point. Similar to hedge funds most of these instruments are accompanied by a serious health warning to potential investors that they may potentially lose their shirts or even worse. The commentator further contends that investors knew what they were buying and knew the methodologies used by the rating agencies to rate these instruments. Due to these facts it was not misleading for the rating agencies to rate treasury bills and subprime underpinned structured products the same rating. One might argue that the role of the rating agency was merely to make these structured products 'legal' investments for investors that could only invest in investment grade securities, the investors still had the obligation to ensure that the investments were appropriate for them and or their clients. In other words you cannot buy a security merely because it carries the highest investment rating, bestowed on it by one of the respected rating agencies. If this is true one must question the purpose and/or value of an investment rating, expressed by an institution that get paid handsomely by the issuer of the rated instrument, using questionable mathematical models.

In an article in Wellesley Investment Advisor's newsletter of December 2007, Moody's the role of the rating agencies is also questioned (15). Remarks by a senior Moody's economist, indicates a serious lack of introspection. Mr Zandi from Moody's is quoted as identifying a number of 'other' culprits responsible for this financial 'pickle' we find ourselves in: Who's to blame? That is, who is at fault for the mess in the nation's mortgage and housing markets, which continues to weigh on global financial markets and threatens the economic expansion? While answering this question is important for apportioning legal blame, it is vital for formulating an appropriate policy response. Policymakers can't determine how to make the financial system better without knowing whose actions are responsible for the systems current disarray. So who is to blame? Lenders, absolutely, borrowers, those who committed fraud, they've contributed. Wall Street, those firms involved in taking the loans and turning them into financial securities, yes, investors who bought the securitized loans without due consideration of their risk, undoubtedly (16). Most importantly is the blame the regulatory process itself should bear. Current oversight of the mortgage market is composed of a hodgepodge of regulators, including the Federal Reserve, the OCC, the FDIC, the OTS, the NCUA and a plethora of state agencies. At last we have this problem solved. If we lock this motley crew up we've got this problem licked. Not so fast says the commentator from Wellesley Investment Advisors, what about the role of Moody's? (17). Could it be that these mighty rating agencies that can make or break companies and even countries be the biggest culprit of them all?

The argument can however be made that the rating agencies were merely rating instruments constructed by their clients, i.e. the banks and financial service providers. This argument deserves some further investigation. Satyajit Das, questions the sustainability of the profits generated by the banking and investment banking industries. This relentless pursuit of ever greater returns has led to banks relying not on better service to their clients but on what Das termed "Voodoo banking" .This new strategy pioneered in the 1990's by JP Morgan and Bankers Trust, focused on risk adjusted returns. At the root of this phenomenon is a change in business strategy away from the long term relationship approach that Alan Greenspan expected of the banking industry, to an impersonal "originate and sell" strategy. This change in strategy could be detected in a change in attitude by Bankers Trust officials as described by Frank Partnoy (18). He describes how valuable Bankers Trust clients become "pigeons" that were "hammered" in order to maximize profits. An illustration of the culture is reflected in an extract from a training video were a Bankers Trust official made the following comment while describing a hypothetical derivative transaction; "What Bankers Trust can do for Sony and IBM is get in the middle and rip them off - take a little money" (19). This sentiment was echoed by a former managing director and senior derivatives saleswoman at Bankers Trust who described the culture at the firm as "amoral" because of questionable practices where senior managers were rewarding practices that made a lot of money for the bank even though it was not in the best interest of the bank's clients. The following phrase attributed to a Bankers Trust derivative salesman captures the spirit of the culture; "Funny business you know. Lure people into that calm and then just totally fuck'em." I believe that these strategies and culture so aptly described by Partnoy is not dissimilar to the attitudes of those that created the sub prime circus.

Against this backdrop an article by two "Financial Stability Specialists" from the Bank of England helps us in gaining a greater understanding of why stress testing by banks failed on a global scale (20). Tree key areas of failure are identified. The first two are "disaster myopia" and "network externalities". The first is a bias towards underestimating the probability of "adverse outcomes" otherwise known as disasters. Subjective evaluation of probabilities, were given a rational veneer convincing everyone including the modelers that they had nothing to fear. This allowed the decision makers to justify the risk they were taking on board. The second factor identified is the role of "network externalities". This term refers to the complexity added to risk assessment modeling that takes into account not only the financial viability of your counterparty but the viability of your counterparty's counterparties. Put simply your counterparty may default due to no fault of its own but because one of its counterparty's defaulted. With the added elements brought about by globalization the accurate assessment of risk becomes a highly complicated exercise that should always be regarded as an indicator rather than an absolute.

The third element that deserves our attention is misaligned

incentive structures. Such misalignment may be within firms and between firms and regulators. There is little incentive for executives to curtail uncontrolled risk taking and other forms of extreme opportunism if they know that such curtailment might threaten their bonuses. As we have seen with the NYSE 'market makers' and the Salomon bond market manipulation incidences of extreme opportunism is often widespread and by no means isolated events that can be attributed to the failings of an individual. Together with such one directional incentive structures the 'too big to fail' mindset forms a powerful climate for extreme opportunism. What incentive is there for executives to control risk if they believe they will be bailed out by government if their risk taking policies backfire and they will suffer no serious sanction or personal financial loss? This dangerous psychology is clearly demonstrated by the results of a Bank of England/SFA stress testing seminar held with UK banks. During a survey it became apparent that the participants only tested very moderate stress scenarios. Their explanation for this apparent oddity captures the essence of the problem, "…there was no incentive to run severe stress tests and show these to management. If there were such a severe shock, they would very likely lose their bonus and possibly their jobs. And in that event, the authorities would have to step-in anyway to save the bank and others suffering a similar plight."

The most terrifying of this is the fact that when disaster struck these guys were absolutely correct. Do I have to say anything more?

EPILOGUE

For the purposes of this book, extreme opportunism has been defined as the 'extreme pursuit of self-interest by individuals and groups'. Structural conditions refer to those variables most likely to influence the strategies and rules prevalent in a particular sub-culture. The origin of these structural factors may be normative or interests based or even a combination of the two. The roles of these structural factors are principally to act as motivators, facilitators or inhibitors of opportunistic behavior. An imbalance between these factors was observable in the incidences of extreme opportunism that were analyzed. Managing levels of opportunism should therefore be possible through the manipulation of one or more of these factors. By conceptualizing structural factors, underlying incidences of extreme opportunism in financial markets as forces with counterbalancing potential, one is forced to analyze these factors relative to one another and not in isolation. Through a thorough analysis of the role of these structural factors underlying incidences of extreme opportunism in financial markets, sufficient evidence was found to support the hypothesis that we are therefore not dealing with an unforeseeable or unmanageable aberration, or a 'rogue' phenomenon. Extreme opportunism should much rather be regarded as a very important and potentially very hazardous element of modern business. Clients and shareholders should therefore ensure that it receives as much shareholder, management and regulatory attention as other facets of business, for example making profits. In an environment in which highly geared financial products are used by highly incentivised actors, inexperienced regulatory and oversight actors using outdated and low-budget control systems have little chance of effectively inhibiting extreme opportunism. The magnitude of the problem increased exponentially with an ever greater reliance on mathematical modeling to not only design these products but also to identify, quantify, monitor and manage the risks associated with them. As we have seen with the LTCM collapse and the sub prime disaster mathematical skill is no substitute for common sense. Eminent economists warned against the fact that "…in recent years economics has turned virtually into a branch of applied mathematics, and has become detached from real-world institutions and events." (1). As we have seen the rating agencies and the risk managers tasked with quantifying the risks associated with highly geared and intricate financial products are all highly reliant on mathematical modeling. If these models and or the assumptions used by those that design or use them are flawed, the results can be catastrophic. Proponents of blanket financial market deregulation should also ask themselves if an industry that deeply affects the lives of current and future generations could really be left to its own devices. As former derivatives trader, Satyajit Das put it "fund managers are performance junkies. Like athletes, there is a significant incentive to cheat" (2). If you want to manage other people's money, effective oversight and controls should be a given.

One of the most promising regulatory responses in recent years is the introduction of the Sarbanes Oxley legislation in the United States. Of primary interest to me is the fact that responsibility is focused where it is supposed to be, at the top. Company executives are held directly responsible for, among other things, the accuracy of information disseminated to regulators, shareholders and the investor public at large. The legislation is also very clear with regard to the sanctions attached to breaches of the terms set out in the legislation (3). Some of the measures introduced in the legislation states that "CEO and CFO must review all financial reports"; "financial report does not contain any misrepresentations"; "information in the financial report is 'fairly presented'"; "CEO and CFO are responsible for the internal accounting controls"; "CEO and CFO must report any deficiencies in internal accounting controls, or any fraud involving the management of the audit committee"; and "CEO and CFO must indicate any material changes in internal accounting controls" . The Act furthermore requires that "All annual financial reports must include an Internal Control Report stating that management is responsible for an 'adequate' internal control structure, and an assessment by management of the effectiveness of the control structure. Any shortcomings in these controls must also be reported. In addition, registered external auditors must attest to the accuracy of the company management's assertion that internal accounting controls are in place, operational and effective." Section 409 of the Act states "Companies are required to disclose on an almost real-time basis information concerning material changes in its financial condition or operations". There is little doubt about where the concerns of the lawmaker are focused, most definitely not on 'rogue traders'.

Sarbanes-Oxley also came under severe criticism, especially due to the costs associated with compliance. A very striking argument made is that shareholders are prepared to live with a certain amount of fraud (4). It is argued that "…shareholders will find such regulation valuable only if the benefit from reduced fraud is greater than the cost of regulatory compliance. SOX's attempt to create a perfect world with zero fraud goes too far. Moreover, it is well accepted in financial economics literature that the costs and benefits of securities regulation should be evaluated from the perspective of typical shareholders who can avoid some costs of fraud by investing in diversified portfolios of shares. By imposing the costs of eliminating fraud on all firms in investors' portfolios, the SOX mandates are a terrible deal for the ordinary investors it purports to protect."

One of the shortcomings of this argument is the fact that it appears to single out fraud and its cost to shareholders as the only problem. In my view, the cost to shareholders of the culture of extreme opportunism that plagues the financial markets is much greater than the cost of implementing

Sarbanes-Oxley type regulation. Fraud is but one element of the manifestation of extreme opportunism. It must be duly noted that most cases of spectacular losses or corporate collapses started with apparently insignificant actions. The concealment of a loss or a profit was often the first step. There is no difference between overcharging a client through inflated service charges on his savings account and causing an investor to lose money by front-running him. Was the AIB management's overcharging of their thousands of clients less wrong than the actions of John Rusnak? The argument can be made that the intent to defraud in the AIB overcharging example may have been there from the start, while in the majority of so-called 'rogue trader' cases analyzed, there was no initial intent to defraud. If one would add up the hidden cost of transactions and actions that result in losses but never make the headlines, the billions of USD paid in fines every year by large corporations, and the silent losses suffered by clients when they are being misled by analysts or are traded against by their brokers and portfolio managers, to name but a few, one might find the cost of implementing SOX much more palatable. If Sarbanes-Oxley is viewed as a concerted effort to temper the opportunistic culture prevalent in the financial markets, its benefits over the long term would be immeasurable. If we view fraud as only the visible tip of extreme opportunism we quickly realize that what is viewed by some observers as overkill might in reality be the bare necessity. A case in point is the costs, direct and indirect, resultant from the most recent sub-prime related financial meltdown. Nouriel Roubine's quoted estimate of potential losses overall, exceeding USD 2 trillion is a stark reminder of the magnitude of the cost attributable to uncontrolled extreme opportunism.

An interesting phenomenon highlighted by Abolafia is the fact that clients expect traders to be opportunistic in order to achieve as much profit as possible (5). The way in which you make money is much less important than the making of money. It is therefore of little surprise that, even after Salomon Brothers admitted that they manipulated the Treasury securities market, their clients kept trading the same securities with them. Extreme opportunism does not deter clients or shareholders and it appears that, as long as the potential profit outweighs the perceived risks, little informal restraint can be expected from these two groups. The culture of opportunism is therefore perpetuated through reinforcement from at least two fronts, shareholders and clients. Other than formal regulation, there appears to be very little to restrain extreme opportunism in financial markets and, as we have shown in this book it is in all probability a much more universal and common phenomenon than previously thought. In order to deal with this phenomenon, the "collective moral hazard" approach used by James Dow (6) has definite merit. A combination of factors like inappropriate incentives for staff and management, encouragement of extreme opportunistic behavior, weak or passive internal control structures, erratic and partisan regulatory and judicial behavior, all contribute to the creation and maintenance of a culture of extreme opportunism.

The solution to the problem would therefore require a holistic approach that would include, among other things; changes to the way legal systems operate internationally, the way in which audit firms conduct their business and the mandatory psychological testing of individuals who are employed in positions of trust in the financial service and corporate environments and use potentially hazardous instruments. The limitations of self-regulation and the exclusion of certain products from efficient regulation deserve our attention. In an environment with very strong motivators, like extreme salaries, the balance between motivators and inhibitors should be maintained vigorously. Industry bodies tasked with self-regulation could come under severe pressure from their principals to be as lenient as possible, unless the sanctions they face for not being effective are as extreme as the profits and the rewards at stake. Another problem one faces is situations in which a product or service is less regulated because the users are deemed to be wealthy enough or skilled enough to be able to 'handle' the risks associated with the product. This phenomenon is not limited to the financial markets and is quite common in extreme sports. A hedge fund is one such example, where weak regulation is justified by limiting those who may use it. The problem, as we have seen in the Long Term Capital Management (LTCM) event, is that the actions of hedge funds affect a very large segment of the financial markets and can lead to systemic failure. Furthermore, derivative instruments, collective investment schemes and exotic products like "Absolute Return' products used by ordinary investors and pension funds often belie their exposure to hedge fund activity. The mere name "Hedge" fund is extremely misleading, as hedge fund managers can follow virtually any investment strategy with virtually limitless gearing levels. There is a real need for hedge fund strategies to be monitored for extreme gearing levels through independent oversight, as it is fast becoming one of the largest asset classes available to investors. According to the FSA, the US hedge fund market in the US exceeded USD 1 trillion in 2005 (7). Its lure of high returns for investors and even higher returns for its managers, coupled with little or no regulation and oversight, creates an environment with a high extreme opportunism potential. This problem is further exacerbated by the fact that consultants that should provide their clients with unbiased advice are often handsomely incentivised by hedge fund managers to promote their funds. Hedge fund contracts are often designed to exploite legal loopholes allowing retirement funds to invest disproportionate amounts into highly illiquid products that in many instances allow for investment managers to deduct hefty 'performance bonuses' from their clients' portfolio's while losing them billions.

The August 2009 SEC fine of USD 33 million paid by Bank of America is another stark reminder of the culture of extreme opportunism that plagues Wall Street. Merril Lynch & Company paid USD 3.6 billion in bonuses at the end of 2008 despite the fact that it recorded a record loss of USD 27.6 billion in 2008 (8). This loss followed their 2007 loss of USD 7.8 billion for 2007. A further USD 2.2 billion in 'other' bonuses were also paid to the executives of Merrill. The fine paid by Bank of America will affect no-one other than perhaps the shareholders and maybe appease some critics. The amount is insignificant compared to the bonuses paid to executives that managed their company into the ground while enriching themselves at the cost of their shareholders and the US taxpayers. Even if the recipients of the bonuses had to pay the fine themselves they would still be left with more than USD 5 billion in bonuses. As a deterrent to others, this type of regulatory enforcement means very little.

Another glaring shortcoming of financial markets is the lack of effective and objective oversight of financial transactions, through the proper use of advanced transaction monitoring and evaluation systems. The benefits of such systems is their ability to monitor and audit vast amounts of transactions on a near-real-time basis, allowing auditors, executives and regulators alike to detect anomalous transactions in time. These systems would also be capable of tracking and evaluating transactions in most of the world financial markets on a continuous basis and could be programmed to autonomously report anomalous transactions to regulators. As mentioned earlier such systems like the "ELECTRONIC TRUSTEE" system were developed to provide high-speed transaction monitoring and audit capabilities to those charged with the responsibility of managing investments These systems allow for investment transactions to be audited as they are executed and not months or years after the fact. The development and implementation of such systems needs to become a priority. Unfortunately, these systems are often viewed as unnecessary overheads by those in authority. This is a view not dissimilar to those apparently held by the management teams and regulators tasked with overseeing Daiwa, Sumitomo, Barings, AIB, Kidder Peabody, NAB and Societe Generale. It is therefore not surprising that the anatomy of the events of extreme opportunism events analyzed over the period of 25 years, are remarkably similar. As long as we have limited oversight and ineffective formal and informal controls in an environment where rewards are massive and instantaneous, extreme opportunism will manifest itself with devastating regularity.

Another major concern is the apparent inability of regulators to design and implement useful and effective regulation. All too often, regulation takes the form of forcing companies to submit thousands of pages of information, which is stored without anyone actually analyzing it. If this information cannot be converted into useful 'intelligence' it means nothing. If anomalies cannot be detected, the scarce resources of regulators cannot be directed efficiently to areas where it is needed. With the ever-present poaching of top quality staff by the private sector, the use of technology can also play a crucial role in maintaining continuity and standards of oversight. It must, however, be emphasized that there is no substitute for having the 'will' to manage extreme opportunism. As Mr Iguchi pointed out, his superiors had no "will" to see his mistakes. Professor Irene Finel-Honigman points out that once we look through the apparent individualism associated with 'rogue traders' we realize they are "...part of a system that allows these transactions to take place, due to negligence, complacency, lack of oversight or collusion." (9). One can only hope that the SEC under leadership of its Chairman Mary L. Shapiro will be able to put in effect the very necessary "Financial Stability Oversight Council" and other regulatory measures to improve our ability to detect and manage extreme opportunism in financial markets (10). The mere fact that she publicly identified the incestuous relationship between investment advisors and broker-dealers/money managers, the lack of transparency associated with hedge funds and over-the-counter (OTC) derivatives as well as questionable practices like "rating shopping" as key areas of concern, is already a step in the right direction. It is an unfortunate reality that regulation without a strong and consistent political 'will' to manage extreme opportunism will have little chance of success. Political 'will' on the other hand is often entirely dependent on public opinion. Every individual therefore has a responsibility to ensure the creation and maintenance of an environment where 'extreme opportunism' is effectively controlled.

REFERENCES

COMMENTS

1. *Yahoo News July 21 2009*
2. *Levitt 1997:2*
3. *Levitt 1997: 6*
4. *Leeson e-mail*
5. *Dow et al. 2009:1-3*

PROLOGUE

1. *Weidlich & Scheer2009: 1-2.*
2. *Bloomberg Aug 12 2008*

INTRODUCTION

1. *Taleb 2008:17*
2. *Investopedia*
3. *NYSE 2005: 1-2*
4. *Weidner 2003: 1-3*
5. *Carhart, Kaniel, Musto & reed 1999: 2,7*
6. *Ni, Pearson& Poteshman 2004:1-7*
7. *Ni, Pearson& Poteshman 2004: 24*
8. *Abolafia 2001: 1-2*
9. *Partnoy 2003: 94-95*
10.*Partnoy 2003: 83*
11. *Lowenstein 2002: 19*
12. *Business Times 1997: 1-4*
13. *FSA Japa. 1998: 1-2*
14. *Partnoy 2003: 321-330*
15. *Crenshaw 2005: 1-3*
16. *Treanor 2006: 1-2*
17. *Lie 2006b: 1-13*
18. *Abolafia 2001: 2*

19. Abolafia 2001: 9-11
20. Ardut 2005: 22

CHAPTER 1

1. Kennedy, Rositer & Seib 2008: 1-4
2. Simmons 2005: 1-10
3. Simmons 2005: 3
4. Simmons 2005: 7
5. Wikipedia
6. Bloomberg 2008: 1-2
7. SGGID 2008:2
8. Tradersnarrative February 2008
9. Schwartz & Bennhold 2008: 4
10. Oprisk & compliance 2007
11. SEC 2005, 2006 & 2007
12. Clark 2008: 2
13. Schwartz & Bennhold 2008: 1-4
14. AMF 2008: 1-2
15. Timesonline 21 February 2008
16. Seeking Alpha 21 February 2008
17. Wikipedia
18. SGGID 2008: 49
19. SGGID 2008: 49
20. SGGID 2008: 50
21. SGGID 2008: 56
22. SGGID 2008: 58
23. SGGID 2008: 60
24. SGGID 2008: 25
25. SGGID 2008: 65-68
26. Societe Generale Special Committee Report 2008: 1-7
27. SGGID 2008: 8
28. SGGID 2008: 8
29. SGGID 2008: 46-47
30. Kircher 2009: 1-2
31. Lichfield 2008:1-2
32. Dow et al. 2009:1-3

CHAPTER 2

1. *Hills 1998: 1-3*
2. *Hills 1998: 1-3*
3. *Bruce 2004: 96-101*
4. *Hills 1998: 3*
5. *Farukawa 1999: 1-2*
6. *Tschoegl 2000: 103- 121*
7. *Weston 2003: 1-5*
8. *Farukawa 1999: 1-2*
9. *Farukawa 1997e: 1-2*
10. *Farukawa 1997d: 1-2*
11. *Farukawa 1997d: 1*
12. *Farukawa 1997a: 1*
13. *Farukawa 1997b: 1*
14. *Farukawa 1997c: 1*
15. *Verity 1998: 1*
16. *CFTC Release 1999: 1-2*
17. *CFTC Release 1999: 1-2*
18. *CNN Money 30 June 1999: 1-2*
19. *SFA 2000: 1-2*
20. *SFA 2000: 7*
21. *SFA 2000: 1-7*
22. *Killick 2002: 1-4*
23. *Weston 2003: 1-5*
24. *Weston 2003: 1-5*
25. *Weston 2003: 1-5*

CHAPTER 3

1. *Jameson 2001b: 1-4*
2. *Nanto, Jackson & Wells 1995: 4*
3. *Time 1997: 1*
4. *Asieweek.com 1995: 1*
5. *Time 1995: 1-3*
6. *Investopedia*
7. *Kattoulas 1997: 1*
8. *Time 1997: 1*

9. *Time 1997: 1*
10. *Kane & De Trask 1998: 19*
11. *USA v. Daiwa Bank 1995: 1-21*
12. *USA v. Daiwa Bank 1995: 7*
13. *USA v. Daiwa Bank 1995: 8*
14. *USA v. Daiwa Bank 1995: 9*
15. *Krane & De Trask 1998: 19*
16. *Time 1997: 1-3*
17. *Krane & De Trask 1998: 24*
18. *Krane & De Trask 1998: 24*
19. *Krane & De Trask 1998: 24*
20. *Krane & De Trask 1998: 24*
21. *Nanto, Jackson & Wells 1995: 4*
22. *Nanto, Jackson & Wells 1995: 5*
23. *Asiaweek.com 1995:2*
24. *Time 1997: 2*
25. *Time 1997: 2*
26. *Asiaweek.com 1995: 1*
27. *Time 2006: 1*
28. *Wikipedia*

CHAPTER 4

1. *Freedman & Burke 2001: 5,8*
2. *Partnoy 2003: 174, 181*
3. *Freedman & Burke 2001: 4*
4. *Partnoy 2003: 176*
5. *Freedman & Burke 2001: 4*
6. *Partnoy 2003: 176*
7. *Freedman & Burke 2001: 10*
8. *Partnoy 2003: 175*
9. *SEC 2008: 8*
10. *Freedman & Burke 2003: 3-6*
11. *Freedman & Burke 2003: 10-11*
12. *Freedman & Burke 2003: 7*
13. *Laudon & Laudon 2004: 5*
14. *Investopedia*

15. *Freedman & Burke 2001: 10*
16. *Freedman & Burke 2001: 10*
17. *CSFI 2003: 9*
18. *Partnoy 2003: 175-180*
19. *Partnoy 2003; 175-180*
20. *SEC 1998: 11*
21. *Freedman & Burke 2001: 9*
22. *Partnoy 2003: 176-177*
23. *Freedman & Burke 2001: 9*
24. *Partnoy 2003: 179*
25. *Laudon & Laudon 2004: 5*
26. *Laudon & Laudon 2004: 4*
27. *Freedman & Burke 2001: 9*
28. *SEC 1998: 14-15*
29. *Partnoy 2003: 180-181*
30. *Laudon & Laudon 2004: 5*
31. *Freedman & Burke 2001: 7-8*
32. *Partnoy 2003: 181*
33. *Freedman & Burke 2001: 1-8*
34. *Freedman & Burke 2001: 13*
35. *SEC 2004: 2*
36. *SEC 2004: 21-23*
37. *Freedman & Burke 2001: 13-14*
38. *Laudon & Laudon 2004: 1*
39. *Laudon & Laudon 2004: 9*
40. *Freedman & Burke 2001: 12*
41. *Freedman & Burke 2001: 6*

CHAPTER 5

1. *Fay 1997: 70-73*
2. *Fay 1997: 52*
3. *Singapore Report 1995: 65*
4. *Singapore Report 1995: 65*
5. *Fay 1997: 68*
6. *Leeson 2005: 60*
7. *Leeson 2005: 53*

8. *Leeson 2005: 52-53*
9. *Fay 1997: 95-98*
10. *Brown & Steenbeek 2001: 5*
11. *Fay 1997: 97-101*
12. *Fay 1997: 99*
13. *Fay 1997: 101*
14. *Leeson 2005: 60*
15. *Leeson 2005: 85*
16. *Leeson 2005: 87*
17. *Fay 1997: 106-107*
18. *Brown & Steenbeek 2001: 5-8*
19. *Brown & Steenbeek 2001: 6-8*
20. *Leeson 2005: 173*
21. *Leeson 2005: 181*
22. *Fay 1997: 144*
23. *Leeson 2005: 84-85*
24. *Singapore Report 1995: 179*
25. *ERisk 2005: 1-3*
26. *Singapore Report 1995: Bx*
27. *Fay 1997: 135-136*
28. *Fay 1997: 136*
29. *Singapore Report 1995: 10-11*
30. *Leeson 2005: 79*
31. *Risk Institute: 4*
32. *Leeson 2005: 337*
33. *Singapore Report 1995: 179*
34. *Leeson 2005: 333-334*
35. *Investopedia*
36. *Leeson 2005: 83*
37. *Leeson Interview 2006*
38. *Risk Institute: 1-3*
39. *Risk Institute: 3*
40. *Brown & Steenbeek 2001: 1-44*
41. *Investopedia*
42. *Investopedia*
43. *Brown & Steenbeek 2001: 7*
44. *Brown & Steenbeek 2001: 44*

45. Risk Institute: 2
46. Fay 1997: 145
47. Fay 1997: 157
48. Lowenstein 2002: 3-5
49. Fay 1997: 159
50. Risk Institute: 2
51. Risk Institute: 3-4
52. Risk Institute: 1
53. Risk Institute: 3-7
54. Risk Institute: 1-7
55. Fay 1997: 187
56. Fay 1997: 131
57. Fay 1997: 133
58. Fay 1997: 133
59. Singapore Report 1995: 118
60. Reyes 1995: 1-7
61. Fay 1997: 107
62. Fay 1997: 167
63. Reyes 1995: 3-4
64. Fay 1997: 160-170
65. Fay 1997: 168-169
66. Singapore Report 1995: 118-148
67. Fay 1997: 149-153
68. Fay 1997: 180
69. Leeson 2005: 175
70. Fay 1997: 187
71. Fay 1997: 127
72. Fay 1997: 137
73. Fay 1997: 124
74. Fay 1997: 133-134
75. Fay 1997: 136
76. Fay 1997: 139
77. Fay 1997: 147
78. Finkelstein 2003: 1-3
79. Fay 1997: 140
80. Risk Institute: 2-4
81. Leeson 2005: 297-299

82. Fay 1997: 231
83. Fay 1997: 231
84. Drennan 2004: 5
85. Leeson 2006: Interview
86. Drennan 2004: 5
87. Drennan 2004: 7-8
88. Leeson 2005: 335
89. Leeson 2005: 208
90. Leeson 2005: 282
91. Leeson 2005: 248
92. Leeson 2005: 181
93. Fay 1997: 125
94. Leeson 2006: Interview
95. Leeson 2005: 87
96. Risk Institute: 2-4
97. Leeson 2006: Interview
98. Leeson 2005: 88
99. Riskglossary.com
100. Partnoy 2003: 179
101. Fay 1997: 62
102. Fay 1997: 64
103. Leeson 2006: Interview
104. Leeson 2005: 339
105. www.electronictrustee.com
106. Leeson 2006: e-mail

CHAPTER 6

1. BBC: 2002
2. McNee 2004: 1-6
3. Ludwig 2002: 32
4. USA v. John m. Rusnak 2002: 1-7
5. BBC 24 October 2004: 1-2
6. Dresser 2004: 1-2
7. Washington Times 30 May 2004
8. Dresser 2004: 1-2
9. Associated Press Newswires 2004: 1

10. *Associated Press Newswires 2004: 1-2*
11. *Associated Press Newswires 2004: 1-2*
12 *Associated Press Newswires 2004: 2*
13. *Washington Times 2004: 1-3*
14. *Washington Times 2004: 2*
15. *Burke 2003: 1-22*
16. *Burke 2003: 2*
17. *USA v. John M. Rusnak 2002: 1-7*
18. *Burke 2003: 2*
19. *Investorwords.com*
20. *Partnoy 1999: 32*
21. *Ryan 1998: 71*
22. *Ryan 1998: 71*
23. *Partnoy 1999: 32*
24. *USA v. John M. Rusnak 2002: 1-3*
25. *Kearney & Hutson 2002: 1-4*
26. *Kearney & Hutson 2002: 1-4*
27. *Ryan 1998: 99*
28. *Ryan 1998: 116*
29. *Ryan 1998: 94*
30. *Kearney & Hutson 2002: 3*
31. *Ryan 1998: 65*
32. *Kearney & Hutson 2002:4*
33. *Ludwig Report 2002: 13*
34. *Ludwig Report 2002: 9*
35. *Ludwig Report 2002: 7*
36. *Ludwig Report 2002: 7-8*
37. *Ludwig Report 2002: 15*
38. *USA v. John M. Rusnak 2002: 8*
39. *USA v. John M. Rusnak 2002: 9*
40. *Burke 2002: 11*
41. *Federal Reserve 2006: 1-41*
42. *USA v. John M. Rusnak 2002: 10*
43. *USA v. John M. Rusnak 2002: 10*
44. *USA v. John M. Rusnak 2002: 11*
45. *Ludwig Report 2002: 29*
46. *Ludwig Report 2002: 1*

47. *Burke 2002: 13*
48. *Ludwig Report 2002: 31-43*
49. *Ludwig Report 2002: 19*
50. *Luwig Report 2002: 9*
51. *Bruce 2004: 46*
52. *Ludwig Report 2002: 20*
53. *Ludwig Report 2002: 21*
54. *Ludwig Report 2002: 22-23*
55. *Ludwig Report 2002: 23*
56. *Ludwig Report 2002: 23*
57. *Ludwig Report 2002: 24*
58. *Ludwig Report 2002: 25-26*
59. *Ludwig Report 2002: 25*
60. *Ludwig Report 2002: 31*
61. *Partnoy 1999: 103*
62. *Ludwig Report 2002: 25*
63. *Ludwig Report 2002: 39*
64. *Ludwig Report 2002: 31*
65. *Ludwig Report 2002: 8*
66. *Burke 2002: 15*
67. *Lowenstein 2002: 14*
68. *Lorenz & Politzer 1990: 17*
69. *Lorenz & Politzer 1990; 19-21*
70. *Ludwig Report 2002: 21*
71. *Lewis 1999: 150*
72. *Partnoy 1999: 1-9*
73. *Partnoy 1999: 108*
74. *Partnoy 1999: 259-260*
75. *Ludwig Report 2002: 7*
76. *SEC v. Victor R. Gomez 1996: 1-2*
77. *Partnoy 1999: 191*
78. *Ludwig Report 2002: 21*
79. *Ludwig Report 2002: 20*
80. *Ludwig Report 2002: 27*
81. *Ludwig Report 2002: 4*
82. *Partnoy 1999: 108*
83. *Lorenz & Politzer 1990: 22*

84. BBC News 26 September 2002
85. Washington Times 30 May 2004
86. Washington Times 30 May 2004
87. Wikipedia

CHAPTER 7

1. Turnbull 2006: 1-2
2. Bell 2006: 1-2
3. AAP 2006: 1-3
4. AFP 2004: 1
5. AAP 2004: 1
6. APRA Report 2004: 14
7. Investopedia
8. Investopedia
9. Investopedia
10. Investopedia
11. APRA Report 2004: 14
12. Reily & Brown 2000: 1031
13. APRA Report 2004: 14-18
14. APRA Report 2004: 14-18
15. US Treasury 2000
16. Investopedia
17. Investopedia
18. Wood 2006: 2
19. APRA Report 2004: 14
20. APRA Report 2004: 17
21. Woolrich 2005: 1-2
22. APRA Report 2004: 5
23. APRA Report 2004: 5
24. APRA Report 2004: 5
25. PWC Report 2004: 43-45
26. APRA Report 2004: 55
27. Garnaut & Hughes 2004: 1-2
28. Cornell 2004: 4
29. ACSI 2004: 4
30. PWC Report 2004: 25

31. PWC Report 2004: 25
32. Trader 2004: 6
33. PWC Report 2004: 5-7
34. Mackenzie 2001: 1-6
35. Trader 2004: 4-5
36. APRA Report 2004: 5-7
37. APRA Report 2004: 5
38. APRA Report 2004: 6
39. APRA Report 2004: 72
40. APRA Report 2004: 22
41. APRA Report 2004: 23
42. Leeson 1996: 53
43. APRA Report 2004: 37
44. APRA Report 2004: 20
45. ABC 2004: 1-4
46. Woodrich 2005: 2
47. Cornell 2004: 1-4
48. Singh 2004: 1-6
49. Kemp 2004: 1-2
50. Wood 2006: 1-3
51. Kohler 2004: 1-4
52. Cornell 2004: 4
53. AFP 2004: 1
54. Newman 2005: 1

CHAPTER 8

1. Fligstein 2001: 203
2. Stilitz 2003: 36-40
3. FDIC 2002: 1-5
4. Stiglitz 2003: 103
5. Curry & Shibut 2003: 31
6. Wood 1990: 1
7. Fischel 1995: 197-199
8. Fischel 1995: 200
9. Fischel 1995: 164-167
10. Partnoy 2003: 107-110

11. *Partnoy 2003: 96*
12. *Partnoy 2003: 99-102*
13. *Partnoy 2003: 108*
14. *Partnoy 2003: 110*
15. *Partnoy 2003: 155- 167*
16. *Stiglitz 2003: 164-167*
17. *Stiglitz 2003: 143*
18. *Stiglitz 2003: 167*
19. *Partnoy 2003: 97*
20. *Stiglitz 2003: 167*
21. *Wood 1990: 1-3*
22. *Wood 1990: 2*
23. *Fischel 1995: 167, 151*
24. *BBC News 2004: 1-2*
25. *SEC 2004b: 3*
26. *SEC 2004a: 9-10*
27. *SEC 2004b: 2*
28. *SEC 2004a: 19-21*
29. *SEC 2004: 1*
30. *Wikipedia 2006b: 1-10*
31. *Dow Jones/AP 2006: 1*
32. *FinanzNachrichten.de 2006: 1-2*
33. *SEC 2004a: 17*
34. *Steward & Waldie 2006: 1-3*
35. *Pantesco 2006: 1-2*
36. *USA v. Jeffrey K. Skilling & Kenneth L. Lay 2004: 1-43*
37. *Ipsen 1993: 1-2*
38. *FTC 1999: 1-3*
39. *Lie 2006a: 1-6*
40. *Lie 2006b: 2*
41. *Lie 2006a: 3*
42. *Lie 2006a: 5*
43. *Lie 2006a 4*
44. *Ardut 2005: 213-235*
45. *Ardut 2005: 216*
46. *Lie 2006: 1*

CHAPTER 9

Onaran 2008: 1-2
2. Investopedia
3. Investopedia
4. Partnoy 2003:66-67
5. International Herald Tribune 29 April 2008
6. Das 2008:22-24
7. Investopedia
8. Uchitelle 1991: 1
9. Uchitelle 1991: 1
!0. Das 2008: 22-24
11. Lowenstein 2008: 1-8
12. Beal 2008: 1-3
13. Derman & Wilmott 2009: 1-2
14. International Law Review May 2008
15. Limited Risk Investor December 2007
16. Limited Risk Investor December 2007
17. Limited Risk Investor December 2007
18. Partnoy 2003: 55
19 Partnoy 2003: 55
20. Coppins & Haldane 2009: 6-8

EPILOGUE.

1. Dow et al. 2009:1-3
2. Das 2006: 83
3. Sarbanes Oxley 2006: 1-2
4. Butler & Ribstein 2006:1-4
5. Abolafia 2001: 370
6. Dow 2002: 32-39
7. FSA 2005
8. Weidlich & Scheer2009: 1-2
9. Finel-Honigman 2008: 1
10. Schapiro 2009:1-10

SOURCES & BIBLIOGRAPHY

PRIMARY SOURCES

AAP. 2004. "Whistleblower revealed NAB rogue trading".
http://www.smh.com.au/articles/2004/01/14/1073877863243.ht
ml?from=storyrhs
AAP. 2006. "Ex-NAB traders jailed over $326m scandal".
http://news.ninemsn.com.au/article.aspx?id=65348
ACI. "Association for Collective Investments".
http://www.aci.co.za/
ACSI. 2004. "A culture of Blame- NAB" in Corporate
Citizenship.no.17.
http://www.acsi.org.au/documents/...
AFP. 2004. "Rogue trading loss at Australia's NAB balloons to
277 million dollars".
http://findarticles.com/p/articles/mi_kmafp/is_200401/ai_kepm
361170/print
Agence France Press. 2000. "Yamaichi Securities: Former
head jailed for money hiding".
http://bankrupt.com/TCRAP_Public/000330.MBX
AMF. 2008. "Enforcement Committee decision concerning
Societe Generale, Amber fund (Cayman) Limited.
http://www.amf-france.org/documents/general/8241_1.pdf
Answers.com. "Yamaichi Securities".
http://en.wikipedia.org/wiki/Yamaichi_Securities
APRA Report. 2004. "Report Into Irregular Currency Options
Trading at the National Australia Bank". 23 March.
http://www.nabgroup.com/vgnmedia/downld/APRAreport_24m
arch04.pdf#search=%22apra%20national%20australia%20bank
%22
ASIAWEEK.COM.1995. "Anatomy Of A Scam".
http://www.asiaweek/95/0825/biz1.html

ASIAWEEK.COM. 1995 b. "Japan's $1-Billion Scam".
http://www.asiaweek.com/asiaweek/95/1027/biz2.html
ASIAWEEK.COM. 1996. "Perils of Profit. The Sumitomo
debacle underscores the need for risk management".
http://www.pathfinder.com/Asiaweek/96/0705/ed2.html
Associated Press Newswires 19. 10. 2004. "Leaders of
Ireland's largest bank testifies about ' awful and embarrassing'
charging scandals".
http://www.cbba.co.uk/links_alliedirish.html
Associated Press. 2006. "Feds hike ex-Enron boss fine to $183
million". MSNBC.com 13 Aug.
http://www.msnbc.msn.com/id/14334725/
Baltimore Business Journal- May 2004. "Allied Irish Banks
overcharged customers, report says".
http://www.bizjournals.com/baltimore/stories/2004/05/03/daily
31.html
Bank of England report. 1995. "Report of the Board of
Banking Supervision Inquiry into the Circumstances of the
Collapse of Barings 18 July 1995".
http://www.numa.com/ref/barings/bar00.htm
Barron, C. 2002. "Leslie Frankel: Stockbroking giant linked to
market crook". Sunday Times 30 Jun 2002.
http://www.sudaytimes.co.za/2002/06/30/insight/in12.asp
Barry, S. 2004. "Sumitomo, CLR make peace in last act of
Hamanaka affair" October 2004.
http://www.findarticles.com/p/articles/mi_m3MKT/is_43-
3_112/ai_n6276716
BBC News. 26 March 1998. "Copper trader jailed for $2.6bn
fraud".
http://news.bbc.co.uk/1/hi/oldbusiness/69960.stm
BBC News. 6 February 2002a. "Rogue traders of our time".
http://news.bbc.co.uk/1/hi/business/1804410.stm
BBC News. 7 February 2002b. "Leeson blames chiefs for
trader's losses".
http://newsbbc.co.uk/1/hibusiness/1806095.stm
BBC News. 7 February 2002c. "The fraud step by step".
http://news.bbc.co.uk/1/hi/business/1807497.stm

BBC News 7 February 2002d. "Rogue trader "Mr Middle America'. http://news.bbc.co.uk/1/hi/business/1805777.stm
BBC News 26 September 2002e. "AIB clinches Allfirst merger". http://news.bbc.co.uk/2/low/business/2282790.stm
BBC News 24 October 2002f. " 'Rogue' AIB trader pleads guilty to fraud".
http://news.bbc.co.uk/1/hi/business/2358463.stm
BBC News 19 April 2004. "Shell bosses 'fooled the market'".
http://news.bbc.co.uk/1/hi/business/3640781.stm
Beal, D. 2008. " Credit Crunch Visionary"
http://www.tcbmag.com/ideasopinions/capitalbeat/104375p2.as px
Bell, L. 2006. "NAB rogue traders jailed". The World Today Tuesday, 4 July. ABC Online .
http://www.abc.net.au/pm/stories/s357092.htm
Born, B. 1998. "Testimony of Brooksley Born, Chairperson Commodity Futures Trading Commission, Concerning Long-Term Capital Management before the U.S. House Of Representatives Committee on Banking and Financial Services October 1, 1998".
http://www.cftc.gov/opa/speeches/opaborn-35.htm
Botha, E. 1998. "Taped recordings of Gensec instructions handed to auditors". Dispatch Online November 27,1998.
http://www.dispatch.co.za/1998/11/27/business/BUS6.HTM
Botha v Gensec Asset Management (Pty) Ltd, 1999.
http://www.lawlibrary.co.za/resources/judgments/index.htm
Bowers, S. 2004. "UK metal brokers accused of rogue complicity". The Guardian Monday October 4.
http://www.guardian.co.uk/japan/story/0,7369,1319126,00.html
Bullen, D. 2004. "NAB clams up as trader meets the press". Radio Interview with Tim Lester ABC News.
http://www.abc.net.au/pm/content/2004/s1032635.htm
Business Report, 1998. "When conspirators unload, front-runners must watch out". November 3, 1998.
http://www.busrep.co.za/general/print_article.php? fArticled=60126&fSectionId=650...

Cagan, P. 2002. "Making A Scene...". ALGO Research Quarterly, Vol. 5, No.2.
http://www.algorithmics.com/solutions/opvantage/docs/Making AScene.pdf#search=%22making%20a%20scene%20cagan%22
Cameron, J. 2002. "10 things your asset manager won't tell you".
http://hobbes.ict.ru.ac.za/csae/jse/021122confessionsofanassetm anager.html
Cameron, B. 2006. "Secret profits can be made in many ways". Personal Finance April 8.
http://www.persfin.co.za/index.php? fSectionId=652&fArticleId=3194570
CBC News. 2005. "The WorldCom story". CBC News Online, July 13. http://www.cbc.ca/news/background/worldcom/
CFTC. 1998. " CFTC Files and Settles action Against Sumitomo Corporation for Manipulating the Copper Market in 1995-96". CFTC release #4144-98 May 11.
http://www.washingtonpost.com/wp- srv/business/longterm/asiaecon/stories/diet021798.htm
CFTC. 1999a. "CFTC Enforcement Proceeding Filed Against Global Minerals and Metals, R. David Cambell, Carl Alm, Merrill Lynch & Co., Merrill Lynch International Inc., and Merrill Lynch Pierce Fenner and Smith (Brokers & Dealers) Limited in connection with 1995 Manipulation and attempted Manipulation of the Copper Market; Global, Cambell, and Alm Charged in the Administrative Proceeding with Direct Participation in the Conduct; Merrill Lynch Entities Charged with Aiding and Abetting". CFTC Release #4265-99 May 20. http://www.cftc.gov/opa/enf99/opa4265-99.htm
CFTC. 1999b. "Merrril Lynch International, Inc. And Merrill Lynch Pierce Fenner & Smith (Broker & Dealers), Ltd. Pay $15 Million to Settle Charges Of Aiding And Abetting Manipulation Of The Copper Market". CFTC Release # 4284- 99 June 30.
http://www.cftc.gov/opa/enf99/opa4284-99.htm

Choa-Eoan, H. 1995. "Lending a Hand to Godzilla". TIME October 30.
http://jcgi.pathfinder.com/time/magazine/printout/0,8816,98363
4,00.html

Clark, N. 2008. " Document Says Trader's Rogue Bets Began in Summer".
http://www.nytimes.com/2008/02/20/business/worldbusiness/20
socgen.html?pagewanted=print

CNNMoney.com. 1999a. "Sumitomo sues Chase, UBS".
June 3.
http://www.washingtonpost.com/wpsrv/business/longterm/asiae
con/stories/diet021798.htm

CNNMoney.com. 1999b. "Merrill settles copper suit". June 30.
http://archives.econ.utah.edu/archives/a-
list/2002w25/msg00031.htm

Cobbet, J 2005. "Mystery player moves market". Moneyweb.
15 sep 2005.
http://www.yieldx.co.za/media_centre/moneyweb_transcripts/2
0050915a.aspx

Cohan, P.S.2005. "Wanted: a Better Ringmaster".
http://www.suite101.com/print_message.cfm/investing/79810/1
135163

Coppins, G. & Haldane, A. 2009. " Why gobal banks failed the stress test" In Finance v123n02 June 2009.

Cornell, A. 2004. "Prophets of Loss". Financial Review, 28 May.
http://w4.stern.nyu.edu/emplibrary/Australian_Financial_Revie
w_Magazine.pdf#search=%22prophets%20of%20loss
%20financial%20review%22

Cray, C. 2002. "Letter to Senate Banking Committee". January
9 2002.
http://www.enronwatchdog.org/PDFs/DonaldsonSEC.pdf#searc
h=%22cray%20c%20senate%20banking%20committee%22

Creaton, S. 2004. " Bank's Culture Has To Be Eliminated".
http://www.iboa.ie/press_re_conference_oct_04.htm

Crenshaw, A.B. 2005. "Study Hints At Bias of Advisors on Pensions". Washington Post. 16 May 2005.
www.washingtonpost.com

CSFI (Centre for the Study of Financial Innovation). 2003. "The CSFI's annual survey of the risks facing banks".
www.csfi.org.uk

Curry, T. & Shibut, L. 2000. "The Cost of the Savings and Loan Crises: Truth and Consequences". In FDIC Banking Review.
http://www.fdic.gov/bank/analytical/banking/2000dec/brv13n2_2.pdf

Dail, J.B. 1996. "Remarks of Joseph B. Dail, Commissioner U.S. Commodity Futures Trading Commission Panel on Oversight of Exchanges and Clearing Houses Asia Pacific Futures Regulator's Forum Sydney, Australia December 4, 1996".
http://www.cftc.gov/opa/speeches/opadial-621.htm

Daiwa Indictment. 1995. "11/95 Criminal Complaint & Indictment Against Daiwa Bank".
http://www.lectlaw.com/files/cas60.htm

Dalglish,B & Wallace, B. 1995. " Barings Bank Collapses". The Canadian Encyclopedia.
http://www.thecanadianencyclopedia.com/PrinterFriendly.cfm?Params=M1ARTM00

Das, S. 2006. "The secret world of Hedge Funds". ASIA INC July- August 2006.
http://www.asia-inc.com/money.html

Das, S. 2008. "Voodoo Banking". inFinance October 2008 v122n04

Dattatreya, R. 2006. "Daiwa: Lack in segregation of duties leads to losses of $1.1 billion". Banker Middle East. March edition.
http://www.bankerme.com/bme/2006/mar/risk_management.asp

Derman, E. & Wilmott, P. 2009. " The Financial Moddelers Manifesto"
http://www.financialmodelingguide.com/financial-modeling-tips/tips/financial-modelers-manifesto/

Dial, J. B. 1995. "Status Report on Regulatory and Self-Regulatory Responses to the Barings Bankruptcy".
http://www.cftc.gov/opa/speeches/opachic95s.htm

Dispatch Online. 1997. "Mixed market follows poor performance".
http://www.dispatch.co.za/1997/09/23/page%206.htm

Dow, J. 2002. "What is Systemic Risk? Moral hazard, initial shocks and propagation". Institute for Monetary and Economic Studies of Japan.
http://www.imes.boj.or.jp/english/publication/edps/edps2000_index.html

Dow, S. C. *et al*. 2009. " Letter to Her Majesty the Queen".
www.feed-charity.org/user/image/**queen**2009b.pdf

Dresser, G. 2004. "Allied Irish tax evasion sparks uproar". Thisismoney.co.uk 28 May 2004.
http://www.thisismoney.co.uk/news/article.html?in_article_id=319430&in_page_id=2

Die Burger, 1998. "Gensec man maak beweringe van witboordjiemisdaad". 29 Oktober 1998.
http://152.111.1.251/argief/berigte/dieburger/1998/10/29/1/6.html

Die Burger, 1998b. "Beurs 'kry talle klagtes oor binnetransaksies". 10 November 1998.
http://152.111.1.251/argief/berigte/dieburger/1998/11/10/6/7.html

Efrat, Z. 1996. "Societe Generale buyout of Frankel surprises". Sunday Times Business Times.
http://www.btimes.co.za/96/1013/comp/comp2.htm

Efrat, Z. 1998. "How futures close-out affect the value of your shares". Sunday Times Business Times.
http://www.btimes.co.za/98/0208/btmoney/money8.htm

Ellis. G. 2006. SABC Radio Interview. RSG Channel 21/01/2006

Epstein, R. 2004. " NAB rogue trader not surprised by losses".
ABC Online Tuesday, 27 January, 2004.
http://www.abc.net.au/pm/content/2004/s1032635.htm

Evans-Lombe, Justice. 2001 Barings Liquidation, 2001. In the
High Court of Justice Chancery Division. Case No: 1996 B
No.477& CH1998 B No 5286.
http://www.ewi.org.uk/files/Barings%20Plc%20v%20Coopers
%20&%20Lybrand.doc

Fahrer, M. 2009. " Linking executive pay with risk
management" In Finance v123n02 June 2009.

FDIC. 2002. "The S&L Crises: A Chrono-Bibliography".
Federal Deposit Insurance Corporation.
http://www.fdic.gov/bank/historical/s&l/

Federal Reserve. 2006. "Japan – Spot Exchange Rate,
YEN/US$".
http://www.federalreserve.gov/releases/h10/hist/dat96_ja.txt

FinanzNachhrichten.de 2006.
http://www.google.co.za/search?
hl=en&source=hp&q=finanznachrichten&meta=&aq=1&oq=fin
anz

FSA 1998. "Financial Supervisory Agency Statement by the
Commissioner. Administrative actions against financial
institutions involved in recent bribery cases". July 31.
http://www.fsa.go.jp/p_fsa/danwa/danwae/dan-e-731.html

FSA 2005. "Current State of Hedge Funds in Japan".
http://www.fsa.go.jp/en/newsletter/2006/03c.html

Finel-Honingman, I. 2008. "Societe Generale 2008: Rogues in
the   Trading   Room,   Knaves   in   the   Boardroom".
web.gc.cuny.edu/Eusc/activities/paper/FinelHonigman08.pdf

Finkelstein, S. 2003. "Jayson Blair Meet Nicholas Leeson". The
Wall Street Journal. May 20, 2003.
http://online.wsj.com/article/0,,SB105339346632871500,00.ht
ml

Fletcher, F. & Shameen, A. 1996. "Sumitomo's Shokko: How
a star copper trader ran up a $1.8-billion loss".
ASIAWEEK.com
http://www.asiaweek.com/asiaweek/96/0628/biz5.html

FOXNews. 2006. "Three Banks Settle Suit Stemming from Enron Collapse for $6.6B".
http://www.foxnews.com/story/0,2933,196794,00.html

FTC. 1999. "Shell and Castrol Settle FTC Charges". Federal Trade Commission Release 15 September.
http://www.ftc/oa/1999/09/shellcastrol.htm

Furukawa, T. 1997a. "As trial continues, Hamanaka copper role is uncovered – Yasuo Hamanaka, former copper trader for Sumitomo Corp". March 11.
http://www.findarticles.com/p/articles/mi_m3MKT/is_n48_v10 5/ai_19204084

Furukawa, T. 1997b. "Hamanaka defence is lax Sumitomo control – ex-copper trader Yasuo Hamanaka". March 18.
http://www.findarticles.com/p/articles/mi_m3MKT/is_n48_v10 5/ai_19220274/4

Furukawa, T. 1997c. "Sumitomo trail probes letters – trail of Yasuo Hamanaka". May 12.
http://www.findarticles.com/p/articles/mi_m3MKT/is_n48_v10 5/ai_19397552

Furukawa, T. 1997d. "Hamanaka's ex-boss has his day in court- Yasuo Hamanaka and Saburo Shimizu of Sumitomo Corp., the copper trading trail". June 9.
http://www.findarticles.com/p/articles/mi_m3MKT/is_n48_v10 5/ai_19495038

Furukawa, T. 1997e. "Hamanaka says he followed his leader; worked with Shimizu to cover losses- Yasuo Hamanaka of Sumitomo Corp., Saburo Shimizu, copper trading losses". July 10.
http://www.findarticles.com/p/articles/mi_m3MKT/is_n48_v10 5/ai_19580293

Furukawa, T. 1997f. "Prosecutors utilize Hamanaka notebook to trace money trail – Yasuo Hamanaka of Sumitomo Corp". December 12.
http://www.findarticles.com/p/articles/mi_m3MKT/is_n48_v10 5/ai_20065885

Furukawa, T. 1999. "Hamanaka to start prison term soon –
Yasuo Hamanaka case". June 30.
http://www.findarticles.com/p/articles/mi_m3MKT/is_n48_v10
5/ai_55109319
Garnaut, J. & Hughes, A. 2004 "NAB board was warned a
year ago".
http://www.smh.com.au/articles/2004/02/19/1077072783866.ht
ml?from=storyrhs
Gibson, R. 1997. "Prisoner of Power. The Greg Blank story".
Zebra Press. Sandton.
Gleason, D. 1998. "The lower the tax base". Daily Mail &
Guardian.
http://server.mg.co.za/mg/features/gleason/18dec-gleason.html
Gleason, D. 1999. "When does 'having the edge' become
'insider trading'".
http://www.server.mg.co.za/mg/features/gleason/29jan-
gleason.html
Global Policy Forum (GPF). 2003. Bloomberg News: "IMF
Report Cites Errors in Handling of 3 Crises".
htpp://globalpolicy.org/socecon/bwiwto/imf/2003/0730report.ht
m
Greenspan, A. 1998. "Mr Greenspan testifies on private-
sector refinancing of the large hedge fund, Long Term Capital
Management".
B.I.S. Review 77/1998.
Greenwald, J. 1995. "A Blown Billion". TIME October 9.
http://timeproxy.yaga.com/time/magazine/printout/0,8816,9835
31,00.html
Hasenfuss, M. 1999. "Gensec clears window-dressing
suspects". Business Report June 23, 1999.
http://www.busrep.co.za/general/print_article.php?
fArticleId=64906&fSectionId=563…
Heard, J. 1998. (1) "Dealer claims wide market malpractice".
Sunday Times Business Times.
http://www.btimes.co.za/98/1101/comp/comp.htm

Heard, J. 1998. (2) "Tapes in dealer row handed back to Gensec". Sunday Times Business Times.
http://www.btimes.co.za/98/1122/comp/comp06.htm
Hills, B. 1998. "The Financial Monster that Tried to Eat Australia". Sydney Morning Herald December 11, 1998.
http://www.globalpolicy.org/socecon/bwi-wto/normura.htm
Horvat, A. 1998: "Say Goodbye to Yamaichi". Euromoney February.
http://www.cic.sfu.ca/horvat/yamaichi.html
IBOA 2004.
http://www.iboa.ie/press_re_conference_oct_04.htm
International Law Review. 2008. " Stop persecuting rating agencies" May 2008.
http://www.iflr.com/Article/1976590/Stop-persecuting-ratings-agencies.html
Investorwords.
http://www.investorwords.com/3827/Primary_Dealer.html
Ipsen, E. 1993. "Shell Gains Despite Currency Fiasco".
International Herald Tribune. February 26.
http://www.iht.com/bin/print_ipub.php?
file=/articles/1993/02/26/shel_1.php
Irish Parliament Debates. . 21 March 2002
http://www.irlgov.ie/debates-02/s21march/sect3.htm
Irish Parliament Debates. 6 February 2002
http://www.irlgov.ie/debates-02/6feb/sect1.htm
Irish Parliament Debates.7 February 2002
http://historicaldebates.oireachtas.ie/S/0169/S.0169.200202070
003.html
Irish Parliament Debates. 19 February 2002
http://historicaldebates.oireachtas.ie/D/0548/D.0548.200202190
012.html
Jackson, B. 2002. "Enron execs hid losses, made millions". CNN.com February 2.
http://archives.cnn.com/2002/LAW/02/02/enron.report/
Jolly, D. 2009. "Ex-trader tells how he lost so much for one bank" International Herald Tribune Thursday, January 22.
http://www.iht.com/bin/printfriendly.php?id=19606400

Kattoulas, V. 1997. "Daiwa Bond Trader Has His Say".
International Herald Tribune. Wednesday January 8.
http://www.iht.com/articles/1997/01/08/daiwa.t.php
Kearney, C. & Hutson, E. "The AIB's Treasury Management
Debacle". http://www.internationalbusiness.ie/AIB
%20Independent.pdf
Kemp, S. 2004. "NAB paid $200,000 bonuses to traders".
January 16.
http://www.theage.com.au/cgibin/common/popupPrintArticle.pl
?path=/articles/2004/
Kennedy, S. Rositer, J & Seib, C. 2008. "Rogue Traders'
profit haul lifted bonusses at Societe Generale' claims lawyer"
TimesOnline February 16 2008.
http://business.timesonline.co.uk/tol/business/industry_sectors/b
anking_and_finance/article3378665.ece
Killick, M. 2002. "Sumitomo's Scandal: Secret payment link to
JP Morgan loan". Financial Times June 14.
http://archives.econ.utah.edu/archives/alist/2002w25/msg00031
.htm
Kirchner,T. 2009: " Kerviel Speaks Out: Far from the Typical
Rogue Trader story".
http://seekingalpha.com/article/119519kerviel-speaks-out-far-
from-the-typical-rogue-trader-story
Kohn, K. 18 June 1996. "Managers of rogue traders share
blame for huge losses". Bloomberg Business News:
http://chron.com/content/chronicle/business/96/06/19/rogues.2-
0.html
Kohler, A. 2004. "My appointment no risk: Kraehe".
http://www.abc.net.au/insidebusiness/content/2004/s1050534.ht
m
Langley, M. 2002. "Commission of Inquiry into the rapid
depreciation of the exchange rate of the rand and related
matters: Final Report 30 June 2002".
http://www.polity.org.za/polity/govdocs/commissions/2002/ran
d/part_g.pdf

Laudon, K.C. & Laudon, J.P. 2004. "Essentials of Management Information Systems". Organization and Technology Second Edition.
http://www.prenhall.com/divisions/bp/app/laudon/exercises/case05.html
Leeson, N. 2005. "Rogue Trader". Time Warner. London.
Leeson, N. 2006. "Personal Interview at Galway in Ireland"
Leeson, N. Official Website. http://www.nickleeson.com/
Lichfield, J. 2008. "French bank hit by EUR 600m rogue trading scandal". The Independent Oct 18, 2008.
http://www.independent.co.uk/news/business/news/french-bank-hit-by-euro600m-rogue-trading-scandal-965657.html
Leith, W. 2002. "How to lose a billion". Guardian. October 26.
http://business.guardian.co.uk/story/0,3604,818620,00.html
Levitt, A. 1997. "A Good Year for the Markets, A Busy Year for the SEC". Remarks by Chairman Arthur Levitt United States Securities and Exchange Commission SIA Regional firms Committee Chicago, Illinois – May 6, 1997.
http://www.sec.gov/news/speech/speecharchive/1997speech.shtml
Lie, E. 2006a. "Testimony of Erik Lie" "Before U.S. Senate Committee on Banking, Housing, and Urban Affairs". September 6 2006.
http://www.biz.uiowa.edu/faculty/elie/TestimonyErikLie.pdf
Lie, E 2006b. "Backdating of Executive Stock options".
http://www.biz.uiowa.edu/faculty/elie/backdating.htm
Lieberman, J. 2002 . "Rating the Raters: Enron and the Credit Rating Agencies'. Senate Committee on Governmental Affairs March 20, 2002.
http://hsgac.senate.gov/032002lieberman.htm
Limited Risk Investor 2007.
http://www.wellesleyinvestment.com/ourviews_topintro.asp?SPID=64250&LinkID=70031&Title=This%20Month's%20Issue&preview
Lords Hansard. 1995. July 18. "Barings".
http://www.parliament.thestationeryoffice.co.uk/pa/ld199495/ldhansrd/vo950718/text/50718-10.htm

Lords Hansard. 1995b. July 21. "Banking Supervision".
http://www.parliament.thestationeryoffice.co.uk/pa/ld199495/ld
hansrd/vo950721/text/5072111.htm
Lorenz, V.C. & Politzer, R. M. 1990. "Final report of Task
Force on Gambling Addiction in Maryland".
http://www.nyu.edu/its/socsci/task_force_contents.html
Lowenstein, R. 2008. " Triple-A Failure" New York Times
April 27, 2008.
http://www.nytimes.com/2008/04/27/magazine/27Credit-
t.html?_r=1&pagewanted=print
Ludwig, 2002. "Report to the Boards of Directors of Allied
Irish Banks, Plc., Allfirst Financial Inc., and Allfirst Bank
concerning Currency Trading Losses submitted by Promontory
Financial Group and Wachtell, Lipton, Rosen & Katz March
12, 2002".
http://www.ireland.com/newspaper/special/2002/aib/ludwig.pdf
MacDonald, A. & Donovan, D. 2006. "No SEC charges for
Shell ex-executive". FinanzNachhrichten.de. 30.08.2006.
http://www.finanznachrichten.de/nachrichten-2006-08/artikel-
6920586.asp
Mackenzie, S. 2001. "Nightmare on Bourke Street".
crikey.com.au. http://www.crikey.com.au/articles/2001/12/02-
nbhomeside.print.html
MacMillan, S.G.R. "Report of the Inspectors of Barings
Futures (Singapore) Pte Ltd.".
http://www.sgrm.com/art41.htm
Malkin, L. 1995. " U.S. Attorney's Office Following Paper
Trail on Huge Trading Loss: Prosecutors Go after Top Daiwa
Executives". International Herald Tribune. Saturday October
21.
http://www.iht.com/articles/1995/10/21/daiwa.t.php
McCarthaigh, S. 2002. "Most of Euro 789m losses not
recoverable". Irish Examiner March 15.
http://archives.tcm.ie/irishexaminer/2002/03/15/story24843.asp
McCurrie, W. 2007. "Investing 101- 30 March 2007".
Moneyweb.

http://www.moneyweb.co.za/mw/view/mw/en/page57?
oid=83919&sn=Detail

McNee, A. 2004 . "Barings Case Study". eRisk.com. February
2004. eRisk. 12 March 2005.
http://www.erisk.com/Learning/CaseStudies/ref_case_barings.a
sp

Milner, M. 2003. "Delotte & Touche negligent in Barings
audit, rules judge".
http://business.guardian.co.uk/0,3858,4689137-108725,00html

Mizruchi, M S & Stearns, L B. 1994. "Money Banking and
Financial Markets". The Handbook of Economic Sociology,
edited by M J Smelser, & R Swedberg. Princeton: Princeton
University Press.

Moneymax. 13 August 2004.
http://www.moneymax.co.za/email/newsletter/market update
html.asp?DayID=904

Moore, J. 2004. "Mr Copper's brokers earned $8.4m bonuses".
October 9.
http://www.smh.com.au/articles/2004/10/08/1097089569712.ht
ml?from=storylhs

Morris, R. 1998. "Conflicting versions of enquiry at Gensec".
Business Report. December 8, 1998.
http://www.busrep.co.za/general/print_article.php?
fArticleId=61084&fSectionId=561

Morrissey, B. 2002. "WorldCom's Day of Reckoning".
InternetNewsBureau.com. July 22.
http://www.internetnews.com/bus-news/article.php/1430361

Murphy, D. 2002. "'Unholy' friendship with boss gave trader
free reign". Irish Independent. 15 March.
http://www.unison.ie/irish_independent/index.php3?
issue_id=7066

Murphy, D. & Aughney,J. 2002. "Lies, fraud and betrayal".
Irish Independent. 15 March.
http://www.unison.ie/irish_independent/index.php3?
issue_id=7066

Murray, M. 2004. "How Rusnak changed AIB". THE
POST.IE 18/01.
http://archives.tcm.ie/businesspost/2004/01/18/story91203543.a
sp
Nanto, D.K. Jackson, W.D. & Wells, F.J. 1995. "Daiwa Bank
Problem: Background and Policy Issues".
http://digital.library.unt.edu/govdocs/crs//data/1995/uplmetacrs
202/951164e_1995Nov30.txt?
PHPSESSID=b9299893e0d9e30fcff6f223e059bdc1
Newman, G. 2005. "National admits to $80m fee-asco".
http://www.news.com.au/business/story/0,23636,160816261433
4,00.html#
Niskanen, W. 2003. " Enron, WorldCom, and Other Disasters"
CATO Handbook for Congress. Crane, E. H. & Boaz, D Eds.
Cato Institute Washington, D.C.
NYSE: "Types of Members".
http://www.nyse.com/about/members/1022221394057.html
NYSE, 2005. "NYSE Regulation Charges 17 Former Specialist
Members with Securities Fraud". April 12 2005.
http://www.nyse.com/press/1113302993163.html
O'Donnell, J. & Willing, R. 2003. "Prison Time Gets Harder
for White-Collar crooks". USA Today March 12.
http://www.cjcj.org/press/white_collar.html
Oneran, Y. 2008. " Banks' Subprime Losses top $500 billion
on Writedowns (Update 1). Bloomberg.com August 12 2008
http://www.bloomberg.com/apps/news?
pid=20670001&sid=a8sW0n1Cs1tY
Oprisk & Compliance. 2007.
http://www.opriskandcompliance.com/
Oxford Dictionary. 1994. Oxford University Press.
Pantesco, J. 2006. "Skilling sentenced to 24 years in prison in
Enron fraud case". Jurist- Paper Chase Newsburst. October 23.
http://jurist.law.pitt.edu/paperchase/2006/10/skilling-sentenced-
to-24-years-prison.php
Perry, M. "Coopers fined in Barings disciplinary".
http://www.accountancyage.com/articles/print/2029722

Pravda, 2002-02-09. "John Rusnak became scapegoat".
http://english.pravda.ru/world/2002/02/09/26320.html
Perry, M. 2002. "Coopers fined in Barings disciplinary".
Accountancy Age 29 Apr 2002.
http://www.accountancyage.com/articles/print/2029722
PWC Report. 2004. "Investigation into foreign exchange
losses at the National Australia Bank". 12 March 2004.
http://www.nabgroup.com/vgnmedia/downld/pwcreport.pdf
PWC Report. 2008. " Summary of PWC diagnostic review and
analysis of the action plan". 23 May 2008.
http://www.societegenerale.com/sg/file/fichierig/documentIG_5
197/pricewatercooper.pdf
Reuters 1997. "Japan racketeer admits payoff charges
(Yamaichi Securities case)".
http://vikingphoenix.com/news/archives/1997/jp970005.htm
Reuters 2008. " Societe Generale fined for breaches of internal
controls" International Herald Tribune. Friday July 4.
http://www.iht.com/bin/printfriendly.php?id=14248786
Reyes, A. 1995. "Uncovering the Cover-up". Asiaweek.com
http://www.asiaweek.com/asiaweek/95/1027/biz1.html
Riskglossary.com
http://www.riskglossary.com/
Risk Institute.
http://riskinstitute.ch/137560.htm
Ritholtz, B. 2009. "Fix What's Broken" welling@weeden
Volume 11, Issue 12 June 26 2009.
http://www.ritholtz.com/blog/wpcontent/uploads/2009/06/rithol
tz-06-09.pdf
Robarts, G. 2005. "White collar fraud costs firms billions".
BBC News 21 November 2005.
http://www.bbc.co.uk/1/hi/business/4456260.stm
Robertson, D. 2006. "The Times: Former Shell chief is pleased
but he may sue his accusers". August 31.
http://www.timesonline.co.uk/article/0,,200-2335870.html
Rodriguez, L. 2003. " Financial Deregulation" CATO
Handbook for Congress. Crane, E. H. & Boaz, D Eds. Cato
Institute Washington, D.C.

Rose, R. 2006. "Life assurers silent on 'secret profits'".
Business Day 28 March.
http://www.businessday.co.za/articles/specialreports.aspx?
ID=BD4A176612

Rowland, M. 2001. "Accounting error forces bank to $3b
write-down".
http://www.abc.net.au/pm/stories/s357092.htm

Rowland, M. 2004. " ACRA accused of weakness in
supervisory role".
http://www.abc.net.au/cgibin/common/printfriendly.pl?
http://www.abc.net.au/pm/co

Rutten, L. 2003. "A Primer on New Techniques used by the
Sophisticated Financial Fraudster". UNCTAD Report.
http://www.unctad.org/en/docs/ditccom39_en.pdf

Ryan, C. 1989. "McGregor's Dictionary of Stock Market
Terms". Juta & Co Ltd. Cape Town.

Sage, A. 2008. " Societe Generale expects further heat with
release of internal Jerome Kerviel report" . Timesonline May
24.
http://business.timesonline.co.uk/tol/business/industry_sectors/b
anking_and_finance/article3994694.ece

Sarbanes-Oxley 2006. "Sarbanes Oxley Compliance".
http://www.sarbanesoxley101.com/sarbanesoxleycompliance.ht
m

Schapiro, M.L. 2009: "Regulatory Perspectives on the Obama
Administration's Financial Regulatory Reform Proposals"
http://www.sec.gov/news/testimony/2009/ts072209mls.htm

Schwartz, N & Bennhold, K. 2008. "A Traders's Secrets a
Bank's Secrets" New York Times February 5 2008.
www.nytimes.com/2008/02/05/business/.../05bank.html

SEC. 1996. "Securities and Exchange Commission v. Victor R.
Gomez, United States District Court for the Southern District of
new York". 96 Civ. No 96-2056 (LMM).
http://www.sec.gov/litigation/litreleases/lr14851.txt

SEC. 1998. "Initial decision of an SEC Administrative Law
Judge In The Matter of Orlando Joseph Jett". Admin. Proc. File
No 3-8919.

http://www.sec.gov/litigation/aljdec/id127cff.htm
SEC. 2004. " In the Matter of Orlando Joseph Jett".
http://www.sec.gov/litigation/opinions/33-8395.htm
SEC 2004a. "Securities and Exchange Commission v. Royal Dutch Petroleum Company and The "SHELL" Transport and Trading Company Plc.". Complaint H-04-3359.
http://www.sec.gov/litigation/complaints/comp18844.pdf
SEC. 2004b. "Royal Dutch Petroleum Company and the "Shell" Transport and Trading Company, P.L.C. Pay $120 Million to Settle SEC Fraud Case Involving Massive Overstatement of Proven Hydrocarbon Reserves".
http://www.sec.gov/litigation/litreleases/lr18844.htm
SEC. 2006. "In the Matter of Guillaume Pollet" SEC Release No. 54924/December 12, 2006.
http://www.sec.gov/litigation/admin/2006/34-54924.pdf
Seib, Christine. 2008. " Societe Generale missed 75 warnings on trader Kerviel. Timesonline February 21.
http://business.timesonline.co.uk/tol/business/industry_sectors/b anking_and_finance/article3407991.ece
Seeking Alpha 2008. seekingalpha.com/article/65432-socgen-chart-of-theday-jerome-**kerviel**-s-p-l
Serrill M. S. 1996. "Billion Dollar Loser". Time International June 24 Volume 147, No.26.
http://www.time.com/time/international/1996/960624/japan.htm l
Seward,S. & Waldie, P. 2006. "Canadian Enron Executive Sentenced to 2 1/2 years". Globeadvisor .com September 19.
https://secure.globeadvisor.com/servlet/ArticleNews/story/gam/ 20060919/RENRON19
SFA. 2000. "Disciplinary Action Rudolf Wolff & Co. Ltd, Tadayoshi Tazaki, William Harker and John Wolff". Board Notice 540 .1 March.
http://www.fsa.gov.uk/pubs/additional/540.pdf
SGGID 2008. " Mission Green: Summary report" May 20 2008.
http://www.socgen.com/sg/file/fichierig/documentIG_5197/rap portmissiongreen.pdf

Shah, A. 1999. "Price limits: Time for surgery".
http://www.mayin.org/ajayshah/MEDIA/1999/pricelimits.html
Singapore Report. 1995. "Barings Futures (Singapore) Pte
Ltd. The Report of the Inspectors appointed by the Minister for
Finance". National Library Singapore.
http://www.fsa.gov.uk/pubs/additional/540.pdf#search=%22sfa
%20board%20notice%20540%22
Singh, K. 2004. "How to Lose Millions in Speculative
Currency Trading". THAISTOCKS.COM
http://www.thaistocks.com/currency-trading.htm
Societe Generale 2008. "Explanatory notes about exceptional
fraud" Paris January 27th 2008.
http://www.socgen.com/sg/upload/comm24012008/en/fraudnot
e.pdf
Societe Generale Special Committee Report 2008. "Report of
the Board of Directors to the General Shareholders Meeting" 22
May 2008. http://www.socgen.com
Sugawara, S. 1998. "Japan Approves Bank Rescue Plan".
Washington Post. February 17.
http://www.washingtonpost.com/wpsrv/business/longterm/asiae
con/stories/diet021798.htm
Taipei Times. 2005. "Ten years after fiasco, problems remain".
Feb 28 2005.
http://www.taipeitimes.com/News/biz/archives/2005/02/28/200
3224944/print
Terence, P. & Welsh, T. 1994. "Jack Welch's Nightmare on
Wall Street. The Welch legacy will be scarred by the
management fiasco at Kidder Peabody. Here is General
Electric's brutal lesson how not to run a business."
CNNMoney.com.
http://money.cnn.com/magazines/fortune/fortune_archive/1994/
09/05/79703/index.htm
The Washington Times. 30/05/2004. "Aer Lingus chairman
resigns over scandal".
http://washingtontimes.com/business/20040530-103657-
8356r.htm

Thoma, M. "An Option to Be Manipulated?". Economist's view. May 7 2006.
http://economistsview.typepad.com/economistsview/2006/05/o ptions_to_be_m.html

Thornton, P. 2005. "Missing trader leaves China with $823m bill and copper at record high". November 16.
http://www.findarticles.com/p/articles/mi_qn4158/is_20051116 /ai_n15835912

TIME. 1997. "I didn't set out to rob a Bank". Iguchi Interview. February 10 VOL. 149 NO. 6.
http://www.time.com/time/magazine/1997/int/970210/interview .i_didnt_set.html

Trader, T. 2004. "All the NAB forex angles". crickey.com.
http://www.crikey.com.au/404.aspx? aspxerrorpath=/articles/2004/01/15-0005.html

Tradersnarrative. Feb 8 2008.
http://www.tradersnarrative.com

Treanor, J. 2006. "Watchdog warns listed companies of crackdown on stock market malpractice". Guardian September 26.
http://www.guardianweeklyquiz.co.uk/

Turnbull, J. 2006. "Rogue NAB traders found guilty".
NEWS.com.au. 27-05-2006.
http://www.news.com.au/story/print/0,10119,19275686,00.html

Uchitelle, L. 1991. "Calling Bank Supervision Archaic, Greenspan Seeks Major Change". New York Times February 10 1991.
http://www.nytimes.com/1991/02/10/us/calling-bank-supervision-archaic-greenspan-seeks-major-change.html

United States of America v. John M. Rusnak. 2002.
SMS/SD/USAO # 2002R00205.
http://www.usdoj.gov/dag/cftf/chargingdocs/allfirst.pdf

United States of America v. Jeffrey K. Skilling and Kenneth L. Lay, Defendants. 2004. Cr.NO. H-04-25 (S-2).
http://images.chron.com/content/news/photos/06/05/18/final-redactedindictmentforjury.pdf

USDOJ, 2005. "Former Managing Director of SG Cowan Securities pleads guilty to "PIPE" Insider trading scheme" http://www.usdoj.gov/usao/nye/pr/2005/2005apr21.html

Verity, A. 1998. "Sumitomo pays pounds 5m to UK regulator". http://findarticles.com/p/articles/mi_qn4158/is_19980512/ai_n14155794/print

Walker, J. 1997. "Looming futures close-out stirs up volatility in share prices". Sunday Times Business Times. http://www.btimes.co.za/97/0921/markets/markets.htm

Walsh, D. 2003. "Mass jobs destruction at US retailer Kmart". 18 January.wsws.org http://www.wsws.org/articles/2003/jan2003/jan2003/kmar-j18.shtml

Walsh, C. 2005. "Few escaped unscathed from glittering class of 1995". Guardian Unlimited February 20, 2005. http://observer.guardian.co.uk/business/story/0,6903,1418359.00.html

Weidlich, T. & Scheer,D. 2009. " Bank of America Fined $33 Million by SEC Over Merrill (Update 1). Bloomberg.com. August 2009. http://www.bloomberg.com/apps/news?pid=20601087&sid=ak_7l7vmBs.g#

Weidner, D. 2003. "More Hefty Payments For NYSE Bigs". CBS News. http://www.cbsnews.com/stories/2003/10/10/national/printable577573.shtml

Werdigier, J. 2008." Trading scandal diverts attention from Societe Generale's subprime losses". International Herald Tribune. Tuesday January 29. http://www.iht.com/bin/printfriendly.php?id=9585235

Wikipedia. 2006a ."Savings and Loan crises". 30 September. http://en.wikipedia.org/wiki/Savings_and_Loan_crisis

Wikipedia. 2006b. "Royal Dutch Shell". 25 October. http://en.wikipedia.org/wiki/Royal_Dutch_Shell

Wood, K. 1990. "The Sentencing of Mike Milken". http://www.cortland.edu/polsci/milken.html

Woolriche,N. 2005. " Rogue trader tells of NAB culture". ABC
Online Monday 1 August, 2005.
http://www.abc.net.au/pm/content/2005/s1427581.htm
Yahoo News. 2009. "Obama hits out at Wall Street" Monday
July 20, 2009.
http://news.yahoo.com/s/nm/20090720/bs_nm/us_obama_walls
treet

SECONDARY SOURCES

Abju, R. 2004. "The Orange County Bankruptcy".
http://rajuabju.com/literature/oc_bankruptcy.htm
Abolafia, M Y. 1998. "Markets as cultures: an ethnographic
approach". "The Laws of the Markets", edited by M Callon:
Blackwell publishers.
Abolafia, M.Y. 2001. "Making Markets: Opportunism and
Restraint on Wall Street". First Harvard University Press
paperback edition, 2001. London.
Abolafia, M Y. 2002. "Making Markets: Opportunism and
Restraint on Wall Street". "Readings in Economic Sociology",
edited by N Biggart: Oxford Blackwell.
Adut, A. 2005. "A Theory of Scandal: Victorians,
Homosexuality, and the Fall of Oscar Wilde". American
Journal of Sociology. Volume 111, Number 1 July 2005.
Boden, D. 2000. "Worlds in Action: Information,
Instantaneity and Global Futures Trading". "The risk society
and beyond, critical issues for social theory", edited by B
Adam, U Beck and J van Loon: Sage Publications.
Bodurtha, J. 2002. "Derivatives "Events""
http://bodurtha.georgetown.edu/enron/derivatives_events.htm
Brown, J. S. & Steenbeek,O.W. 2001. "Doubling: Nick
Leeson's trading Strategy".
http://pages.stern.nyu.edu/~sbrown/leeson.PDF

Brown, P. 2003. "Four rogue traders". Accamail.
http://www.accaglobal.com/publications/fsr/67/963970
Bruce, J.C. 2005. "Trust and Risk in the Context of Securities Lending a
Sociological Analysis". Masters Dissertation UNISA
Bruck, C. 1989. "The Predators' Ball". Penguin Books. New York.
Burke, S.2003. Volpert, K. Ed. "Currency Exchange Trading and Rogue Trader John Rusnak".
http://www.publications.villanova.edu/
Concept/2004/John_Rusnak.pdf
Burton, D. 2000. "The Use of Case Studies in Social Science Research". "Research Training for Social Scientists" Burton, D. (ed). Sage Publications. London.
Butler, H. & Ribstein, L. 2006. "The Sarbanes-Oxley Debacle: What We've Learned; How to Fix It".
http://papers.ssrn.com/sol3/papers.cfm?
abstract_id=911277#PaperDownload
Burrough, B & Helyar, J. 2001. "Barbarians at the gate". Random house business books. London.
Burton, E T. 1996. "Derivatives: Is There Any Future for Them in Pension Funds?".
http://www.people.virginia.edu/~etb6d/deriva.htm
Carhart,L. Kaniel, R. Musto, D.K. & Reed,A. 1999. "Mutual Fund Returns and Market Microstructure". The Wharton School.
http://knowledge.wharton.upenn.edu/paper.cfm?
paperID=800&CFID=8691394&CFTOKEN=67049295&jsessi
onid=a830ffb85f61224c1921
Collins, R. "The Multiple Fronts of Economic Sociology".
http://www.gsm.uci.edu/econsoc/Collins.html
Cuber, J. F. 1968. "Sociology, A Synopsis of Principles". Appleton – Century-Crofts, 6th Edition. New York.
Das, S. 2006. " Traders , Guns & Money". Ft Prentice Hall. Henry Ling Ltd Dorchester.

Digenan,J. Felson, D. Kelly, R. & Wiemert, A.
"Metallgeselchaft AG: A Case Study".
http://www.stuart.iit.edu/fmtreview/fmtrev3.htm
Drennan, L.T. 2004. "Ethics , Governance and Risk
Management:- Lessons from Mirror group Newspapers and
Barings Bank" . www.caledoniancrag.com/documents/ISBEE
%Drennan%20paper.doc
Fay, S. 1997. "The Collapse Of Barings".
W. W. Norton & Company. New York. London.
**Fenton-OÇreevy, M. Nicholson, N. Soane, E. & Willman, P.
2005** "Traders risks, decisions, and management in financial
markets". Oxford University Press. New York.
Ferguson, N. 2008. " The Ascent of Money" Allen Lane. Clays
Ltd, St Eves plc.
Fischel, D. 1995. "Payback. The Conspiracy to Destroy Mike
Milken and His Financial Revolution". HarperBusiness. A
Division of HarperCollinsPublishers. New York.
Fligstein, N. 2001. "The Architecture of Markets". Princeton
University Press. New Jersey.
Freedman, R. D. & Burke J. R. 2001. "Kidder Peabody &
Co". New York University Stern School of Business.
http://www.stern.nyu.edu/mgt/private_file/mo/rfreedma_ca/kid
der.pdf#search=%22Kidder%20stern%20%22
Galbraith, J K. 1992. "The Great Crash 1929". Penguin
books. London.
Granovetter, M. 2000. "A Theoretical Agenda for Economic
Sociology".
http://www.santafe.edu/files/workshops/dynamics/granovetter.p
df
Hamilton, S. & Micklethwait, A. 2006."Greed and Corporate
failure; The lessons from recent disasters". Palgrave Macmillan.
Herring, R. J. 2005. "BCCI & Barings: Bank Resolutions
Complicated by Fraud and Global Corporate Structure".
http://fic.wharton.upenn.edu/fic/papers/05/0518.pdf#search=
%22herring%20bcci%20barings%22

Hoch, S.J. & Kunreuther, H. C. 2001. "A Complex Web of Decisions".
http://media.wiley.com/product_data/excerpt/77/04713824/047 1382477.pdf#search=%22a%20complex%20web%20of %20decisions%22

Ingham, J. January 2004."The Nature of Money". Economic Sociology –European Electronic Newsletter Vol. 5, No. 2

Jameson, R. 2001a. "Orange County". An ERisk.com Case Study. June 2001.
http://www.ERisk.com

Jameson, R. 2001b. "Daiwa Bank". An ERisk .com Case Study. August 2001.
http://www.ERisk.com

Jameson, R. 2002. "US Savings & Loans Crises". August 2002.
http://www.ERisk.com

Johnson, H.M. 1971. "Sociology: a systemic introduction". Routledge & Kegan Paul Ltd. London.

Jorion, P. "Citron's Track Record".
http://www.gsm.uci.edu/~jorion/oc/track.gif

Kane, E.J. & De Trask, K. 1998. "Covering up of Trading Losses: Opportunity–Cost accounting as an Internal Control Mechanism". National Bureau of Economic Research, Cambridge. http://papers.ssrn.com/sol3/papers.cfm? abstract_id=141400

Knorr Cetina, K & Bruegger, U. 2000. "The Market as an Object of Attachment: Exploring Postsocial Relations in Financial Markets". Canadian Journal of Sociology 25, 2 (2000): 141 – 168.
http://www.cjsonline.ca/articles/knorr.html

Kooi, M. 1996. "Analysing Sumitomo". Risk Institute.
http://riskinstitute.ch/134800.htm

Kothari, V. 2000. "Credit Derivatives".
http://www.credit- eriv.com/creprime.htm

Krawiec, K.D. 2000. "Accounting for Greed: Unraveling the Rogue Trader Mystery". Oregon Law Review Summer 2000-volume 79, Number 2.
http://www.law.uoregon.edu/org/olr/archives/79/79olr301.pdf#search=%22second%20hand%20books%20toshihide%20iguchi%22

Krawec, K.D. 2009. " The Return of the Rogue". Arizona Law Review, Volume 51: 879.
http://works.bepress.com/cgi/viewcontent.cgi?article=1009&context=kimberly_krawiec

Krugman, P. 1996. "How Copper Came a Cropper. Sumitomo's rubber-baron tactics make the case for regulation". The Dismal Science July 19.
http://web.mit.edu/krugman/www/copper.html

Lewis, M. 1999. "Liars Poker". Coronet Books. Hodder & Stoughton. London.

Lewis, M. 2009." Panic".Penguin Books. Clays Ltd. St Evesplc.

Lie, J. 1997. "Sociology of Markets". Annual Review of Sociology.

Logue, D.E. & Rader, J.S. 1997. "Managing Pension Plans: A Comprehensive Guide to Plan Performance" Harvard Business School Press. Boston, Massachusetts.

Lowenstein, R. 2002. "When Genius Failed". Clays Ltd.: St Ives plc London.

Mackenzie, D & Millo, Y 2001. "Negotiating a Market, Performing Theory: The Historical Sociology of a Financial Derivatives Exchange".
http://papers.ssrn.com/sol3/papers.cfm?abstract_id=279029

Mackenzie, D. 2002. "Risk, Financial Crises, and Globalisation; Long-Term Capital Management and the Sociology of Arbitrage". International Network for Economic Method (IWEM) Biennial Conference, September 1st / 2nd 2002.
http://www.econ.stir,ac.uk/Conferences/INEM%20program%20April.htm

Marwah, S. & Deflem, M. 2006: "Revisiting Merton: Continuities in the Theory of Anomie-and-Opportunity-Structures". Pp 57-76 in Sociological Theory and Criminological Research: Views from Europe and the United States, edited by Mathieu Deflem. Amsterdam: Elsevier.

Mathewson, G. n.d. "Operating a Global Financial Institution in the 21st Century: Risk and Rewards". http://www.baft.org/content_folders/83rd%20Annual %20Meeting/418_0815_Operating_a_Global_Financial_Institut ion_in_the_21st_Century_Risks_and_Rewards__Sir_George_ Mathewson.ppt

Mayer, M. 2003. "Risk Reduction in the New Financial Architecture: Realities, Fallacies and Proposals". http://www.levy.org/docs/wrkpap/papers/268.html

McNee, A. 2004 . "Barings Case Study." eRisk.com. February 2004. eRisk. 12 March 2005. http://www.erisk.com/Learning/CaseStudies/ref_case_barings.a sp

McNee, A 2002. "Allied Irish Banks Case Study". April 2002. http://www.erisk.com/Learning/CaseStudies/ref_case_aib.asp

McWilliams, D. 2002. " Trying to feel sorry for Rusnak". http://www.davidmcwilliams.ie/Articles/view.asp? ArticleID=178

Merton, R.K. 1957. "Social Theory and Social Structure". Revised and Enlarged Edition. The Free Press, Glencoe, Illinois.

Miles,M. & Huberman, M. "An Expanded Sourcebook. Qualitative Data Analysis". (2nd edition). Sage London.

Mouzelis, N. 1974. "Social and System Integration: Some Reflections on Fundamental Distinction". The British Journal of Sociology, Vol. 25, No.4. (Dec.,1974),pp. 395-409.

Mouzelis, N. 1991. "Back to Sociological Theory". Macmillan. London.

Ni, S. X, Pearson, N. D. and Poteshman, A. M., "Stock Price Clustering on Option Expiration Dates". August 27, 2004. Journal of Financial Economics 00 (2002) 000-000.

http://sophiexni.googlepages.com/NiPearsonPoteshman.Jan200
5.pdf

Parsons, T. 1951. "The Social System". The Free Press.
Glencoe, Illinois.

Partnoy, F 1999. "FIASCO". Penguin Books. London.

Partnoy, F. 2003. "Infectious Greed". Profile Books .
London,

Punch, K, F. 2005. "Introduction to Social Research". Sage.
London

Puplava J. J. 2000. "Rogue Wave – Rogue Trader". Financial
Sense Online October 26.
http://www.financialsense.com/series2/rogue.html

Ragin,C. C. 1994. "Constructing Social Research". Pine Forge
Press. California.

Reily, F.K. & Brown, K.C. " Investment Analysis and
Portfolio Management". Sixth Edition. Hartcourt College
Publishers. New York.

Ribstein, L. 2006. "The Paulson report and the costs and
benefits of regulation".
http://busmovie.typepad.com/ideoblog/2006/11/the_paulson_re
p.html

Richter, R. 2001. "New Economic Sociology and New
Institutional Economics". http://www.uni-
saarland.de/fak1/fr12/albert/mitarbeiter/richter/institute/revise4.
pdf

Riskmanagement. 2006. "Gamblers no longer anonymous".
October 9.
http://www.riskmanagementmagazine.com.au/articles/19/0c03c
919.asp

Rochlin,.G. 1997. "Chapter 6: Jacking into the Market" in
"Trapped in the net".
http://www.pupress.princeton.edu/books/rochlin/chapter_06.ht
ml

Ryan, H. 1995. "The Orange County Bankruptcy and
California's Fiscal Crises".
http://www.howardryan.net/orange.htm

Smelser, N J. 1976. "The Sociology of Economic Life". Prentice-Hall Inc: Englewood Cliffs.
Spillman, L. 1999. "Enriching Exchange: Cultural Dimensions of Markets". American Journal of Economics and Sociology.
http://www.findarticles.com/cf_0/m0254/458496772/print.jhtml
Steward, J.B. 1992. "Den of Thieves". A Touchstone Book. Published by Simon & Schuster. New York.
Stiglitz, J. 2003. "The Roaring Nineties". Penguin Books. London.
Suprynowicz, V. 1998. "Armed Robbery".
http://www.enterstageright.com/archive/articles/0598milken.ht m
Sutherland, E. H. 1924. "Criminology". Philadelphia and London, J. B. Lippencot Company.
Sutherland, E H. 1947. "Principles of Criminology". Philadelphia and London. J. B. Lippencot Company
Sutherland, E. H. & Cressey, D. R. 1978. "Criminology". Philadelphia and London. J.B. Lippencot Company. 10th Edition.
Taleb, N.N. 2008. "The Black Swan". Penguin Books. Clays Ltd, St Eves plc.
Thackray, J. "Leeson's Story Rings True". Derivatives Strategy.com.
http://www.derivativesstrategy.com/magazine/archive/1995-1996/0496play.asp?print
Tschoegl, A. E. 2004. "The Key to Risk Management: Management".
The Wharton School of the University of Pennsylvania, Philadelphia.
http://fic.wharton.upenn.edu/fic/papers/99/9942.pdf#search=%22Tschoegl%20the%20key%22.
Van Zyl, C, Botha, Z & Skerritt, P. 2003. "Understanding South African Financial Markets". Van Schaik Publishers. Pretoria.

Visano, B.S. 2002. "Financial manias and panics: a socioeconomic perspective". American Journal of Economics and Sociology. Oct, 2002.
http://www.findarticles.com/p/articles/mim0254/is461/ai94336
733/print

Von Mises, L. undated. "Michael R. Milken vs. The Power Elite".
http://www.mises.org/econsense/ch49.asp

Warde, I. 1998. "Crony Capitalism: LTCM, a hedge fund above suspicion". Le Monde diplomatique, November 1998.
http://mondediplo.com/1998/11/05warde2

Weston, R.2003. "The Sumitomo Copper Fraud: Were there signs?".
http://www.econ.mq.edu.au/cjes/research/Weston_2003_5.pdf#
search=%22The%20Sumitomo%20copper%20fraud%20%3A
%20were%20there%20signs%22

Wood, D. 2004. "A Link Between Option Selling and Rogue Trading?".
Financial Engineering News.
http://www.fenews.com/fen40/one_time_articles/rogue-
trading/rogue-trading.html

ABBREVIATIONS

ACI	Association for Collective Investments
ALCO	Asset and Liability Committee (Barings)
APRA	Australian Prudential Regulation Authority
ASX	Australian Stock Exchange
AUD	Australian Dollar
BB&Co	Barings Brothers & Co Limited
BFS	Baring Futures Singapore
BIB	Barings Investment Bank Group
BNP	Banque Nationale de Paris
BNZ	Bank of New Zealand Limited – NAB's banking subsidiary in New Zealand
BoE	Bank of England
BSJ	Baring Securities Japan
BSL	Baring Securities Limited
CEO	Chief Executive Officer
CFTC	Commodities Futures Trading Commission (US)
C & L	Coopers & Lybrand
Deloittes	Deloitte & Touche Auditors
ETB	European Trust and Banking Co.
FCT	First Continental Trading
FDIC	Federal Deposit Insurance Corporation
FPG	Financial Products Group (Barings)
FX	Foreign Exchange
GAAP	Generally Accepted Accounting Principles
GBP	British Pound
G-7	Group of Seven Major Industrial Democracies
IPO	Initial Public Offering
IT	Information Technology

JGB   Japanese Government Bonds
JPY   Japanese Yen
JSE   Johannesburg Stock Exchange

LIFFE   London International Financial Futures and Options
             Exchange

MANCO   Management Committee (Barings)
MBS   Mortgaged Backed Securities

Nikkei 225   Nikkei 225 Stock Average Index
NYSE   New York Stock Exchange
NZD   New Zealand Dollar

OSE   Osaka Securities Exchange
OTC   over-the counter (transaction)
OUB   Overseas Union Bank

P & L   profit and loss

Repo   Repurchase Agreement
RRR   Reserves Replacement Ratio

SARB   South African Reserve Bank
SBC   Swiss Bank Corporation
SEC   Securities & Exchange Commission
SFA   Securities and Futures Association (UK)
SFO   Serious Fraud Office
SG   Societe Generale
SGGID   Societe Generale General Inspection Department
SIB   Securities Investment Board (UK)
SIMEX   Singapore International Monetary Exchange
SLK   Spear, Leeds & Kellogg

TSE   Tokyo Stock Exchange

USD   United States Dollar

             VaR Value at Risk, a quantitative method to
             calculate possible losses within a defined interval
             and time period

| YEN | Japanese Currency |
| ZAR | South African Rand |

GLOSSARY

ARBITRAGE: The exploitation of temporary price differences in the same security on different markets.

BACK OFFICE: The section of a financial services institution tasked with settling transactions.

CALL OPTION: A contract which gives the owner the right but not the obligation to buy from the writer a specified security or securities at a specified price at a specified date, or within a specified time period.

CREDIT RISK: The risk that a counterparty will not settle an obligation fully when due.

FRONT RUNNING: The taking of a position in a security ahead of a buy or sell action, a trader knows will be taken by his firm or one of its clients, that will influence the price of the security he took a position in.

FUTURES CONTRACT: A contract to buy or sell a currency, commodity or security at some future date at a fixed price.

GEARING: The debt equity ratio of a company (or Leverage).

HEDGING: The process through which an investor can offset the risk that the price of one financial instrument will rise or fall, by buying or selling another financial instrument.

LEVERAGE: From a speculative point of view, the opportunity for a large profit at a small cost. It implies high risk.

LONG POSITION: A position taken by a trader in expectation of a price rise in a particular security.

NAKED POSITION: A position in securities not protected from market risk through hedging. One example is where a trader sells an option over a security, without holding a position in the underlying security as protection.

PUT OPTION: A contract that gives the holder the right but not the obligation to sell to the writer of the option specified securities at an agreed to price at an agreed to time.

SETTLEMENT: The process by which balances arising from the buying or selling of securities is paid off.

SHORT POSITION: A position normally established in expectation of a drop in the price of the relevant securities.

STRIKE PRICE: The prearranged price at which the buyer of an option may buy or sell the securities specified in the options contract.

VOLATILITY SMILE: A common graphical shape that results from plotting the strike price and implied volatility of a group of options with the same expiration date.

www.ingramcontent.com/pod-product-compliance
Lightning Source LLC
Chambersburg PA
CBHW071400170526
45165CB00001B/124

* 9 7 8 1 4 4 9 5 9 5 2 1 0 *